Associational anarchism

Manchester University Press

CONTEMPORARY ANARCHIST STUDIES

A series edited by
Laurence Davis, *University College Cork, Ireland*
Uri Gordon, *University of Nottingham, UK*
Nathan Jun, *Midwestern State University, USA*
Alex Prichard, *Exeter University, UK*

Contemporary Anarchist Studies promotes the study of anarchism as a framework for understanding and acting on the most pressing problems of our times. The series publishes cutting-edge, socially engaged scholarship from around the world – bridging theory and practice, academic rigor and the insights of contemporary activism.

The topical scope of the series encompasses anarchist history and theory broadly construed; individual anarchist thinkers; anarchist informed analysis of current issues and institutions; and anarchist or anarchist-inspired movements and practices. Contributions informed by anti-capitalist, feminist, ecological, indigenous and non-Western or global South anarchist perspectives are particularly welcome. So, too, are manuscripts that promise to illuminate the relationships between the personal and the political aspects of transformative social change, local and global problems, and anarchism and other movements and ideologies. Above all, we wish to publish books that will help activist scholars and scholar activists think about how to challenge and build real alternatives to existing structures of oppression and injustice.

Recent books in the series

Anarchism and eugenics
Anarchy in Athens
The autonomous life?
Black flags and social movements
Cooking up a revolution
The politics of attack
No masters but God

Associational anarchism

Towards a left-libertarian conception of freedom

Chris Wyatt

MANCHESTER UNIVERSITY PRESS

Published by Manchester University Press
Oxford Road, Manchester M13 9PL

www.manchesteruniversitypress.co.uk

British Library Cataloguing-in-Publication Data
A catalogue record for this book is available from the British Library

ISBN 978 1 5261 7128 3 hardback
ISBN 978 1 5261 9153 3 paperback

First published 2023
Paperback published 2025

The publisher has no responsibility for the persistence or accuracy of URLs for any external or third-party internet websites referred to in this book, and does not guarantee that any content on such websites is, or will remain, accurate or appropriate.

EU authorised representative for GPSR:
Easy Access System Europe – Mustamäe tee 50, 10621 Tallinn, Estonia
gpsr.requests@easproject.com

Typeset
by Deanta Global Publishing Services, Chennai, India

Contents

Introduction

This book presents a new conception of liberty.[1] Liberty is one of the most contested ideas in both ancient and modern political thought, and my approach is to think about it primarily as an organisational problem. A full and progressive conception of liberty, I will contend, unifies liberty with the conditions of its profitable exercise. This is because a society cannot claim to be free if large sections of its inhabitants lack the resources to do or become something they desire and which is not beyond their capabilities. The underlying task is to mount a defence of a left-libertarian political economy, which can be thought of as a meeting between Karl Marx's (1818–83) critique of capitalism, the guild socialist writings of G.D.H. Cole (1889–1959) and the sub-schools of social anarchism. In this sense, the project attempts to bring together in theoretical dialogue a range of various perspectives, and in doing so it contributes towards the healing of a major historical schism in socialist theory. The outcome is a newly formed anarchist constitution, which is hereafter referred to as 'associational anarchism'. It will become clear as my argument unfolds the precise ways in which an original account of both liberty and its realisation has been articulated. Liberty, this book will claim, can be attained without passing through the mediation of self-interested employers, career politicians or state planners.

If people were asked to consider what they deem to be amongst the most favourable values of their society, it may well be that security, longevity and social order would rank highly. Freedom is not necessarily the core value. That said, the vast majority would surely agree that freedom, in common with other popular ideals like democracy and social justice, is in general something to be thought of approvingly – that regardless of its prioritisation in the scale of desired characteristics, it is a vital component of the good society. This much seems fairly uncontroversial. But here, on the most basic of levels, the consensus ends. The critiques, defences and counter-critiques of the numerous and competing notions of freedom ensure that debates on its precise nature continue to rage in a conceptual battlefield. The result of these often-complex controversies is that freedom is still interpreted in so many different ways by so many different protagonists. Contentions about the meaning of liberty go back at least to the dawn of the modern era. In the liberal tradition, John Locke's (1632–1704) *Two Treatises on Government* (1689) is a canonical text, as are J.S. Mill's (1806–73) *On Liberty* (1859) and John Rawls's (1921–2002) *A Theory of Justice* (1971). J.J. Rousseau (1712–78) is widely regarded as one of the most influential of the early modern thinkers on liberty in the republican sense of self-rule. Then there are the numerous outpourings from Marxist and anarchist scholars who, in their various ways, argue that freedom is incompatible with a capitalist mode of production; for these thinkers, only the abolishment of market economies and the complete eradication of the wage-labour relation can engender real freedom. As the subsequent chapters unfold, there will be recourse to return to many of the ideas first laid out in these texts. So in presenting a particular conception of liberty, this book adds to an enormous body of literature; in addition, with regards to the recent surge in anarchist studies (Kinna, 2014a: 3–4), it also offers something new to current anarchist discourse.

It will be instructive at this point to offer a few concise words on the specific constellations through which my argument has been constructed; a more detailed account is then provided in the following chapter. The interlinking of social anarchism and Marxist-humanism is, most immediately, a complete renunciation of capitalism. As section two of Chapter 2 will indicate, although the classical anarchists rejected authoritarian forms of socialism, in the main they had no fundamental disagreement with Marx's account of capital. What is new in this book are the ways in which the latter has been affiliated with an adaption of certain guild socialist ideals, revised along a social anarchist path, in order to form a redesigned class struggle anarchism. Its core premise is that Marx's call to move beyond capitalist society must point towards a decentralised and libertarian constitution, rather than a communist state. For reasons that are explained in Chapter 1, this concept is called 'freedom as Marxian-autonomy', which, I will suggest, can be understood as a continuation of the wider twentieth-century anarchist project of 'advanced selfhood'. It will become evident how associational anarchism socialises the means of production through a newly formed mode of organisation, and in the process makes every effort to universalise what we may think of as self-actualising forms of labour, expressed within a system of workplace democracies, where every cooperator has the opportunity to fully develop and refine their critical and intellectual capabilities. Throughout the subsequent chapters, these labour processes will also be referred to as de-alienated, multi-skilled, creative and aesthetic, depending on the context.

To very briefly summarise, my principal claim is that self-determination, through self-mastery of one's material life, can only manifest through an equal and democratic access to productive resources. Seen in this light, freedom equates chiefly with the opportunity to evolve in enriching and altruistic terms as both productive and consumptive agents, whilst simultaneously protecting a measure of freedom as non-restraint. Work of some kind is the most fundamental component of human existence. No society that is at present imaginable could ever be at liberty to avoid reproducing continuously its means of subsistence. The hours of the working day may be reduced to allow people more time to pursue their goals outside the workplace, but necessary labour will remain for the foreseeable future. It is reasonable to presume that wherever possible producers would naturally like their essential activity to be a creative, fulfilling and meaningful experience. Likewise, for a society to be considered genuinely free, it must also protect a comprehensive sphere of unpreventedness within which individuals are sovereign over their own affairs. In what follows, these two maxims are coherently combined in a conceptual framework that does not posit negative (non-coercion) and positive (self-direction, self-development) ideals in perpetual contradiction.[2]

Perhaps the most immediate objection here from liberal quarters would be that prioritising the collective side of individuals – or a sub-set of the desires of individuals to be more precise – elevates the good of the community above the good of the private side of the individual, which in effect threatens the right of individuals to determine their own conceptions of the good. In response, my proposal that self-actualisation must be pursued democratically in both the productive and consumptive spheres will challenge the ideological belief that only liberalism protects negative liberty.[3] But my contention goes a stage further. It makes the bolder claim that there are very good reasons why a pluralised left-libertarian economy offers optimum assurance of individual liberty. Its key objective is, through a more auspicious approach to what has been termed 'instrumental participation', to engender the social relations within which the equal political liberties will be of fair value to all citizens, whilst the other main subjective liberties will be of lesser unequal value. These conditions could never be sustained in neo-liberal societies. This is because the strong centralising tendencies of global capital reduce freedom largely to the wielding of corporate power in the unrelenting quest to maximise profit, which leads inevitably to the formation of economic cartels dominated by perennial and self-centred oligarchies, all of which desolate both formal and effective freedom. I will therefore be highly critical of the standpoint advocated by theorists of negative liberty like Isaiah Berlin and F.A. Hayek. It is true that social liberals have addressed the problematic consequences of huge financial inequalities through redistributed means, in John Rawls's case extensively. Adopting a more radical approach, associational anarchism removes the main cause of inequalities at a deeper fundamental level.

A basic starting point on which the argument of this book rests then is that hard market forces must lose their ascendancy in much the same way socialist planning agencies must be stripped of their unaccountable authority. As Chapter 3 will explain, the associational anarchist combination of social planning with a guild-regulated market system is one attempt to achieve precisely this. Hence, this theoretical attempt to unite the private sphere of production with the public sphere of citizenship within a newly constructed system of communal ownership presents a viable decentralised alternative to both liberal democracy and state socialism. The outcome is an organisational schema of horizontalised networks, which are held together through what I will argue are libertarian politics. Although there is no role for a centralised state, there is a pluralist self-governance to fulfil the functions of coordination and administration. Political intermediation proceeds via a complex web of interrelating functional associations, which operate within a system of revitalised communities. As routine methods of management are carried out through modes of self-regulation that embody the key anarchist values of equality, solidarity and mutual aid, this specific configuration of functional devolution adds formative detail to the guiding anarchist principle that coercive and authoritarian structures must be replaced with voluntary and libertarian alternatives. These then in outline form are the core institutional contours that are filled out and developed in the various expositions that follow. The sequence of the forthcoming chapters can now be explained in more depth.

Structure of the book

The book is divided into three parts. Part I, 'A new genre of social anarchism', consists of four chapters, all of which raise controversial and provocative questions. Although they contain some preliminary discussions, in the main they establish the prerequisites for the evaluative and argumentative chapters that make up the remainder of the book. Part II, 'Libertarian politics: social coordination through functional decentralisation', breaks down into three chapters (5, 6 and 7), which together demonstrate the robustness of associational anarchism's unusual mixed-economy. Here I argue that regular patterns of social arrangements can be securely ordered in the absence of both state planning and impersonal market forces. Finally, Part III, 'The associational anarchist conditions of liberty in the realm of necessity', has four chapters (8 to 11). These chapters make the case that a free constitution can only be attained by extending democracy into a certain kind of egalitarian economy.

Chapter 1, 'Freedom as Marxian-autonomy', details at length the foundational elements that, when constellated in a particular way, form the core of this book's conception of freedom. Chapter 2, 'Social anarchism: classical to contemporary', begins by showing why Cole's guild socialist writings provide, once suitably revised, solid grounds upon which to frame a new configuration of class-struggle anarchism. It then provides a full exposition of the social perspective in the anarchist doctrine, and in doing so identifies the areas of overlap between certain forms of anarchism and certain forms of Marxism, especially as anarcho-syndicalism has methods centred on production. It is true that differences between the two schools of socialist thought remain, especially regarding political organisation. Through its paradigm mode of organisation, associational anarchism straddles this divide. The central Marxian tenet that social class is the foundational inequality through which capitalism systematically reproduces itself is retained; likewise, anarchism's distinguishing principle that the authoritarian and oppressive structures of the modern state must be abolished and replaced with localised alternatives is also espoused. Upon these two pivotal premises, an original synthesis between anarchism and Marxism is forged.

Chapter 3, 'Anarcho-constitutionalism as associational anarchism', introduces the organisational contours of associational anarchism in full. At the core, there is democratic control over one's productive life. I will explain how a federation of quasi-independent guild cooperatives, within which associated producers share resources on a democratic basis, will meet the demands of efficiency through self-governing means. The primary agencies that will regulate the product range are not the state or the market, but a system of consumer councils. The product mix is determined by an unconventional combination of participatory planning and what may be termed 'market-pluralism'. But although good use is made of a public collective proviso as well as private market exchange in terms of consumptive goods, they are entirely distinct from the central planning of command socialism or the mixed-economy of social democracy. The method of democratic planning and the delineation of the guild market system are both original and are hence unique to associational anarchism. Finally, the chapter draws to a close by indicating how these specific structural arrangements will institutionalise a self-actualising mode of labour universally. As these first three chapters cover a wide range of themes and perspectives, Chapter 4, 'Bridging the Marxist–anarchist divide', will take stock of the newly formed premises upon which my argument rests. Here the organisational innovations associational anarchist theory introduces into a specific Marxist-anarchist conceptual amalgamation are summarised concisely.

Part II is made up of three chapters. Chapter 5, 'Legal authority beyond state imposition', provides an exposition of associational anarchist jurisprudence. Here I suggest new ways of addressing the problems that emerge when an anarchist understanding of freedom is reconciled with the claim that anti-social behaviour can be restrained in the absence of a statist codified system of law. From this book's perspective, it is not the actual act of legislation that in itself is oppressive. What makes law-making an imposition on freedom is when it passes through a detached chamber, and when laws are enforced by the coercive institutions of the state. There are two interrelating constituents of associational anarchism's plural legal framework that are the most central. Firstly, the guilds will be self-legislating bodies. Uniform systems of laws, each one applying only to the jurisdiction of an individual guild, will only be made by those who have an obligation to obey them, and as the guilds are voluntary organisations, adherence to one's own laws is not compulsory. In these senses, the control of legal mandates is under popular control. Secondly, drawing from the intriguing political thought of J.J. Rousseau, these direct forms of democracy internal to each local guild will embody general will deliberations. I will argue that his thesis on participation and collective sovereignty provides, once revised along a non-statist path, a sound platform upon which to construct real democratic structures. Following this, through a discussion of the natural law theories of Michael Bakunin and Peter Kropotkin, the chapter shows how inter-personal conflicts at the wider community level can be solved in the absence of a statist administration of law enforcement.

Chapter 6, 'Free federation', introduces the federated forms visualised by Bakunin and Kropotkin, which are juxtaposed to Cole's functional federation. From here the chapter will address the critique that in the absence of central authority, the productive and distributive functions of neighbourhoods and regions cannot be coordinated. The charge is that an anarchist federation contains an irresolvable contradiction between voluntarism and decentralisation, on the one hand, and the imperatives of welfare and the redistribution of rare natural resources, on the other. Associational anarchism answers this demanding question by placing control of the latter into the hands of the guilds, rather than the local communities themselves, and by proposing a system of interacting federal bodies whose delegated authority is structurally checked in an important way. The functional principle of demarcation will in effect limit the scope of the jurisdiction of each component, and in doing so procures the organisational contours that assure, to a reasonable extent, the autonomy of the local community. The second section of the chapter completes my defence of a functional federation by indicating how the associational anarchist method of democratic investment planning brings economic and political decision-making into harmony, and as such enables a general adherence to an accepted common good in the public sphere.

At this point, the more radical form of republicanism, which incorporates both the labour-republican and the anarchist republican traditions, is introduced. This perspective is hostile to the wage-labour contract, and it recognises systemic modes of domination. In calling for an equal access to productive assets, labour-republicanism seeks to radically reconstruct economic relations. This will entail new forms of participation and deliberation, which thoroughly restructure the internal relations of the workplace. As a transformative principle, 'freedom as non-domination' stands as a normative benchmark. Yet in recasting it outside the confines of liberal-republicanism, contemporary anarcho-republicanism goes a stage further – its move beyond the institution of private property seeks a non-statist constitutional politics. My contention is that a 'democratic republicanisation of property' leads straight to associational anarchism. This claim is reinforced in Chapter 9, where the move beyond systemic domination is theorised. Filling out in finer organisational detail the demands of the radical republicans re-establishes the fierce rejection of capitalism into the heart of anarchism, which dovetails neatly with the content of section one of Chapter 2.

The context of the seventh chapter, 'The organisational contours of an unorthodox mixed-economy', is situated largely around a prolonged discussion with F.A. Hayek, whose combined writings expound arguably one of the most sophisticated defences of a market forces economy in twentieth-century literature. His work raises important questions, not least of which is how a socio-economic order can sustain regular patterns in the absence of a central coordinating body. In *The Road to Serfdom* (first published in 1944) he builds a strong case that the centralised planning of state socialism will, quickly and inevitably, degenerate along inefficient and totalitarian lines. This seemingly accurate prediction (prophesied some sixty to seventy years earlier by the leading social anarchist thinkers) strongly suggests that any theory of economic planning must offer a mandatory response to his critique of social engineering. For Hayek, markets are telecommunication systems which digest and disseminate pieces of information more swiftly than any rational design ever could. They achieve this through the price mechanism, which is said to be a sophisticated device for transmitting data on supply and demand curves. There is, however, an immediate problem that free-market liberalism inevitably encounters. This is the omnipresent tendency for capital and wealth to agglomerate in monopolistic corporations. These self-perpetuating oligopolies are, as a matter of organisational necessity, themselves administered through central panning. It follows that the only solution to this impasse is a decentralised method of democratic planning that, whilst meeting the requirements of social coordination, has built-in mechanisms to prevent the planning agencies from escalating in scope to the degree that centralising tendencies could not be restrained. This is a devilishly difficult task, but as this chapter will show, it is not insurmountable. Two immediate interrelated propositions arise. Can market relations be redefined and curtailed without giving rise to a huge and oppressive bureaucracy? Conversely, can the latter be avoided without assigning free reign to enterprise autonomy and commodity production? Associational anarchism theorises a positive answer to both these questions. The interacting functional agencies will not be burdened with the impossible task of understanding all the entrails of national or corporate plans. This has important implications that throw up a number of contentious points, many of which call into doubt some of the main conjectures through which Hayek critiques economic planning. As we shall see, there are solid reasons why the feared metamorphosis of positive liberty into absolute tyranny is, in the appropriate context, far from inevitable. For these reasons, I conclude emphatically that associational anarchism is the road to freedom, not serfdom.

Turning now to Part III, Chapter 8, 'Self-determination, self-realisation and negative freedom', engages with the contentions surrounding the intrinsic and instrumental values of participation. Through a critical appraisal of John Rawls's work on social justice, I will argue it is legitimate to increase the magnitude of the intrinsic content. The reason for this is that participation is more meaningful, and hence more easily invoked, when it rests upon a creative and aesthetic value. Only then can political participation serve its instrumental function of alerting citizens to the early stages of tyrannical rule. This claim is reinforced by turning to a closely related theme discussed in contemporary liberal-republican political theory, where a link is established between the civic virtue gained through public service and the preservation of negative freedom. I will contend that in associational anarchism, the coveted acts of civic virtue will not need to be forced through a centralised political authority. As it is the context of participation, not just its content, that is decisive, a system of workers cooperatives is the essential ingredient. The general idea is that the required public service and knowledge of political processes will be a consequence of the democratisation of economic life. My argument follows this logic. If political participation is a precondition for the preservation of negative freedom, and as economic democracy is indispensable to effective participation, then it is the self-realisation and self-determination components of freedom as Marxian-autonomy that afford negative freedom optimal protection.

Chapter 9, 'Freedom in the guild system', continues with the general theme of Chapter 8, only now the debate picks up once again the discussion with Hayek. Here I argue that a system of workers cooperatives, monitored by decentralised consumer councils, can attain individual freedom far more effectively than the typical wage-labour enterprise. Hayek contends that a coercive act must always be both inter-agential and intentional. When goal-seeking agents cannot fulfil their plans due to insufficient material resources, they may lack power or ability, but as long as their choices have not been deliberately determined by the arbitrary will of an external party, they purportedly suffer no loss in freedom. In his hands, negative liberty draws a clear demarcating line between freedom and ability, distinguishes freedom from the conditions of its practice and has a strict definition of coercion. I will argue that he is severely wrong on these most pivotal points. Simply being left alone is an insufficient standard upon which to base a conception of freedom. The problem with equating interference with only human agency is that it rules out coercion at the systemic level, where it is often hidden, unintentional, indirect and experienced through unpremeditated means. My argument is substantiated by contrasting Hayek's minimalist account of coercion with the radical republican critique of structural domination, the outcome of which is a vindication of the latter. In my opinion, the opportunities for individuals to develop the capabilities they value are dependent upon an equal and democratic access to material resources. Otherwise, the non-owners of the means of production will have little choice but to sell their only productive asset, labour-power, and to risk accepting disadvantageous and heavily unequal terms. The worker–capitalist contract cannot be founded upon real freedom when the former is threatened with unemployment, insecurities and other hardships that follow in the wake of capital strike/flight. In these conditions, the surface equality of the wage-labour relation shields a deeper structural inequality. A hugely unequal distribution of the material means of life has to fall, therefore, within the category of coercive impediments. It is not the alliance of freedom with the conditions of its gainful exercise that impoverishes the value of freedom; it is their separation that does this. I will conclude this chapter by indicating why Hayek, along with Berlin, is in grave error when drawing this distinction.

Chapter 10, 'Freedom in the guild system and beyond', develops an argument that although the usual set of negative freedoms has been recast, freedom as Marxian-autonomy maintains a general condition of non-interference. It will then explain the reasons why a self-employed sector and the cooperative nature of the guild system will be congruous. Due to an egalitarian access to productive assets, inequalities of outcome between the guild cooperatives and the small firms who seek to labour on their own account will fall roughly within the same range. Crucially, where there is no elitist appropriation of surplus and therefore no powerful economic conglomerates, the telecommunication system of the price mechanism may assume a new form. As the information that influences purchasing behaviour will no longer be under the spell of private corporations, the signals that match supply with demand will reflect the autonomous nature of consumer choice, rather than its induced character. I will conclude that in the absence of controlling oligopolies, the self-employed sector may self-coordinate more effectively. To complete this third part of the book, Chapter 11, 'The civic functional bodies', offers a very concise account of the organisational forms in associational anarchism's realm of freedom, the rationale of which is explained at the time.

The conclusion, 'Associational anarchism and human emancipation as developed selfhood', reiterates the key argument of the book. As political power will not, indeed cannot, concentrate to the point where it becomes exclusive, unaccountable or what Cole calls non-functional, there is no reason why the move beyond an oppressive economic leviathan is predestined to end with an equally oppressive political leviathan. Whilst there are historical examples that warn against the totalitarian dangers of positive liberty, it is a fallacy to extrapolate that all forms of perfectionist politics are certain to suffer the same fate. As a feasible addition to the social anarchist creed – one whose elevation of self-developing and meaningful forms of labour is diametrically opposed to the twin evils of the gulag system and the contemporary global sweatshop economy – associational anarchism strengthens the argument against both authoritarian states and unaccountable private corporations.

Notes

1 As there is no significant difference between the terms 'liberty' and 'freedom', I will follow most other commentators and, in the interests of convenience, use them interchangeably and to denote the same thing.
2 These terms are fully explained in Chapter 1.
3 It is also true that liberals have not always focused only on freedom *from*. As Gray points out, neither Locke nor Kant nor J.S. Mill can be referred to as unequivocal negative libertarians (1984b: 342).

Part I

A new genre of social anarchism

This first part consists of four chapters. As liberty cannot be separated from the conditions of its meaningful exercise, these chapters provide a detailed account of the left-libertarianism structures that are essential to its realisation. Chapter 1, 'Freedom as Marxian-autonomy', lays out in full the specific conception of freedom pieced together and defended in this book. Chapter 2, 'Social anarchism: classical to contemporary', covers the theories of class-struggle anarchism, paying particular attention to their constitutional forms, and their congruence with certain strands of democratic Marxism. Chapter 3, 'Anarcho-constitutionalism as associational anarchism', provides a complete exposition of the particular genre of anarchism presented in this book. Finally, as these three chapters cover a great deal of theoretical ground, Chapter 4, 'Bridging the Marxist–anarchist divide', will bring together in summary form the innovations introduced into this particular Marxist-anarchist conceptual amalgamation.

1

Freedom as Marxian-autonomy

The main purpose of this lengthy chapter is to establish the various elements that when integrated in certain ways constitute freedom as Marxian-autonomy in its conceptual completeness. The formal scheme and the various political perspectives, upon which associational anarchism's more specific propositions rest, are defined through their logical sequence. This explanatory treatise will proceed through nine distinct yet interrelated discussions, the interlinking of which will be explained as the chapter unfolds.

The conventional negative–positive dichotomy, or the triadic relation

The most appropriate place to begin is with arguably the two most influential positions on how to conceive freedom. The first is Isaiah Berlin's (1909–97) much-acclaimed distinction between 'negative' and 'positive' liberty, and the second is Gerald MacCallum's (1925–87) triadic formula. This section will explain why it is a version of the latter that pervades the entire constitution of associational anarchism. I will conclude that this newly formed conception has something significant to offer the more general anarchist theory of 'developed selfhood'.

In his canon essay 'Two Concepts of Liberty' in *Four Essays on Liberty* (originally published in 1958), Berlin identifies two concepts of liberty, 'negative' and 'positive'. Negative liberty answers the question "What is the area within which the subject – a person or group of persons – is or should be left to do or be what he is able to do or be, without interference by other persons?"; and positive liberty answers the question "What, or who, is the source of control or interference that can determine someone to do, or be, this rather than that?" (1991: 121–2). The former is usually associated with a private domain within which a condition of unpreventedness is protected. Whether individuals cannot achieve their ends for any other reason, or whether their ends are laudable, is regarded as irrelevant to negative liberty. Positive liberty is the desire of people to be their own masters; here the emphasis is on self-determination or self-actualisation, rather than non-coercion. Berlin contends that initially it may have seemed there was little logical distance between these two concepts, but as they developed historically they very quickly polarised, to the point that they now stand in mutual outright conflict. As a consequence, the freedoms of movement, speech, thought, association, arbitrary arrest, etc. are in grave danger if the state holds the power to crush the ways of life it sees as irrational or immoral. Perfectionism in politics and totalitarianism are, Berlin concludes, dangerously affiliated, in which case it is only the negative concept that deserves the title freedom (1991: 121–2, 131–4; Swift, 2001: 51).

Berlin's division between negative and positive liberty establishes categories that are helpful to the analyses in Part III of this book. But his claim that they are in universal contradiction is suspect for a number of reasons. Chiefly, as his notion of positive freedom is not specified with clarity, it fails to capture the full remit of distinct forms of liberty, and as such obscures real differences. It first appears as self-mastery; individuals may be considered free when they assert control over their lives, as opposed to being under the command of another. But as he develops the concept, it is expanded to include (a) an actual capacity to act, (b) rational self-direction (what he calls 'liberation by reason', and what often gets labelled 'freedom as autonomy' by others) and (c) collective self-determination (Miller, 1991: 9–11). Commentators have, unsurprisingly, pointed out that it is a fallacy to identify all positive concepts with one subcategory.[1] As soon as positive liberty is defined with tighter precision, it becomes apparent that it has been theorised in very different ways by Marxists, feminists, republicans, left-liberals and, as we shall shortly see, especially by anarchists. Nor is this all; there is a further critique that leads straight to the triadic approach.

The conventional reading of Berlin's essay identifies negative liberty with freedom *from*, i.e. constraints or interference, and positive liberty with freedom *to do* or *become* (1991: 126–7, 129–31). Yet as the above indicates, this distinction is misleading. The freedom *from–to do/become* criteria is, as Swift puts it, a red herring. It is more accurate to say that as all liberties involve both conceptions, they imply each other (Swift, 2001: 52–3). MacCallum also believes that as the distinction between negative and positive freedom is unclear and based upon "serious confusion" (1991: 100), and is "both clumsy and misleading" (1991: 115), Berlin was mistaken to separate liberty into these two concepts, and equally mistaken to claim any difference between freedom *from* and freedom *to/become*. This characterisation "cannot distinguish two genuinely different kinds of freedom; it can serve only to emphasize one or the other of two features of every case of the freedom of agents" (MacCallum, 1991: 106).

Taking the format '*x* is (is not) free from *y* to do (not do, become, not become) *z*', *x* ranges over agents, *y* ranges over such 'preventing conditions' as constraints, restrictions, interferences, and barriers, and *z* ranges over actions or conditions of character or circumstance. (MacCallum, 1991: 102)

For MacCallum, then, there is only one concept of freedom, the triadic relation of agency ('X'), interference or obstacle ('Y') and goal or purpose ('Z') (1991: 100–2, 106–8).

So rather than focus on particular defences of either negative or positive ideals, the contentions over the presence or absence of liberty revolve around how exactly the X, Y, Z schema should be applied. This implies that all disagreements will hinge upon the ways in which the three variables captured in the triadic relation are open to interpretation, and, to be more precise, the degree of extension granted to each one. The negative camp views *agency* as individuals complete with all their empirical beliefs and desires. The positive camp views the agent in more extensive terms, yet, in a different sense, in less extensive terms. It is in larger terms when the 'true' desires and goals of the agents are identified with the collective they are affiliated with. It is in lesser terms when the 'true' agents are identified with just a subset of their beliefs and desires, those that are seen as rational, moral and virtuous.[2] Furthermore, the positive camp has a *wider* understanding of what constitutes a *constraint*. The range of potential obstacles is larger because it incorporates more than just inter-agential interference. It also includes indirect systemic forces as well as internal factors like uncontrolled desires, irrational fears and ignorance. It is because there is so much disagreement about what counts as an agent, what should be regarded as a constraint and what constitutes a goal, that Berlin's attempt to differentiate the categories of liberty into negative and positive terms is, for Swift and MacCallum, specious (MacCallum, 1991: 100–2, 106–8, 110, 115; Swift, 2001: 61, 53–4; Carter, 2003: 9–10).

MacCallum's approach makes available an array of different interpretations. In order to illustrate the difference between the political left and right, it will be instructive to take a closer look at the constraints on freedom, the second variable in his triadic relation. Theorists within the negative camp commonly acknowledge that as there are differences in external obstacles, they usually have in mind only those that stem from other agents. This criterion can be restricted even further by inferring that only the obstacles engendered *deliberately* through inter-agential relations may pass as a restriction on freedom. On this understanding, impersonal economic forces that manifest unintentionally cannot be said to restrict people's freedom. This is the standpoint defended by the theorists of the new right like F.A. Hayek (1899–1992). Critics have responded that unintended obstacles must also count as a constraint on freedom. Along with anarchists, socialists typically adhere to a broader understanding; in terms of economic inequalities, the least well-off in capitalist society should be seen as less free than the better-off. This is because without financial resources, freedom has little substantive value; it is merely formal. Socialists of all persuasions then visualise a wider remit than right-libertarians about what constitutes a constraint (i.e. a 'Y') on freedom (Carter, 2003: 11–12; Barry, 1979: 59).

Following suit, I will take it that interference to freedom does not have to be restricted to an inter-agential relation, deliberate or otherwise, to be regarded as a case of unfreedom. The analyses that follow in Parts II and III of this book will indicate why restriction can be caused by far more than deliberate inter-agential imposition. The prevalence of obstacles to freedom can be, as they are in capitalist society, systemic, ideological and frequently unintentional. It is then a particular version of X, Y and Z that is developed in the chapters that follow. It is as well to point out, though, that as authors frequently do present their theories in either negative or positive terms, I will in the interests of convenience also adopt this language. When I say associational anarchist theory respects negative liberty, this will denote opportunities, which implies freedom *from* obstruction and interference, and when I say it implements aspects from the positive camp, this will denote accomplishments, which is clearly freedom *to do/become*.[3] But at all times this will only be one aspect of a bigger picture. In the associational anarchist conception of freedom, there are not two distinct concepts. There is only one conception of the triadic procedure, even though it emphasises different sets of X, Y and Z variables in two interrelating spheres of social life.

How then does my argument converge with the wider historical anarchist project? Anarchism has a long and rich, if often neglected, history of conceptualising freedom coherently. Carissa Honeywell highlights the novel ways in which anarchist political thought has challenged conventional dichotomies, "notably the assumed tension between the individual and the community and between positive and negative versions of the concept" (2014: 112). In particular, she cites the work of five anarchist thinkers – Herbert Read (1893–1968), Alex Comfort (1920–2000), Paul Goodman (1911–72), Colin Ward (1924–2010) and Murray Bookchin (1921–2006) – all of whom were concerned with individual freedom as the development of the self. In their unique ways, they all pointed to the subjective and social contexts through which free personalities could grow, and they sought to show that the commonly mentioned tensions between unrestrained individuals and their association with self-regulating communities are not insolvable. For these five figures, the anarchist components of freedom are the independent capacities of individuals, private judgement and rational deliberation. These characteristic qualities of developed selfhood, an 'inviolate subjectivity', are the basic building blocks for socially cohesive communities. It is clear then that advanced personalities, enriched through the qualities of uniqueness and solidarity, display subjective as well as social imperatives. Understood as such, it is only this type of individual agent who is fit to participate in the kind of inter-personal relations a robust and cohesive community requires. The important point to add is that heavily centralised and administered societies do little to encourage the creative, sensitive and cognitive attributes of the healthy inner-self, and as such they place limitations upon individual development and the opportunity for self-governance (Honeywell, 2014: 111, 113–15, 117, 121–3, 126–9, 130–3).

Of particular relevance to the content of this book, their views cannot in any sense be placed within a concept of freedom that treats negative and positive dimensions as antipathetic. Honeywell notes that the often-cited claim that anarchist freedom is negative overlooks the values of solidarity and self-development that are integral to its conception. The question has been raised that as self-development is a form of Berlin's positive liberty, and as it needs a regulatory political agency to develop the higher capacities of the self, does this place anarchism in a contradictory position with regard to its commitment to freedom? This would involve a tension between a libertarian perspective and a seemingly authoritarian notion of freedom. If so, then anarchism is in a confused predicament with its stance on individual freedom/self-development and its pledge to extirpate political authority. But as Honeywell explains, the anarchist case for freedom incorporates a lack of restraint on the individual human agent (the non-coercion of negative freedom), as an essential foundation upon which to beget the autonomous and developed self, with its vibrant inner life and capacity for responsible judgement (the self-direction of positive freedom). Twentieth-century anarchism infused consistently both conceptions in a way that avoided an 'authoritarian code'. In doing so, the anarchist incorporation of the developed self into its demanding notion of freedom constitutes a rebuttal of Berlin's thesis (2014: 118–20, 134). By developing these themes through the framework of a reconfigured social anarchist political economy, a mode of organisation inspired by an anarchist reading of Cole's guild socialist writings, the argument that unfolds in the following chapters can be read very much as a continuation of this larger anarchist project.

For the more immediate purpose, in order to establish the other essential premises upon which the associational anarchist conception of freedom stands, it is necessary to very briefly introduce the three dominant traditions of political thought that conceptualise liberty in distinct ways. Then, in the two sections that follow the next one, 'Marx and Freedom' and 'Freedom as Marxian-Autonomy in Outline', I will clarify how Marx's notion of freedom can be incorporated into MacCallum's formula and, further, how the former can also be combined with an idealist (see directly below) interpretation of the latter. Only then can the conception of liberty theorised in this book be presented in its fullness.

Liberty and the three main political traditions

The three traditions are the *republican*, the *liberal* and the *idealist* conceptions of liberty. The republican concept argues that citizens gain freedom when they are active within a political community. Positive liberty in this case claims that real freedom is realised through political activity, through participating in cooperative self-governance. The opposite of republican freedom would be despotism, where subjects have no power to defy the dictates of tyrannical rule. As freedom is linked to self-governance, it can be understood as freedom as *self-determination*. We shall see in Chapters 6 and 9 that the form of anarcho-constitutionalism developed in this book has a specific view on what republican self-rule amounts to in organisational terms. The liberal concept stresses that liberty belongs to individuals, who are violated when subject to arbitrary interference by an outside party. Here liberty is protected in a sphere of life within which independent individuals are sovereign. So in contrast to the republican position, freedom as *political participation*, the liberal view claims that freedom *begins where politics ends*, thus protecting liberalism's cherished private sphere. This is the kind of liberty Berlin endorses. Theorists within the liberal camp disagree about the appropriate limits to state intervention in civil society, but they tend to agree that freedom has a direct relation to both the *scope* and the *extent* of government, rather than its particular *character* or *form* (Miller, 1991: 3–4; Swift, 2001: 64–5).

In the third place, there is what Miller refers to as idealist liberty, which has also been termed the 'divided-self' thesis by other theorists. Here attention is not so much on the external social environment, but on the *internal* factors which bear upon individual action. Agents are said to be free when they are autonomous, that is, when they act in accord with their authentic desires and rational beliefs, those of the *higher-selves*. On this account, positive liberty seeks *self-realisation*, articulated as the actualisation of an array of potentialities. The idea here is that certain actions correlate with people's true desires or to a sought-after state of being. Freedom so understood requires the transcendence of momentarily experienced weaknesses, illicit desires and passions, uncontrolled impulses and irrational attitudes, those that correlate with their *lower-selves*. In sum, there is a hypothesised 'higher', 'rational', 'moral', 'true' and 'transcendental' self that is contrasted with a 'lower', 'compulsive', 'irrational' and 'base' self:

The higher-self is the rational, reflecting self, the self that is capable of moral action and of taking responsibility for what one does. This is the 'true' self, since it is what marks us off from other animals. The lower self, on the other hand, is the self of the passions, of unreflecting desires and irrational impulses. (Carter, 2003: 6)

This conception of liberty implies a person may be doing something s/he actually wants (momentarily), but despite having access to the full range of negative freedoms, it may not equate with self-rule (one's longer-term life goal). This is because they are in such cases acting from particular intractable impulses and desires, or what J.S. Mill termed subjection to 'inveterate habits'. So inasmuch as they are slaves to their passions, to borrow Rousseau's striking metaphor, they cannot be considered autonomous (Miller, 1991: 3–5; Swift, 2001: 59–60, 64–5; Smith, 1984: 190).

Although the republican and the idealist positions have frequently been associated with positive liberty, and the liberal perspective with negative liberty, the associational anarchist triadic conception has in certain senses something in common with all three; yet in keeping within the wider social anarchist perspective, it interprets them in specific terms. In particular, a measure of negative freedom is defended within a conceptual framework that moves beyond the bounds of liberal thought, where it exists alongside, and in harmony with, certain positive ideals. MacCallum stresses that as there is such a huge range of potential interpretations of all three variables in the triadic relation, it is crucial that the different views on the range of all three are compartmentalised (1991: 115, 121). It is therefore important to outline the conception of freedom defended in this book in some detail. For this to be possible, it is first necessary to explain what Marx took freedom to be.

Marx and freedom

Only when real, individual man resumes the abstract citizen into himself and as an individual man has become a *species-being* in his empirical life, his individual work and his individual relationship, only when man has recognised and organised his *forces propres* as *social forces* so that social force is no longer separated from him in the form of *political* force, only then will human emancipation be completed. (Marx, 1975: 234, original emphasis)

The Marxist conception of science attempts to penetrate beneath the shield of idealised superficial appearance in order to reveal the concealed essence of things. This includes the entire web of social relations that constitute the genuine foundation of society, rather than the outward manifestations that are merely its external facade. In *Capital* Vol. III, Marx states that 'vulgar' political economy stays at the surface level of economic relations. "But", he immediately adds, "all science would be superfluous if the outward appearance and the essence of things directly coincide" (1977: 494). Starting with the material activity of real individuals, he states what individuals are "coincides with their production, both with *what* they produce and with *how* they produce. The nature of individuals thus depends on the material conditions determining their production" (1977: 161). Due to the increasing development of the forces of production, boundaries placed upon humanity by the natural world are continuously negotiated to the extent that a new era of 'real' freedom will eventually dawn (1977: 509). A key objective is, along with a minimisation of the confines imposed by *natural* conditions, to secure two profound changes in human *social* existence. The first is a radical transformation of labour, which moves beyond the deformation of alienation and into a collective self-expression in the quintessentially human activity of work, 'conscious life-activity' or 'humanising activity' as Marx calls it. Only through meaningful and fulfilling work can people express their social natures. The second is the transcendence of class divides and the final end of minority rule (Marx, 1977: 171–2, 368, 494, 496–7; Heilbroner, 1980: 49, 74, 148–50; Fetscher, 1973: 444–5, 446–7, 450–1).

Put generally, freedom is subjectivity overcoming objectivity, the liberation of people from the domination of things. This progression develops in the realm of physical necessity as well as, in the modern era, reified social relations.[4] There are, then, two aspects of freedom. Firstly, there is the people–nature relation; humans achieve more power over nature via the development of the forces of production. Secondly, there is the individual–society relation; to experience freedom people must consciously shape their social conditions in order to gain liberation from reified social forces. It is here that humanity moves beyond the unfreedom of alienated labour and class oppression. In both cases, freedom is seen as an achievement of reason over external forces. In the first instance, it is the collective subject over a natural objectivity, the physical world, and in the second it is an individual subject over an artificial objectivity, the social world (Marx, 1977: 160, 166–7, 180–1; Walicki, 1984: 217, 220; Heilbroner, 1980: 80–1).

With regards to the latter, Marx's rejection of the economic freedom celebrated in bourgeois society – the right of people to enter 'freely' into contractual relations and to accumulate private property and personal wealth – is based upon a critique of the private ownership of productive resources and the wage–labour relation. For Marx, these social arrangements are alienating, exploitative and mystifying at the systemic level. In *Capital* Vol. I, he stresses that as non-owners of the means of production, the only commodity workers own is their labour-power. Yet they are said by proponents of capitalism to stand in the marketplace opposite the owners of capital, one

a seller, the other a buyer, with the freedom to enter into contractual relations of their own choosing.[5] Marx swiftly rejects this claim:

> The bargain concluded, it is discovered that he was no 'free agent', that the
> time for which he is free to sell his labour-power is the time for which he is
> forced to sell it, that in fact the vampire will not lose its hold on him 'so long
> as there is a muscle, a nerve, a drop of blood to be exploited'. (1977: 475)

He also points out that capitalists, even though they may be spared the
drudgery of alienation, are themselves no freer than the workers. Capitalism
is driven not just by profit, but by the maximisation of profit. Ruthless competition establishes "the inherent laws of capitalist production, in the shape
of external coercive laws having power over every individual capitalist"
(Marx, 1977: 475).[6] Elsewhere, when discussing alienation in the productive process, he reiterates that "the creation of surplus value ... is the determining, supreme, and dominant aim of the capitalist, the complete motive
and content of his actions ... which demonstrates that the capitalist is in the
same slavish relation to capital as the worker" (1977: 509). So for Marx,
there are no free agents in capitalist society.

Along with the critique of alienated labour developed in his early work,
one of the main themes in his mature writings is class exploitation, which
due to the compulsion of competitive accumulation and the subsequent
antagonisms both within and between classes, is endemic to the system.
Drawing from his key distinction between labour and labour-power, he
identifies a division within the working day, which is termed *necessary* and
surplus labour time. During part of their time at work, workers produce
the value of their labour-power, what Marx calls their 'means of subsistence'. Workers do not directly produce all the goods they need in order to
survive. Rather, they produce a given commodity which is equal in value to
those goods. It is this portion of the working day that he terms 'necessary
labour time'. Yet for the remainder of the day, workers continue to expand
labour-power, but as it is no longer necessary labour, they create no value
for themselves; hence the expression 'surplus labour time'. The owners of
the means of production, the capitalist class, are in a position to appropriate
the surplus produced by surplus labour, which in effect is rendered unpaid
labour. Due to contractual agreements this proportion of the working day
Marx calls forced labour, and the rate of surplus value correlates exactly
with the exploitation of labour-power by capital (1977: 473–4). In sum, as
formal freedom in bourgeois society masks a deeper structural unfreedom,
there is no real freedom in capitalist society.

Marx notes though that capitalism has played a hugely significant role in
accelerating the unfolding of history. In asserting unparalleled control over

nature, it has facilitated great progress (1977: 225). But, he adds, along with the maximum development of the forces of production, it has also engendered the maximum degree of alienated labour. As labour breaks down into increasingly smaller partial activities, collective labour advances, but so does the monotonous work of the individual worker, who is reduced to a "crippled monstrosity" (1977: 477). Here divided labour produces impersonal products that appear to exist independently in an externalised market, and come to subjugate the workers who produced them. This involves a reification of social relations, as captured in the Marxian term 'commodity fetishism', which results in a distortion of people's personalities.[7] So as the concentrated and alienated power of capital proliferates, then conversely the lives of individual workers become increasingly poorer (Marx, 1977: 223–4, 515–16; Walicki, 1984: 221–2, 217). The causes of this are not, due to the mystifying and concealing effect of fetishism, directly grasped. So for Marx, bourgeois society cannot be equated with real freedom. Let us now see how this critique can be incorporated into a conception of freedom that has the combined premise of MacCallum's triadic formula with a Marxian reading of idealist liberty.

Freedom as Marxian-autonomy in outline

On the Marxian doctrine, the triadic relation asserts that speaking at a generalised level of abstraction, wage-labourers ('X'), are constrained by the capitalist mode of production ('Y') to self-emancipate through revolutionary change ('Z'). Firstly, freedom *from* signals the move beyond the market imperatives of capitalist society. Marxist-socialism seeks to emancipate people from the dire material conditions that condemn wage-labourers to a dehumanised and impoverished life, and it unshackles them from their subjection to mystified social relations and entities. Secondly, in respect of freedom *to do/become*, capitalism's impersonal economy is replaced with rational planning. A complete transformation of economic relations will intentionally install humanised labour universally, and it will provide the opportunity for democratic participation by teams of associated producers. The goal is collective self-actualisation, seen as a self-realised human essence. Freedom is equated with the unobstructed development of the superior capacities inherent within each person, the creative faculties of their species-being. Only self-realisation conceived in these terms can, his argument infers, constitute real freedom. How then does this particular account of the triadic relation express itself in idealist terms?

An idealist conception of freedom, when placed within the triadic approach, proposes that the subject of freedom, agency as the autonomous and rational higher-self ('X'), is free from ignorance, injudicious desires and the uncontrolled impulses of the lower-self ('Y'), to fulfil one's chosen life goals ('Z'). For our purposes, this translates as: workers' higher-selves ('X') are restricted by their lower-selves ('Y') to self-actualise in post-capitalist society ('Z'). This is because the social relations of production in a market forces economy lead individuals to misunderstand their genuine interests. They are induced to identify with the commodities they consume. The Marxist critique identifies the lower-self with pernicious factors like alienated labour and reified social relations. It is the level of confusion, illusion, a distorted perspective and a lack of awareness of one's potential. Conversely, the higher-self includes the desire to work in creative and fulfilling conditions and to participate meaningfully in productive decision-making. At this advanced level, collective self-development is not attained by means of an aggregate avaricious individualism, but through ubiquitous forms of dignified labour (Marx, 1977: 53–4). This particular conception suggests that the lower-self has not moved beyond glorified outward appearance. As the internal workings of the capitalist economy are either inconspicuous or misinterpreted, the lower-self is unable to perceive the real nature of one's social surroundings. By way of contrast, the self-mastery and rational self-direction of the higher-self are able to cut through ideological blind spots, hence initiating the path to self-actualisation. This positive approach may, I propose, be referred to as the 'Marxist-humanist freedom as autonomy conception of liberty', or in the interests of convenience, simply *freedom as Marxian-autonomy*. The precise ways in which this concise outline is located within and then expanded through associational anarchism's specific interpretation of the X, Y, Z relation can only be explained in full towards the end of this chapter. In order to arrive at this point, an exposition of the required mode of organisation will follow shortly. Let us first see what this does not involve.

Liberty beyond liberalism and statism

This section will first outline Marx's critique that the abstract individualism of liberalism cannot, in its strict *laissez-faire* sense, provide an adequate account of the communal relations through which people gain their self-understandings. I will agree that as bourgeois society socially constitutes individuals chiefly through contractual arrangements, a solution cannot be sought within the framework of the modern state. Yet of equal significance, state socialist solutions to the liberal contradiction are also rejected. The liberal and statist paths are both well worn, but they remain equally problematic.

Marx rejected the liberal reverence of economic and political freedoms because he thought they were based upon a false premise, one that recognises chiefly separate and asocial individuals, interlinked only through contractual obligations which regulate their social relations. As the Marxist argument stresses the social nature of human beings, it is highly critical of the atomised individual popularised in liberal-capitalist theory. "Production by isolated individuals outside society ... is as great an absurdity as the idea of the development of language without individuals living together and talking to one other" (Marx, 1977: 346). In the sixth of his 'Theses on Feuerbach', he states that individuals cannot be treated as abstract and detached entities. As they must mutually interact in the course of their material lives, it is more accurate to refer to the human essence as an "ensemble of the social relations" (1977: 157). In bourgeois society, this sociability is formed in a peculiar way, which is perhaps best illustrated through the distinction drawn in his early writings between political (the granting of rights and liberties) and human (full) emancipation.

It is in his seminal essay *On the Jewish Question* (1844) that Marx develops an important critique of the modern divide between the state and civil society. He argues that the granting of equal political rights to religious minorities, or indeed to anyone, will be an incomplete form of emancipation. As he puts it, "*[p]olitical* emancipation from religion is not complete and consistent emancipation from religion, because political emancipation is not the complete and consistent form of *human* emancipation" (Marx, 1975: 218, original emphasis). This is because political emancipation does not in any sense undermine the oppressive conditions that encourage and nurture religious beliefs in all their forms. As such, a discussion about real freedom must concentrate on the dire material surroundings that compel people to take refuge in a metaphysical sedative. It then becomes evident that in the modern state, people experience a double life. In the political community, they act as communal beings, whereas in civil society they are private and egoistic individuals (Marx, 1975: 220–2, 226; McLellan, 1977: 39).

Marx's point is that as individuals in civil society are living disjointed and independent lives, the bond of social unity must be formed in abstraction. Consequently, a unified general interest, ostensibly the state, will be artificial because it can only be contrived by ignoring all the private interests in a fragmented civil society. This ensures that economic divisions are rendered insignificant, and, consequently, the oppressive conditions people experience in their material lives remain firmly intact. Marx's chief concern is that if the state can appear neutral with regard to religion, it can do the same with other particular interests, not least those of capital. But in doing so, it preserves a specific kind of civil society. Along with religion, other factors like exploitation, alienation, competition, domination and subordination are also left unchanged. The result is that the modern state emancipates people in a perplexing way. It asserts that the actual differences between people (the 'non-political' distinctions like wealth, religion, race, etc.) will not block their standing as citizens. Political emancipation therefore does not in any way alter the socio-economic conditions in which people live; it emancipates people *just as they are*. This means that the freedom of the individual is limited to the freedom of detached and isolated individuals, which ensures that underneath the distant state, unsociability and estrangement are left untouched in a civil society riddled with economic inequalities and class oppression. The bizarre outcome is that a *superficial* equality in the legal and political spheres is safeguarded in order that the cause of *real* inequality, private ownership in productive property, can be recognised as basic and absolute. For Marx, emancipatory politics can only advance by developing one's communal, or 'species' essence, in civil society that has at present been usurped by the state (Marx,1975: 218, 220–2, 226, 233–4, 243; Colletti, 1975: 34–6; Schecter, 2000: 63, 128–9; Arthur, 1970: 10–11).[8] It is not so much that bourgeois society overlooks human sociability then, it is more that it accounts for it in very limited terms. Following the young Marx, I will regard the abstract and radically independent individual portrayed in classical and neo-liberal theory as contrary to human nature.[9]

It is important though to offer a word of caution with regard to the centralist and statist themes in certain sections of Marx's writings. He deliberately refrains from providing any elaborate insights into the organisational detail of post-capitalist society. In order to disassociate from the utopian socialists, he makes it clear his intention is to analyse existing facts, and not to "write recipes for cook-shops of the future" (1959: 17). But to the extent that a rough picture can be framed from his scattered comments, Marxist-humanism visualises a society of cooperative production with socialised assets. So an egalitarian ownership of productive resources, providing people with access to their means of subsistence, and the abolishment of the wage-labour relation are indispensable to the move beyond class domination. This much is clear enough. Other than this, Marx is vague on the institutional contours of the fully emancipated society. But when he does address the transformative question in *The Communist Manifesto* of 1848, he explicitly endorses a major role for a revolutionary state. In order to 'win the battle of democracy', the proletariat must become the ruling class. "The proletariat will use its political supremacy to wrest, by degrees, all capital from the bourgeoisie, to centralise all instruments of production in the hands of the State" (Marx, 1977: 237). It is true he hoped this would only be a temporary condition, an intermediate phase between capitalism and real communism. It is also at odds with both the libertarian spirit of his early writings, where the state is portrayed as an aspect of alienation (Karatani, 2005: 169, 181), and his later comments on the Paris Commune (March to May, 1871), which reveal a distinctively non-authoritarian view of proletariat rule (Carter, 1971: 76).[10] But still, his call for a 'common plan' is unrelenting in its statism:

> Centralisation of credit in the hands of the State, by means of a national bank with State capital and an exclusive monopoly ... Centralisation of the means of communication and transport in the hands of the State ... Extension of factories and instruments of production owned by the State. (Marx, 1977: 237)

I will argue in Chapter 2 that this is an inappropriate practical strategy for an otherwise laudable cause. From the outset, socialism rightly opposed the private appropriation of the few, and it loathed the kind of "repugnant drudgery" that produces items which serve only the "dull vanity of the rich", a "monstrous system" as Kropotkin puts it (n.d.: 1, 10, 14, 19, 104). The problem is though that the centralised state of command socialism sought to solve productive and redistributive problems in an exorbitantly authoritarian way, and in the process was prepared to suppress individual liberty. By turning to a non-statist socialisation of the means of production, this book offers a very different route to post-capitalist society.

In sum, whilst the centralist and statist themes in sections of Marx's oeuvre are excessively authoritarian, his probing critique of classical political economy remains a powerful and accurate indictment of liberal theory. As it developed throughout the modern era, liberalism came to assume the inevitability of capitalist institutions.[11] In short, liberal societies typically maintain the right to own, exchange and dispose of private property within a market forces economy. Financial inequalities are not just accepted as unavoidable; they are valued because they purportedly incentivise. Yet in order for liberalism to be true to its word that there is an egalitarian access to a set of key liberties, it will have to move beyond the private property relations that underpin the capitalist mode of production. This is because in bourgeois regimes a dichotomy has always existed between people's personal economic affairs and their lives in the public sphere. Liberalism, in both the 'Lockeian universal rights' and the 'Millian utility-developmental' traditions, may have solid arguments against excessive state intervention, but it has hitherto failed to resolve the problems that stem from economic inequalities and the unequal distribution of power embodied in the private ownership of productive assets. In particular, the abstract equality of liberal theory shields the enormous underlining inequalities in wealth, which in turn guarantee vast inequalities in abilities and opportunities that render liberalism's surface equality effectively meaningless. As a corollary, because liberalism cannot abandon its fierce commitment to possessive individualism, it restricts how freedom can be conceptualised. These are very good reasons for eradicating the mystifying social relations of capitalism. The question now becomes what to replace liberalism's reductive ontology with.

Agency

In associational anarchism, the ascent into shared self-mastery does not take place through organisations that claim to represent associates in their entirety. In terms of its organisational contours, the orthodox political representation of the individual is rejected. This point is pivotal; the generic person has been deconstructed and replaced with functionally demarcated bodies which account only for distinct interests inherent in all people. So the position freedom as Marxian-autonomy starts from is that *agency ('X' on MacCallum's triadic formula) is the collective higher-self expressed in interrelated yet separate spheres.* The general idea is that self-realisation will take place through the imperatives people encounter in their capacities as both producers and consumers. Put succinctly, my argument equates freedom with a personality developed through enriching activities within the workplace, and, in complimentary terms, through reflective and benevolent acts of consumption. Only when self-realisation is achieved in both domains can agents be truly free. Rational self-direction has, then, a double momentum. Whilst the more authentic desires of the higher-self belong to autonomous and sensitised individuals, the transcendental movement occurs through differentiated interests arranged democratically in their respective formations. This, I will contend, is the appropriate path to what the young Marx referred to as human emancipation. The following two sections will take a closer look at what this entails.

Anarchist democracy

Generally speaking, anarchism attempts to radically transform hierarchic institutions and the inequality and domination they perpetuate. As a stateless project, it rejects entirely any notion that the concentrated authority centralised into the institutions of the modern state is an essential prerequisite for a stable social order.[12] Anarchists of all persuasions share a belief that the key values of anti-authoritarianism, non-exploitative production, individual autonomy, solidarity, equal distribution, mutual aid, diversity and self-management can deliver laudable goals like justice and freedom. Anarchism is far from anti-organisational (Raekstad, 2016: 408); neither is it antithetical to rules and institutions (Prichard, 2019: 71), but it is opposed to organisations that assume centralised and unaccountable forms. Yet as one would expect, within anarchist circles there is not a single prescription all adherently conform to. At either end of the continuum are the individualist and social positions, which, as Chapter 2 will show, are often portrayed in sharply conflicting terms (Shantz & Williams, 2013: 101, 125; Raekstad, 2016: 2, 4; Levy & Adams, 2019: 1, 18; Firth, 2019: 493). For Laurence Davis though, the individual and communal strands, which exist in 'dynamic and creative tension', are a key source of strength rather than a sign of incoherence. Of great significance to the argument of this book, he addresses the impact of 'communal individuality' upon anarchism's contested relation to democracy. For some, all democracies, including non-statist forms, entail decisions that bind communities and are coercively enforceable. If so, concerted action in an anarchist community denotes collective expressions of freedom, rather than practices of direct democracy. In contrast, other authors have pointed to the libertarian and egalitarian themes that would mark any anarchist democracy, in which case, anarchism is very much a radical form of participatory democracy without the state (Davis, 2019: 47–8, 56–9).

So although anarchy and democracy invoke common characteristics, especially with regard to inclusive forms of participation in workplace and local community decision-making, the relationship between them remains ambivalent. As the following chapters unfold, it will become apparent the ways in which the genre of anarchism developed in this book incorporates, in all the main spheres of social life, particular modes of direct democracy. Chapter 2 will explain in some detail the social (class struggle) component of the anarchist doctrine, as this is where associational anarchism is most at home. Here, and elsewhere, close attention is paid to the meaning of anarchist democracy, as well as its appropriate ideal. For now, suffice to affirm that as both consensus decision-making and 'agent-neutral' majority rule voting,[13] together with an appropriate principle of representation,[14] all have central roles, the political economy of associational anarchism is democratic to its core, or should I say to its plural cores. It is here that we may turn to Cole. In his guild socialist writings, he not only presents a left-libertarian critique of capitalist society, but he also indicates how the necessary corrective would operate in plural-democratic terms. The following two chapters will explain how the defining characteristics of associational anarchism effectively fill out the demands of the social anarchists, and in a framework that transforms Cole's quasi-anarchism into the genuine article.[15] With this in mind, having now established the triadic nature of freedom as Marxian-autonomy, and that the structural requirements for its attainment will be anarcho-democratic in form, its organisational configuration can now be sketched.

Associational anarchism

One of Cole's key claims is that in order for democracy to be liberal in the pluralist sense, it will have to break with the property relations that underpin capitalist society whilst retaining the liberal emphasis on freedom of speech, expression, thought, assembly, information and representation. This is because the new society will have to evolve beyond both a purely negative understanding of liberty, like the one Berlin defends, and the kind of egoistic-individualism that fuels, and worse venerates, cut-throat competition in a pitiless dog-eat-dog capitalist marketplace. Building upon this premise, Cole pictures a system of self-management within which government functions are devolved into self-regulating bodies. The private sphere is transformed into a domain of cooperation and collective governance. Although the community would own productive property, networks of federated units would possess it collectively. Through a reconstructed political body and a thorough re-politicisation of the institutions in the civil sphere, this plural approach transforms the prevailing divide between the public and private spheres. Productive and consumptive organisations are constructed into the structures of the local, regional and national communes through mechanisms of representation and consultation. Administrative machinery is, simultaneously, distributed to these functionally demarcated spheres of accountably held authority.

Cole's deconstruction of the generic citizen may strike the reader as odd. As such, it will be informative to elaborate on the need for a system of dual representation with regard to production and consumption. Following John Clark, I too believe William Morris was right to insist that the good society will encourage the free expression of all creative capacities. Fulfilling productive activity should be treated as the highest good in itself, and not just as a means to other ends. For this reason, the idea that there must be beauty and joy in the kind of labour processes indispensable to a vibrant community is, along with inclusive forms of productive decision-making, central to the higher-self conceptualised in freedom as Marxian-autonomy. Yet Clark adds that "the dominant system has revolutionized itself as it has moved from the productionist to the consumptionist stage of capitalist society" (2013: 139). The consumptionist dimension has a particular image of what a good life is. Health, beauty, sex and fun are available to everyone; all people have to do is consume the right commodities. The problem is, though, that modern consumers frequently struggle to keep their enjoyment levels on an even footing with the consumptive imperative. This is what Clark is referring to when he states that "[t]he most humiliating moral flaw in late capitalism is a failure to inhabit the imaginary consumptionist utopia" (2013: 139, see also 132, 138–9).

It is for reasons such as these that a return to Cole is pivotal. One of his most original ideas was to show how debates in political economy could steer a path beyond the plan (socialist)–market (liberal) straitjacket by indicating how consumer interests can be aggregated in consumer councils at the individual, household, municipal and regional level. His proposal indicates how the liberal emphasis on political equalities can be institutionalised in relations between producers and consumers so that supply and demand ratios can be coordinated without relying on brute market dictates or the concentrated power of state planners. In these senses, his model undermines capitalist social relations by decoupling consumer choice from individual income and by making consumer representation a right of citizenship rather than a prerogative of private wealth. The result is that associated debates are directed beyond the plan-market impasse. This novel idea must, in my opinion, now assume a more central role in contemporary social anarchist literature.[16] Self-management in the workplace and the hierarchy beyond it are plainly contradictory. This calls for equality of access to consumption goods. Following Cole, in associational anarchism this is realised through continuous dialogue between organised production, the guild cooperatives, and organised consumption, the consumer councils. Here the 'invisible hand' of the market is replaced by the 'visible hand' of the consumer councils. A short account of their specific roles is provided at the end of section three of Chapter 3 after the constitution of associational anarchism has been laid out in its entirety; they are then discussed in much more detail in sections two and three of Chapter 7. For now, it is enough to say that the underlying intention is to engender a new left-libertarian consumer consciousness. As we shall see, in moving beyond the 'imaginary consumptionist utopia' of contemporary capitalism, acts of consumption take on a whole new meaning.

Accordingly, associational anarchism preserves much of Cole's libertarian structures. It is worth noting though that significant changes have also been made. I will contend that he concedes too much power to the commune system. In associational anarchism, decision-making is carried out mostly at the local level, and where regional federalism is needed, jointly by the higher-level committees in the guilds and consumer councils. There is still an arbitrating role for the communes, but as Chapter 3 explains, it is reduced to the absolute minimum. At this point, the role of a guild market system is explained; this chapter also provides a full account of the new organisational forms through which investment strategies have been democratised. Then in section one of Chapter 5, self-legislation in what we may think of as guild jurisprudence is outlined and discussed; new agencies in the form of the justice councils have also been introduced in the second section of this chapter. These supplementary configurations move in an anarchist direction, especially with regard to the decentralisation of economic and political decision-making, the establishment of local structures of self-governance and, above all, the universalisation of self-actualising forms of labour. These then are the essential elements of associational anarchism's mode of organisation. Now that they have been traced in these fairly concise terms, freedom as Marxian-autonomy can now be defined in its totality.

Freedom as Marxian-autonomy in full

Firstly, there is a significant point of organisational detail that has not yet been touched upon. Although Marx does not explain in any detail what the organisational bases of the humanly emancipated society would consist of, in *Capital* Vol. III he does draw an important distinction between the 'realm of necessity' and the 'true realm of freedom'. The former realm is inescapable labour, where freedom equates with the transcendence of class domination and alienation. In people's working lives this is an end in itself, yet in another sense, it serves as the main and indispensable condition of authentic freedom in the latter realm. So in the realm of necessity, there are instrumental as well as intrinsic values. The realm of freedom begins where material production breaks off, now energies can be channelled into pursuits that are, in a manner of speaking, ends on their own terms. But freedom in the realm of necessity, consisting of producers associated within conditions most worthy of their creative nature, is the basic prerequisite for freedom to be experienced in the realm of freedom (Marx, 1977: 496–7; Walicki, 1984: 223–5). Marx's decoupling of the realms of necessity and freedom informs associational anarchism's mode of organisation.

Generally speaking, anarchists have usually held that a person has freedom only in affiliation with others, and they have developed innovative and elaborate institutional constructs to articulate their communities. Alex Prichard points out that contemporary anarchist expressions of individual and collective freedom imply three main types of freedom. Along with the negative and positive forms, there are substantive claims about appropriate organisations; the latter may be referred to as 'freedom in', which suggests that whilst autonomy and empowerment are important, they must be addressed in relation to constitutional demands (Prichard, 2019: 72–3). The chapters that follow can, in much the same way they develop the twentieth-century anarchist conception of advanced selfhood, be read as one attempt to continue this project. Two interrelated conceptions of liberty are framed, one for the realm of necessity and one for the realm of freedom, both of which contain elements of freedom *from* and freedom *to do/become*. The realm of necessity upholds a significant measure of non-restriction compatible with the material requirements of a fully democratised economy. The realm of freedom goes further, it secures a maximum degree of non-restriction corresponding to the minimum claims of the numerous and heterogeneous 'ends in themselves'. Both realms are, in the way in which they incorporate both opportunities and accomplishments, an interconnecting version of MacCallum's triadic formula. To be more precise, their organisational forms effectively fill out in finer detail the outline account of freedom as Marxian-autonomy provided above. X is now the functionally demarcated rational higher-self, Y is freedom from both political and economic class domination, the causes of which are imperceptible to the lower-self, and Z is the self-actualisation of economic agents in both their productive and consumptive capacities. The realm of necessity is composed of:

a) an egalitarian access to, and equal democratic control over, the means of production.
b) an institutionalisation of self-actualising forms of cooperative labour.
c) a product-mix that is determined by the consumer councils.
d) a maximal degree of non-interference compatible with (a), (b) and (c).

The realm of freedom is a domain comprised of:

a) a maximal degree of non-interference.
b) a content-neutrality with regard to anarchist-sensitive desire-independent aims.
c) functionally demarcated civic organisations that will (a) in terms of plurality and diversity provide a rich cultural fabric, and (b) sustain social spaces through which freely chosen ends may be pursued.

Taken together, these seven features constitute the associational anarchist conception of liberty in its entirety, which now completes the exposition of freedom as Marxian-autonomy.[17] As this book is chiefly concerned with developing a social anarchist political economy, the following discussions are, with the exception of section two of Chapter 5 and the fairly brief content of Chapter 11, very much focused on the realm of necessity. On a preliminary note though, it is worth pointing out that the pursuit of the collective higher-self occurs only in the realm of necessity. Once citizens have self-actualised as fully developed beings in their economic lives, their activities in the realm of freedom occur within the widest possible scale of unpreventedness. This latter realm is non-discriminatory. No distinction is drawn between the internal rankings of desires, and as such they can be regarded as aim- and content-independent. Here there is a more substantial role for negative freedoms, and, moreover, as they are premised upon an egalitarian and non-exploiting realm of necessity, they will be of lesser unequal value to all individuals. But due to word restrictions, little more can be said about life in the realm of freedom here; I include these cursory remarks only to complete this outline sketch.

Conclusion

This chapter has outlined the institutional contours that emerge from associational anarchism's specific Marxist-anarchist conceptual amalgamation. I am of course not the first to suggest the value of coalescing the latter two schools of anti-capitalist thought. But to the best of my knowledge, it has not been attempted through a revitalised and 'anarchised' guild socialism, configured with a Marxist-humanist understanding of the idealist higher-self located within the triadic formula. As a full and progressive conception of liberty cannot be separated from the conditions of its effective exercise, it is not so much that freedom as Marxian-autonomy will be absorbed into whatever structures happen to 'fit'. It is more accurate to say that associational anarchist structures are a key aspect of what the concept actually is. So this new conception of freedom has not been initially framed in isolation from any socio-economic formation, with consideration given at a later stage to the material conditions most suited to its attainment. Rather, as the associational anarchist higher-self has been theorised with its embodiment in the appropriate sets of social relations very much in mind, the latter is an integral part of the overall conception. The following two chapters will annotate more meticulously what this involves in organisational terms.

Notes

1 See for example Miller (1991: 10) and Clark (2013: 54–5).
2 This position is introduced in more depth in the following section.
3 The terms 'opportunities' and 'accomplishments' are taken from Michael Kramer (2003: 2). In his account of the difference between classical and modern liberalism, Benjamin Franks also explains the negative (rejection of coercion)–positive (achieve life goals) distinction neatly (2019: 556–7).
4 In terms of individuality, reification involves representing a person as a material entity dispossessed of personal qualities, the 'thingification' of the subject; this exists alongside the personification of inanimate objects. The fetishism of commodities is a specific instance of reification.
5 In *Capital* Vol. III, Marx stresses that the workers and the capitalists stand face to face as sellers of different commodities. Here he draws out the alienating effect of "the specifically bipolar nature of the commodities that they sell each other" (1977: 508).

6 Marx had made this point earlier in the preface to *Capital* Vol. I, where he refers to individual capitalists as, along with everyone else, "personifications of economic categories". "My standpoint ... can less than any other make the individual responsible for relations whose creature he socially remains, however much he may subjectively raise himself above them" (Marx, 1977: 417).

7 For a detailed explanation of Marx's critique of commodity fetishism, see Wyatt (2011: chapter 1).

8 Bakunin also critiqued liberalism for portraying individuals as anterior to society, who are seen to exist "apart from and outside society". Real individual freedom, he countered, can only exist within society, through networks of social interdependent relations that embody equality and solidarity (1973: 235–6, 238).

9 For the view that liberals do not overlook the significance of the social matrix, see Adam Swift (2001: 149–52).

10 Others have also pointed out the ambiguity in Marx's works around a centrally planned economy, on the one hand, and a decentralised federation of largely autonomous communes, on the other hand. In different texts, Marx supports both (Schecter, 1994: 4, 8–9).

11 For an insightful account on the antithetical relationship between classical liberalism and capitalism, see Noam Chomsky (2013: 36–8).

12 Chapter 2 will explain why the understanding of anarchism as merely anti-statism is incomplete. As Nathan Jun observes, numerous writers have pointed out that such a basic definition establishes neither anarchism's key features, nor how it differs from other doctrines. That said, the active struggle to bring down the modern state remains as central to anarchism as it has always been (2019: 28–9).

13 This is unlikely to impress anti-organisational anarchists. But as Paul Raekstad notes, "the vast majority of past and present anarchist organizations ... have operated by federalist systems involving majority voting and delegation" (2016: 409). Chapters 5 and 6 provide expositions on the specific ways in which associational anarchism organises majority rule voting and how networks of interlinking federations are framed.

14 Rhiannon Firth points out that anarchism has traditionally rejected the idea of political representation, that a person or body can represent another, as the former gain privileged access to various resources, which invokes alienation from decision-making and choice (2019: 498). But providing a more suitable representative ethic is adopted, and in a stateless direction, these problems can, although not easily, be mitigated.

15 That Cole's guild socialist writings have an affinity with social anarchism has been noted in anarchist literature. For example, Chomsky claims that a real democratic social order must be "based on workers' control, free association, and federal organisation, in the general style of a range of thought that includes, along with many anarchists, G.D.H. Cole's guild socialism" (2005: 195).

16 A good example of which comes from Michael W. Howard, who highlights the problem of isolated acts of consumption, which results in ignorance of the

choices of others. "This could be remedied by planning but also by creating institutions that provide information about the producers and other consumers and by strengthening informal networks based on trust that are mediated by neither market nor state" (2000: 107). The congruence with Cole's proposal that such informal networks may take the form of consumer councils will be evident.

17 For a helpful account of the anarchist attempts to develop negative or positive liberty, and the resulting rift between 'philosophical' and 'social' anarchism, see Benjamin Franks (2019: 556–9).

2

Social anarchism: classical to contemporary

There is no horror, no cruelty, sacrilege, or perjury, no imposture, no infa-
mous transaction, no cynical robbery, no bold plunder or shabby betrayal
that has not been or is not daily being perpetrated by the representatives of
the states, under no other pretext than those elastic words, so convenient and
yet so terrible: *'for reasons of state'*. (Bakunin, 1973: 134, original emphasis)

There are two sections to this chapter. Section one, 'Class struggle anarchism: a redesigned foundation', begins by introducing the key ideals and
principles central to social anarchist discourse. It then suggests there are
certain ideas in Cole's guild socialist writings that, suitably revised, offer
a sound base upon which to build a new model of social anarchism. The
task in section two, 'An anarchist-Marxist dialogue: separating Marxian
economics from Marxian politics', is to clarify the new ways in which this
book develops the classical anarchist project. In order to provide historical
context, an account of the Bakuninist and Kropotkinist currents running
through anarchism's social constituent is laid out. Bakunin and Kropotkin
received Marx's argument that the relations within and between social
classes are the foundational inequalities through which capitalism systematically reproduces itself sympathetically, yet at the same time they defined
class more extensively, and they fiercely rejected his prescribed role for a
communist revolutionary state. Here I put forward a rationale for rejecting
state communism whilst retaining Marx's penetrating critique of classical
political economy.

Class struggle anarchism: a redesigned foundation

There are three sub-sections to this first section of the chapter. The first,
'The essential qualities of anarchism', outlines succinctly anarchism's core
beliefs and values. The second, 'Rejections of capitalism', covers a dispute
that addresses anarchism's deeply felt hostility to capitalism. Whilst all contending parties agree that anarchism is, in principle, opposed to capitalism,

the disagreement is whether it should, simultaneously, be seen as something other than a stateless form of socialism. The third sub-section, 'Cole, anarchism and anti-capitalism', will contest that his guild socialist writings convey certain ideals that, in meeting the claims of both accounts, provide a solid starting point upon which to construct a new social anarchist mode of organisation.[1] From here I will go on to argue that this scheme, associational anarchism, can be understood very much as the practical expression of the ideas and values developed by the representative thinkers of classical anarchism, which is to say that the prominent feature of this theoretical continuum, the multiple practices of direct democracy, will be defended purely in class struggle terms.

The essential qualities of anarchism

Although it is frequently claimed that anarchist thought incorporates a diversity of views, there are certain fundamental premises that all versions share. The doctrine of anarchism is commonly portrayed as being in opposition to the state, which is held to restrict individual freedom. The word 'anarchy' literally means no rulers ('an' = without, 'archy' = ruler), which implies a resolute rejection of oppressive authority and domination. By definition, its core principle is a staunch hostility towards administration by all forms of centralisation, whether through state institutions or the private capitalist enterprise. Anarchists typically oppose 'giantism', a term which refers to large organisations whose internal structures enable elites to dominate, and within which popular self-determination is crushed. Megaorganisations are rigidly bureaucratic, and anarchism is intensely opposed to fixed hierarchical relationships. Within these structures power concentrates at the higher echelons of their edifices, where it quickly assumes unaccountable forms; both Bakunin and Kropotkin never tired of pointing out the threat this poses to liberty. For the former, the propensity for corruption is heightened by external conditions. "Take the most sincere democrat and put him on the throne; if he does not step down promptly, he will surely become a scoundrel" (Bakunin, 1973: 91). It was for these kinds of reasons classical anarchism held that in order to be of equal value to all citizens, freedom must be established through a horizontalised socialisation of wealth that places productive resources and the riches of production at the equal disposal of all. "The no capitalist system implies the no-government system", as Kropotkin puts it (1970: 52; see also Kropotkin, 1970: 53–6, n.d.: 116, 123; Bakunin, 1973: 262–3; Schecter, 1994: 46, 52, 61; Schmidt & Van der Walt, 2009: 6; Pepper, 1993: 155).

In the history of modern political thought, anarchism has, as we shall shortly see, much in common with certain strands of Marxism. Yet it has

also been claimed that it accommodates the main ideals upheld in the liberal doctrine. One scheme deployed to classify distinct currents within the
anarchist perspective is to emphasise either individual freedom or participation in communal affairs. The former is *individual* anarchism, and the latter, which includes the communist, collectivist and syndicalist approaches,
is *social* anarchism. The individualists seek maximum non-interference with
the affairs of self-reliant individuals, who fulfil their goals through voluntary
agreements with others in a non-statist setting, rather than the building of
associations. Anarcho-individualism has been critical of the voluntary collec-
tivism of social anarchism. Whether through enforced rules or moral censure,
society can violate freedom just as much as the state. But although social
anarchism is rejected as it would, allegedly, deny workers their autonomy,
as anarcho-individualists traditionally opposed usury and the exploitation
of labour, they self-identified as socialists. This is on the grounds that each
worker should receive the full value of their efforts. Here classical market
theory in the form of commerce and competition between self-interested individuals would, so it was hoped, benefit the greater good in true Smithian
fashion. A system of dispersed property rights, where agents trade as equal
property holders without the opportunity to expropriate the property of others, was regarded as sufficient to prevent the rise of monopolies. In this sense
they were anti-capitalist. As Peter Ryley puts it, the anarcho-individualist
political economy was 'free market anti-capitalism' (2019: 231). Generally
speaking though, individualism has come to assume a very different mantle in
the current form of libertarianism, which, as Deric Shannon explains, is now
in diametric opposition to its original anarchist meaning of "thick antiauthoritarianism" (2019: 91–2). The most extreme form of contemporary
ultra-right libertarianism, where individuals follow their own inclinations in
an unfettered market economy, is supposedly anarchist capitalism. Yet for
the vast majority of anarchists past and present, myself included, the fusing
together of the terms 'anarchist' and 'capitalism' is a ridiculous oxymoron
which is as far removed from genuine anarchism as state socialism (Schmidt
& Van der Walt, 2009: 6, 56–7; Davis, 2019: 49–50; Clark, 1978: 9; Ward,
2004: 2–3, 62; Ryley, 2019: 225–6, 229, 231, 234; Shannon, 2019: 93–6).

Unlike the inappropriately named anarcho-capitalism, social anarchism
directly opposes class inequality, huge concentrations of private wealth and
the institution of wage-labour. It seeks a libertarian socialist order founded
upon common ownership of productive property, self-governance and
bottom-up participatory planning within a system of federated communes.
Production is arranged in local communities along meaningful and fulfilling lines and in the interests of need, rather than profit. Central to this
project is class struggle, which operates outside the clutches of and in opposition to the state. These two forms of anarchism, individualist and social,

are at either end of the anarchist spectrum. What affiliates them is their renunciation of the current political system. They disagree markedly about where their paths beyond statism lead, but anarchists of all kinds regard the modern state as an entity formed through a set of oppressive institutions (Schmidt & Van der Walt, 2009: 6, 56–7; Clark, 1978: 9; Ward, 2004: 2–3, 62; Ryley, 2019: 225–6). With these points in mind, let us now turn to contemporary debates about the anarchist opposition to capitalism.

Rejections of capitalism

A contention within anarchist discourse that bears heavily upon the argument of this book is the question of whether anarchism is, in principle, universally reducible to anti-capitalism. Let us call the first position – that it is – the *restrictive* view, and the second position – that although an account of anarchism has to include a rejection of capitalism it need not be limited to it – the *inclusive* view. As documented below, both positions are open to more than one interpretation. Given that the key points on both sides have been expressed in the wider discussions on the anarchist canon, it is here that the following narrative is, in the main, located. I will conclude that as associational anarchism theorises self-regulation very much through non-statist socialist forms, it stays predominantly within the bounds of the currents running through the restrictive view, the implications of which are flagged up at the end of this first section of the chapter.

Taking the anarchist canon as a set of standard writings that are commonly seen as authoritative for what anarchism stands for, Nathan Jun adds that its definition depends on how its purpose is seen. For some, a thinker or text should be directly affiliated with an actual anarchist movement, which implies that anarchism is strictly historical. For others, a thinker or a text is one that expresses anarchic ideas, which signifies theory or philosophical orientation. The two frequently coincide, but they are not identical (Jun, 2013: 115). If a central purpose of the canon involves establishing the boundaries of historical anarchist movements, then it will preclude thinkers and texts un-associated with these movements. But if anarchism is an idea that is not tied to any given historical movement, the canon becomes a 'repository of anarchist thinking', existing throughout history, that can enhance contemporary perceptions of anarchism. The latter is the position upheld by Jun, and, no doubt, by the inclusive view more generally. A looser version of the former is developed by Michael Schmidt and Lucien Van der Walt, who argue in *Black Flame* (2009) that anarchism, as a libertarian genre of socialism, stood against social and economic inequalities, and it sought a self-regulated stateless order. Jun notes that this unitary denotation of anarchism blurs the 'historical movement–philosophical orientation' distinction. When Schmidt and Van der Walt claim that anarcho-communism *is* anarchism, they are proposing that thinkers and texts may only pass as anarchist if they express ideas which coexist with the nineteenth-century anarchist movement (Van der Walt, 2013: 194; Jun, 2013: 82–5). In order to show why it is within the class struggle tradition that associational anarchism rests, it will be worth taking a closer look at these two distinct positions on anarchism's anti-capitalism.

In defining anarchism sharply, Schmidt and Van der Walt sacrifice breadth for depth. They do not regard individualist anarchism as a current in the broad anarchist tradition. It may hold libertarian ideas, but these are distinct from those in anarchism. They also reject the often-proposed separation of anarcho-communism from anarcho-syndicalism, as it cannot capture adequately the distinct tendencies within the doctrine of anarchism.[2] Like anarchism, which, as a revolutionary movement, arose initially with the emergence of an industrialised working class, the syndicalist tradition is both anti-capitalist and anti-statist. So according to Schmidt and Van der Walt, from the 'seven sages' of the anarchist canon – Godwin, Stirner, Proudhon, Tucker, Tolstoy, Bakunin and Kropotkin – the former five are not really anarchists. As all seven gave different meanings to their opposition to the state, the lowest common denominator that anarchism can be reduced to simply anti-statism, is vague and 'practically meaningless'. Most traditions have, for a variety of reasons, been critical of the state. Anti-statism is certainly a *necessary* component of anarchist theory, but without further elaboration it is not *sufficient*. It is hardly surprising that anarchism has been labelled inconsistent when Striner, the ultra-individualist,[3] Rothbard, the most extreme neo-liberal, and Bakunin and Kropotkin, both of whom are revolutionary libertarian socialists, are grouped together within a single perspective. The result is that the anarchist perspective appears devoid of a 'coherent theoretical corpus', and is prone to 'major internal contradictions'. For these reasons, Schmidt and Van der Walt offer a tighter definition that does not obscure anarchism's class politics and one that coherently delineates the features of its categories from all others. "'Class struggle' anarchism, sometimes called revolutionary or communist anarchism, is not a type of anarchism … it is the *only* anarchism" (Schmidt & Van der Walt, 2009: 19). On this account, only Bakunin and Kropotkin pass as genuine anarchists. For Schmidt and Van der Walt then, the label anarchism should be reserved for a libertarian socialist doctrine, which understands the state chiefly as supporting class privilege, and nothing more than this (Schmidt & Van der Walt, 2009: 9, 15–17, 19–21, 39–43, 123–6).

Before we move on to the inclusive view, it is worth noting that the class struggle perspective is not limited to a singular definition. Like the authors of *Black Flame*, Benjamin Franks agrees that the individual and social anarchist traditions are too distinct to be placed together under one rubric. His focus is also on the social component. But widening the scope somewhat, he identifies the core principles of anarchism as (1) a rejection of all state institutions, (2) a renunciation of the hierarchical relations omnipresent in capitalist societies, (3) a recognition of the social aspect of the active self, who seeks self-emancipation through direct action, and (4) a belief that the means must be consistent with the goals. He adds that these four key principles interlink, so that incorporated into anarchism's anti-statism is an urgent call to devise non-hierarchical social relationships. It follows that the anarchist hostility to the state must be understood with its other core concepts very much in mind. Franks's class struggle anarchism is defined in broader terms than *Black Flame*'s, which is centred exclusively on Bakunin and the First International (1863–77), yet it is still precise enough to distinguish social anarchism from liberal-anarchism and Marxist-Leninism[4] (Franks, 2012: 214–16, 2014: 61–3; Davis, 2014: 213). Let us now turn to the alternative perspective, that there are other plausible accounts of anarchism that are not defined entirely through their hostility to capitalism, what I have termed the inclusive view.

Jun disputes the claim that as anarchist thinkers and texts must correspond to what mainstream nineteenth-century anarchism took it to be, cases that diverge should be rejected as false anarchists. Rather, the anarchist canon is 'a repository of historically-expressed ideas', regardless of where they stem from. He argues that along with a distinct historical tendency, anarchism also encapsulates a theoretical and philosophical orientation that contains a host of intersecting beliefs and ideals that may not refer exclusively to those advocated by the mainstream of the historical anarcho-communist movement. On his understanding, anarchism is "a synergistic fusion of radical antiauthoritarianism and radical egalitarianism" (Jun, 2013: 88). Thinkers and texts can be appreciated as anarchist if they commit to these two components. By anti-authoritarianism, he means a moral opposition to any relation or institution that wields coercion and domination, together with a commitment to abolish them and seek voluntary alternatives based upon mutual aid. Radical egalitarianism denotes a moral opposition to any form of inequality, political, economic or cultural. An anarchist is anyone who adheres to *both* ideals in partnership, a 'synergistic commitment', and who may appear in philosophical contexts that fall outside the revolutionary nineteenth-century anarchist movement. So for Jun, in contrast to the authors of *Black Flame*, anarchism is not solely socialist. "Anarchism as a philosophical or theoretical orientation is defined not by opposition to capitalism, but by opposition to morally unjustifiable forms of authority and inequality" (Jun, 2013: 90–1). If so, then anarchist thought can exist just as much in feudalism as it does in the modern era (Jun, 2013: 82, 88–91, 116). In a similar vein, Robert Graham defines anarchism as anti-authoritarianism, anti-statism and anti-parliamentarianism (rejection of bourgeois politics); and in positive terms, voluntary association, libertarian methods (prefiguration) and direct action (only people themselves can create their own free communities). Taken as a whole, this substantive definition distinguishes anarchism from other perspectives. Importantly, Graham also critiques *Black Flame* for conceptualising anarchism within the parameters of class struggle. His six-point definition allows for conceptual innovations that may not be reducible to socialist anarchism (2017: 1–2, 2018: 32, 38, 41–4, 2013: 189–92).

These, then, are the bases for what I have termed the restrictive and inclusive positions on anarchism's anti-capitalism. In sum, the former stresses that an attempt to include any vaguely libertarian ideal in the doctrine of anarchism risks obscuring core definitions to the extent that the title anarchist becomes virtually meaningless. Coupled with this, anarchism cannot be reduced to simply negating the state. Otherwise perspectives as wide apart as Marxist-Leninism and neo-liberalism, both of whom have been highly critical of the state, albeit for entirely different reasons, could be labelled anarchist (Van der Walt, 2013: 200). In contrast, the inclusive view infers that anarchist ideas can be found in contexts distinct from the class struggle tradition. Denying this is to risk defining anarchist thought in overly narrow terms, which turns anarchism into a "historical relic" (Graham, 2013: 190–1) or a "theoretical echo chamber" (Jun, 2013: 91). As intriguing as these exchanges are, rather than offer direct critical appraisals, my chief concern is to establish the ways in which their common ground facilitates an anarchist interpretation of Cole's left-libertarian writings.

Cole, anarchism and anti-capitalism

It is noteworthy that Cole's guild socialist writings contain ideas that, on the face of it, meet both the inclusive and exclusive definitions, whilst, in one particular aspect of their organisational detail, they fall short of them. He frames a libertarian mode of organisation that, suitably revised, expresses ideas which are very much in accord with classical anarchism. In brief, he agreed that the extra-constitutional power of capitalist organisations, with full economic control at their disposal, represents the same class that holds political authority in the modern state (1920b: 17). For this reason, he referred to capitalism as 'wage-slavery' (1920b: 17), and the modern state as an instrument of class domination (1920b: 22). So along with capitalism, the modern state should be 'destroyed or painlessly extinguished' (1920b: 32). It is true that he was divorced from the nineteenth-century anarcho-communist movement, and although he recognised the influence of Kropotkin on the development of his thought, he did not refer to himself as a strict anarcho-communist. But this alone does not contradict the anarchist position held in *Black Flame*:

> *Black Flame* does not require that anarchism be reduced to 'self-described anarchists': it only requires *ideological and organisational lineage* ... There is no contradiction between a focused, precise definition, and a rich, nuanced, and broad account. (Van der Walt, 2013: 196)

Cole was a staunch opponent of capitalism; he self-identified as a libertarian socialist, his critique of the modern state was class based and in the productive sphere his guild system drew heavily from syndicalism. The *ideological and organisational lineage* between classical anarchist and Cole's guild socialist thought is, therefore, strong.

Simultaneously, he was morally, and fiercely, opposed to both the political and economic inequalities of his day. He stressed that parliamentary democracy is, typically, conceived in a narrow sense, as applying only to a political sphere, and not more broadly to all other acts taken in association. He found this deeply problematic, as "vast inequalities of wealth and status, resulting in vast inequalities of education, power and control of environment, are necessarily fatal to any real democracy, whether in politics or in any other sphere" (Cole, 1920b: 14). So for Cole, true democracy is incompatible with huge economic inequalities:

> if, in the sphere of industry, one man is a master and the other a wage-slave, one enjoys riches and gives commands and the other has only an insecure subsistence and obeys orders, no amount of purely electoral machinery on a basis of 'one man one vote' will make the two really equal socially or politically. (1920b: 15)

Neither did he leave it here. Such was his hostility to inequality that he opposed it in all spheres. In the case of education, for example, he refers to even a loose monopoly as abhorrent (Cole, 1920b: 102). For these reasons then, Cole concluded that only with the abolishment of class distinctions can a society be democratic, and therefore free (1920b: 16). As such, the theoretical orientation of his guild society is very much an attempt to move beyond the binds of parliamentarianism and towards anti-authoritarian and egalitarian structures designed to engender mutual aid, understood as 'free communal service'.[5] In all these senses, Cole is an exemplar of the restrictive and inclusive positions coinciding, the enormous significance of which can now be appreciated.

Given these points, my proposal is that Cole's guild socialist writings contain certain ideals – in particular the combined principles of participatory democracy, economic equality and functional demarcation – which together provide the fertile ground for constructing a new mode of anarchist organisation. However, whilst he calls the idea of parliamentary socialism, where the working class will assume control of state machinery, 'altogether wrong' (1920b: 30–1), the financial and legal tasks ascribed to his commune system are so extensive that, as they stand, they cannot be justified on any of the anarchist accounts covered above, or indeed by any anarchist.[6] Certain qualifications will need to be made, and in developing them associational anarchist theory, which anarchises the kernel ideal of pluralist democracy, is defined in purely anti-capitalist terms. This is to say that my core argument, which at its base is a prolonged defence of a particular 'anarcho-Marxist humanism', will be broken down into a series of smaller contentions, all of which are in stark contradistinction to capitalism. As such, I do not step outside the restrictive view. It is not so much that reasons are given that, in and of themselves, refute the inclusive view; it is just that I do not draw from or add anything to the purported anarchist ideas and texts that fall outside the boundaries of the former. In sum, as my argument is substantiated largely within a class struggle framework, it is here that this book's contribution to contemporary anarchist literature is made.

The final point to add is that whilst I adopt *Black Flame*'s definition of anarchism as anarcho-syndicalism as a general guide, the organisational forms an anti-statist radical democracy will take are developed along new paths. As the following chapter will explain, the self-governing socialist system theorised in this book is set within a particular mixed-economy, which, along with negotiating planning agencies in civil society, includes a pluralised market system for the supply of consumption goods. In this sense, the social relations of production and consumption are expressed through arrangements that may depart somewhat from the visions of other class-struggle anarchists, whether the early progenitors or more contemporary theorists. On the whole though, as my defence of freedom as Marxian-autonomy gathers pace, key ideas are developed in directions that will not stray too far from the central tenets of the tight social anarchist perspective, and even less from its broader forms.

An anarchist–Marxist dialogue: separating Marxian economics from Marxian politics

Both [Bakunin and Kropotkin] were advocates of social revolution through class struggle to abolish state, capitalism, and economic and social inequality, and create a self-managed socialist economy and society, without a state, in which individual differences could flourish on the basis of social and economic equality. (Schmidt & Van der Walt, 2009: 38)

There are three sub-sections to this second section of the chapter. The first, 'Anarchism, Marx and social class', recounts the concordance and the incongruity in the definition of class. Whilst agreeing that existing class relations are exploitative, Marx and Bakunin pointed to different sections of the working classes as the most likely revolutionary agents, and for the latter, class relations are not restricted to production but extend to domination in all contexts. The second sub-section 'Anarchism, Marx and the state', covers the classical anarchist tenet that the principal aim of the state is to protect the capitalist system, which then enables a minority class to appropriate the larger share of surplus wealth. In this sense, the state is the vehicle through which ruling minorities protect their monopolies. So as the state and capitalism are inseparable concepts, they mutually reinforce class privilege. The disagreement with Marx is over the historical mission of the proletarian dictatorship, which led Bakunin and Kropotkin to reject state communism. As the above subject matters interrelate, they cannot be kept apart in every sense. Bakunin makes this very clear. "'Class', 'power', 'state' are three inseparable terms, one of which presupposes the other two, and which boil down to this: *the political subjection and economic exploitation of the masses*" (1973: 280, original emphasis). Sub-sections one and two have been categorised along the lines of social class and the state only for purposes of illustration, in this way the key questions of contention as well as the points of agreement can be singled out more clearly. In the third sub-section, 'The mutual value of unification', the traditional doctrinarian boundaries between anarchism and Marxism are traced in order to show why they have often been overstated.

Anarchism, Marx and social class

Marx argues that there are two *main* classes in modern society, and indeed in all pre-modern modes of production. He acknowledges the presence of other class formations, but they exist on a more temporary basis and are deterministic to a lesser extent. The location of individuals in the class structure is defined by their position within the social relations of production, as essentially owners or non-owners of the means of production. So at its simplest, a person either sells their own labour-power or buys someone else's. This ensures that capitalists have the power to direct flows of investment, to solely determine the location of production and to exert complete dominion over the items produced. They also have full charge over productive processes and can therefore exercise discipline over their workforce.[7] The foremost issue for Marx is the extraction of a surplus by a minority property-owning class, the rate of which corresponds directly with the rate of exploitation. As Chapter 1 explained, due to the effect of intense competition within the capitalist class, he regards exploitation as a systemic feature of inter-class relations (Marx, 1977: 475; Allen, 2011: 56, 60–4). As we shall now see, the classical anarchists held this critique in high regard, yet they defined class in more extensive terms.

Along with Marx, Kropotkin argued that as the enforcement of the 'free' wage-labour contract is accepted from bare necessity, its supposed freedom is merely a 'sad mockery' (1970: 69). The vast masses of people have no choice but to sell their labour-power on adversarial terms, and in a way that renders surplus value an actual possibility (1970: 193). It makes little sense to speak of liberty all the time workers are bound by the wage-labour contract. When viewed from the position of equity, "a contract entered into between a man who has dined well and a man who sells his labour for a bare subsistence ... is not a contract at all" (1970: 268). So for Kropotkin, a private appropriation system contains a great evil. Industry is directed not to the satisfaction of everyone's needs, but towards the maximisation of profit for the few (1970: 124, 127–8). Likewise, Bakunin and Marx were also united in their condemnation of the exploitative wage-labour contract, and they shared the view that laws sanction domination in civil society. In his review of *Capital*, Bakunin stressed that capitalists and workers may be equal in a strictly legal sense, but in economic terms, workers are serfs to capitalists. So the "natural inner core" of socialism is the drive to move beyond the "monstrous contradictions" of capitalist society (1973: 108–9, 116, 161, 191). In sum, all three thinkers sought a new social order with collectivised productive assets.

Class is then central to both Marxism and anarchism, but there are significant differences. Marx thought the primitive peasantry was not, along with the urban *lumpenproletariat*, suited to revolutionary action. Bakunin held the opposite view. He believed these classes were the least corrupted by bourgeois society, whereas the skilled artisans, the 'aristocracy of labour', were tainted by aspirations of upward mobility. The revolutionary impulse is stronger where people have no stake in society and where it is unpolluted by middle-class civilisation. He also had a broader definition than Marx of the *lumpenproletariat*, in which he included the submerged classes of unskilled workers, unemployed, peasant proprietors and landless agricultural labourers. In addition, Marx identified class as a relation of production, based upon ownership and non-ownership of productive resources. For Bakunin, it certainly includes this, yet it also goes beyond economic ownership. Class involves all relations of domination, not just the relations of production, which include the means of coercion and administration in all contexts. In a similar fashion, when discussing class, Kropotkin defines the state as "the mutual insurance company between military, judicial, landlord, and capitalist" (1970: 131). So, from the anarchist perspective, members of parliament, royalty, lords, military officials, mayors and high-ranking civil servants are, along with industrialists and corporate directors, elements of the ruling class (Kropotkin, 1970: 130–2; Bakunin, 1973: 184, 189–90, 294–5, 334; Avrich, 1973: xv–xvi; Dolgoff, 1973: 5, 13–15, 17; Schmidt & Van der Walt, 2009: 108–10).

Anarchism, Marx and the state

Bakunin's proposal in *Statism and Anarchy* (1873) was to reveal the mutual constitutive domination of capital and the state. He depicts the modern state as an entity formed through rigid hierarchical organisations, the purpose of which is to defend the exclusive interests of the possessing class, and is itself a key component of ruling class power. Seen in these terms, the state's system of domination is very much connected to the private ownership of property, whose relations it endorses. Bakunin argued that historically the state appeared for the purpose of establishing monopolies, which supplied the industrial capitalist class with numerous labourers by forcing them out of the land they previously had access to. In this sense the state is the organised authority of the possessing classes over the masses, the historical consecration of all privilege; it assures the capitalist class of the legal exploitation of the workers (Bakunin, 1973: 202, 206, 256, 276–7, 291). So whether relations of domination are reducible to relations of production, as classical Marxism holds, or whether the state pursues its own interests that are in part independent of its formidable ties with the capitalist class (Jun, 2019: 39), Marxists and anarchists agree that the new progressive society will be free from the coercive influence of the modern liberal state and the private corporation, both of whom uphold class inequalities within which wider relations of domination and subordination are perpetuated.

It was on the crucial issue of the revolutionary use of state power, through a proletarian dictatorship, that Bakunin seriously parted company from Marx. The disagreement was, fundamentally, whether workers should seize the political power of the state or destroy it. Bakunin thought Marx had, as mentioned, revealed accurately the true function of the modern state, which was to sanction exploitative economic conditions. But in the sense that Marx had placed too much emphasis on the influence of economic forces in the formation of the state, his account was too narrow. For Bakunin, the state had emerged independently from the form of economic exploitation it served to maintain. In contrast to Marxist theory, Bakunin believed the state was not just the outcome, but also a causal force of economic and political inequalities. In his view, totalitarian states direct their economies to meet their own ends. So, whilst classical Marxism saw the state, once the working class had won the battle of democracy, as a necessary intermediate body, Bakunin argued that the socialist state, whatever its form, would be just another vehicle of domination (1973: 281–4, 284, 319; Dolgoff, 1973: 4–7, 75, 144; Schmidt & Van der Walt, 2009: 24–5, 52–6, 99–100; Kinna & Prichard, 2019: 229–30).

Bakunin had no doubts that the use of a centralised revolutionary state would end only in military dictatorship. He repeated this warning frequently. The masses would be condemned to obedience by decrees of a "new pseudorevolutionary aristocracy" (1973: 151–2, 279). It was when the dictatorship of the proletariat was equated with the truth, embodied in a guiding authoritarian vanguard, that the formula for a new oppressive class system was formed. The dictatorship would exist not 'of' the proletariat, but 'over' it; hence, the organised domination exerted by a minority class would simply be repeated in the proletariat state. The imperious and regimented communist state would concentrate all administrative power into its own prodigious hands. Its central state bank would control commerce, industry and agriculture. Disciplined workers would be organised into agricultural and industrial armies by state engineers, who would form the new privileged political class (Bakunin, 1973: 121, 126, 332–3). These compulsory standing armies would exist in highly-drilled barracks, instilled to "sleep, wake, work, and live to the beat of a drum" (1973: 284). Unsurprisingly, the brutal reign of the new tyranny would be "the most aristocratic, despotic, arrogant, and elitist of all regimes" (1973: 319). So although the forced labour of the gulag system was the diametrical opposite of what Marx had in mind, the repression caused by real-life socialism is the inevitable result of unaccountable statist politics. The contradiction between dictatorship as the means and freedom as the end is that the objective of dictatorship is self-perpetuation, whereas freedom can only be realised through freedom (Bakunin, 1973: 331–2). It is a central tenet of anarchism that the end must be lived through the means.[8] Authoritarian and centralised methods cannot possibly induce a libertarian and decentralised outcome. For these reasons, authoritarian socialism invested with dictatorial power is a 'monstrous alliance'; it would "be the greatest misfortune that could threaten the liberty of the world" (Bakunin, 1973: 125, see also 330–3; Schmidt & Van der Walt, 2009: 24–5, 52–6, 99–100; Kinna & Prichard, 2019: 229–30).

Kropotkin agreed that the state is the main bulwark of capital, and he drew substantially from Marx in his understanding of class exploitation. He too regarded the role of the state as providing the conditions which enable the capitalist class to appropriate the larger share of surplus wealth. The exploitative wage-system is politically expressed in parliamentarianism. It follows that as the state, seen as the personification of injustice and oppression, is the vehicle through which ruling minorities protect their monopolies; it cannot be used to eradicate them (Kropotkin, 1970: 286, n.d.: 33,

35–6). Like Marx, Kropotkin believed that private ownership in productive property must be replaced with common property, which would signal the end of the wage-labour relation. The misery of workers has increased as the chasm between classes has grown progressively wider. As such, the gaining of political rights for workers, without any real change in economic relations, must be seen as delusory concessions. This is why the watchword of socialism must, in accordance with the key message in Marx's essay *On the Jewish Question* (1843), remain "political freedom is futile without economic freedom" (1970: 46–9). Yet along with Bakunin, Kropotkin was concerned that Marx had underestimated the likelihood that socialism could engender a new tyranny if control of state apparatus was placed exclusively under a small band of workers' representatives. The communist state will not just govern its people politically, but also economically. It will require immense knowledge, as it will need to control production, land, factories, commerce and the banking system. As state organisations are the force through which a minority class fortifies its power, they cannot serve as the vehicle through which to destroy privilege. So along with Bakunin, Kropotkin also rejected the proletarian dictatorship, which will inevitably form a colossal centralised power (1970: 169–72).

To sum up these last two sections, we have seen that anarchism is imprinted with certain themes of Marxian economics, and as such the two doctrines are entangled. Both Marxists and anarchists are in principle opposed to capital. They seek a common end, an (initially or ultimately) non-state libertarian communism without exploitation. So as both schools of thought share a view of the ideal society, their normative theories are not mutually exclusive, at least not in terms of their denotation. In terms of difference, anarchists recognise that the interests of political and economic elites may be mutually reinforcing, but they are not identical; state officials do more than merely serve the interests of an external capitalist class (Jun, 2019: 39–40). The main disagreement though is on the question of practical strategies and the means of transformation. In opposition to the Marxists, Bakunin and Kropotkin rejected the centralised power of a guiding authoritarian vanguard, as it will inevitably ossify into an unremitting mode of oppression. Bakunin for example had distinguished between a person being *an authority* on a given subject (bootmaker, engineer), where there is no compulsion to accept her guidance, and *authoritarian*, where decrees are enforced by a political authority through threats of coercive sanctions (1973: 229–30), the latter of which Marx and Engels were prepared to accept in the transitional socialist state. For the anarchists, the correct remedy can only be an enhancement of local initiative and free federation through territorial and functional decentralisation. All productive resources must be transferred away from individual capitalists and towards communities of organised producers and consumers (Grubacic, 2011: 250; Clark, 1978: 4, 8; Carter, 1971: 60; Firth, 2019: 495; Graham, 2018: 39–41). Schmidt and Van der Walt put it neatly when they conclude that anarchism may be influenced by Marxism, but it cannot be reduced to it. It is more accurate to say that the anarchists attempted to separate Marxist economics from Marxist politics (Schmidt & Van der Walt, 2009: 83–7). It is precisely this separation, and the specific way of doing it, that is essential to this book's claim that Marxist economics needs redirecting along a decentralised and non-statist path.

The mutual value of unification

As we have just seen, both anarchism and Marxism are committed to instigating a world beyond inequality and exploitation, where production need not be an alienating experience. Yet the tensions between them have, going back to Marx's bickering with the anarchists of his day, been repeatedly corroborated. Drawing from the above, the task now is to highlight the considerable degree of convergence between certain strands of thought in both doctrines, which, to be more precise, consists of themes central to social anarchism and non-statist communism. It is this amalgamation that permeates the entire constitution of associational anarchism.

Contemporary possibilities for mutually supportive arrangements between the Marxist and anarchist schools of thought are neatly captured in the work of Benjamin Franks. He explains that initially, even before the dominance of Leninist orthodoxy within the Marxist tradition, contentions around the use of a hierarchical centralised party constrained anarchist and Marxist interchange. Strict internal party discipline, with its decontested messages and its prolonging of the revolutionary state, became the spearhead of standard Marxism. Standing as the official medium through which ideas were channelled, the party form impacted upon Marxism's constellation of concepts,[9] whilst anarchist alternatives were disregarded or treated as negligible. By the early 1920s, "organised methods that were shared by anarchists and Marxists, such as revolutionary syndicalism, were rejected in favour of party-building" (Franks, 2012: 221). With full hegemonic control over revolutionary socialism, Marxist-Leninism regarded itself as the only genuine contender to capitalism. By 1921–22, the Bolsheviks were openly persecuting anarchists, who, seeing the Russian regime as a tyranny, had quickly come to self-identify in opposition to it. But with the appeal of the hierarchically organised party in decline, attention refocused upon non-Leninist accounts of Marxism, including those compatible with anarchism. Progressively, "many contemporary anarchists recognize that much can be gained from a thoughtful interaction with a renewed Marxism no longer tied to the regimented interpretations of the Leninist party" (Franks, 2012: 222, see also 217–21).

Recognitions of this kind are now widespread. Rather than continue the established practice of demarcating their doctrinal differences, which only serves to reinforce the existing borderline and to aid ideological ossification, Ruth Kinna and Alex Prichard welcome the theoretical attempt to steer a path towards a "black *and* red" radical politics (2012: 1–6). Likewise, a newly emerging emancipatory politics will need to move beyond what Saku Pinta and David Berry refer to as the "essentialist tribalism" that has characterised the Left for the last 150 years (2012: 294). The argument of this book is very much in line with these appeals. Given the evident overlap covered in the previous two sub-sections, any attempt to schematically partition the two schools of thought is bound to run into analytical difficulties. Indeed, "Marx and Engels wanted a classless, moneyless society, without government and wage slavery: thus in this respect they, too, were 'anarchists'" (Pepper, 1993: 205). And ever since, "it is equally clear that those currents on both 'sides' of the anarchist-Marxist 'divide' most concerned with working-class self-organisation have displayed a remarkable degree of commonality" (Pinta & Berry, 2012: 296). Clark, too, recognises that when left-wing Marxists demand a system of workers' councils, they cannot be easily distinguished from the anarcho-syndicalist wing of anarchism (1978: 7). Chomsky calls this a "sensible blend" (2005: 227). So, what exactly would the drawing together of anarchism and decentralised socialism involve?

Pinta and Berry argue that if the individualist, anti-organisational and market-centred positions of the vast anarchist perspective are omitted, along with the reformist, election-based, centralising, vanguardist and command planning approaches of the two dominant statist expressions of Marxism (popularly referred to as social democracy and Marxist-Leninism), then what remains constitutes a conceivable overlap. The unity would involve an alliance consisting of the anarchist avocation of non-oligarchic organisation and its strict anti-authoritarianism, with the Marxist critique of capitalist social relations and its commitment to eradicating alienated labour (Pinta & Berry, 2012: 294–8).[10] Simon Springer puts it neatly when he infers that "anarchists need to be vigilant against the neo-liberal infection, in the same way that Marxists should be weary of the colonising potential of the state" (2017: 285). Sasha Lilley, who suggests it is beneficial to the "transformative anti-capitalist project" to bury the hatchet that has divided the Marxists and anarchists camps, also regards the combination of the "rich tradition of Marxist political economy" with "anarchism's wariness of the state" as mutually enriching (2011: 21).[11] It would seem then that although there remains a degree of what Springer terms "sibling rivalry" between the two kinships (2017: 281), democratic Marxism and social anarchism are not mutually exclusive schools of thought. There is also much agreement on what both positions do not want. Perhaps most noticeable is the concerted aversion to capitalist consumer culture. Neither Marxists nor anarchists seek a possessive individualistic society which churns out a high volume of superfluous items that provide little fulfilment for producers and no lasting satisfaction for consumers. It is these attempts to couple the progressive components of social anarchism with a libertarian Marxist perspective that informs the institutional contours of associational anarchism.

Conclusion

This chapter has suggested that (a) there are certain anti-capitalist ideals in Cole's guild socialist writings that, upon suitable revision, are ripe for anarchisation, and (b) there are certain maxims from the Marxian and anarchist traditions that can be brought together in order to form a new conceptual amalgamation. Combining these two main premises provides the fertile ground upon which to construct a new genre of anarchism that, following Bakunin, Kropotkin and the subsequent class struggle anarchist tradition, is fiercely anti-capitalist. Having now established the theoretical premises of the voluntarist and egalitarian society, the task of the next chapter is to provide a detailed exposition of its organisational contours, and how it paves the way towards a de-alienated sociality within a system of engaging workplaces.

Notes

1 That there can be such consistency is not at stake in the dispute between the contending parties. Their disagreement is whether ideas that stem from outside the nineteenth-century revolutionary anarchist movement, where there is no ideological linkage, can be read anarchically.
2 Others too have stressed that anarcho-communism and anarcho-syndicalism are not exclusive categories (Raekstad, 2016: 407).
3 For a claim that the authors of *Black Flame* fail to acknowledge Stirner's 'union of egoists' and his overlap with the classical anarchists, see Feiten (2013: 22–3, 127).
4 In his discussion of anarchist accounts of revolution, Laurence Davis points to a further dissemblance within the class struggle outlook. The authors of *Black Flame* call for a decisive rupture, whereas Franks endorses a strategy of multiple smaller and interacting confrontations (2014: 213).
5 This term is discussed in section two of Chapter 9.

6 For a critique that Cole's national commune is actually a pseudo-name for a sovereign parliament, and merely a (poorly) disguised political leviathan, see Elliott (1925: 483–4). Other commentators have made similar critiques, notably Nicholls (1994: 48–9, 87–8); Ellis (1923: 585–6, 590–3); Elliott (1968: 188); Gray (1946: 454–5); Von Mises (1951: 261); Hsiao (1927: 122–3); Glass (1966: 44–5); and Ulam (1951: 90). For a critical discussion on these objections, see Wyatt (2006: 104–14).

7 For a brief yet accurate account of why factory life in an ideal typical wage-labour enterprise resembles a military dictatorship, see DeLeon (1996: 193–4).

8 This is illustrated clearly in the case of anarcho-syndicalism's revolutionary unions, which serve as the productive *means* that will also constitute the desired *end* (Van der Walt, 2019: 250–2).

9 Franks (2012: 17, 208–13, 2014: 59–63) adapts the term conceptual constellation, along with the framing of core, adjacent and peripheral concepts that make up an ideology's conceptual morphology, from Michael Freeden's (1996, 2003) innovative stance on what ideologies actually are. In forming new conceptual morphologies between Marxism and anarchism, this methodological approach would no doubt shed new light on associational anarchism's mode of organisation. Due to space restrictions, I cannot do justice to it here, but it will be the entire subject matter of a future project.

10 Chomsky (2005: 125) and Franks (2012: 208–11) both point to a shared Marxist-anarchist hostility to alienated labour, and a mutual portrayal of the individual as a social creature.

11 During his eco-socialist discussion of the 'red-green' debate, David Pepper makes a very similar point (1993: 1–5, 176).

3

Anarcho-constitutionalism as associational anarchism

> I was against centralism whether it manifested itself in the dictatorship of a class ... or in an overweening advocacy of the claims of the State as representing the whole body of citizens. I believed that democracy had to be small, or broken up into small groups, in order to be real, and that it had to be functional for this to be possible – that is, related to a definite and particular activity and not to an indiscriminate medley of purposes combined in a single body deemed to be superior to and different in its motives from all others. To this conception of democracy I have adhered all my life. (Cole, 1958: vi–vii)

The three sections that make up this chapter will introduce associational anarchism's mode of organisation in full. In transcending the divide between state and civil society, democratic participation is extended into the economic and civic realms and is centred on the various organisations individuals belong to. Self-governance applies both within and between these differentiated formations. The first section, 'The socio-economic foundations of associational anarchism', will explain their associational forms in full. It can then be shown how goods and resources will be allocated democratically, which is the objective of the second section, 'An unconventional plan–market synthesis'. Although both planning and market exchange will continue to have a role, it will not be within the frameworks built into the central planning of command socialism or the mixed-economy typical of social democracy. The method of democratic planning and the delineation of the guild market system are both original and are hence unique to associational anarchism. It is these structural arrangements that make up the organisational aspects of freedom as Marxian-autonomy. Section three, 'Humanised production', will then establish the internal structures the guild cooperatives will need to assume in order to make labour a fulfilling and enriching experience for all associates.

The socio-economic foundation of associational anarchism

It is the organisational contours sketched in Cole's *Guild Socialism Restated* (1920b) that are primarily drawn from in the four sub-sections of this first section of the chapter. His libertarian socialism has three branches of economic and social activity that form the bases of a federal structure: (a) the producers' organisations, the economic guilds, (b) two distinct organisations to represent consumers and (c) the civic services, which account for citizens' non-economic interests. This model is functional throughout, divided into territorial units which are institutionally linked at different levels. The coordinating agency is a commune system, which consists of representatives from the guilds, the consumer councils and the civic bodies.

The principle of functional demarcation

Cole's demanding goal is, in the main, to reconcile democratic planning with individual liberty (1920b: 156). This requires that decision-making must be determined through participatory structures of transparency and accountability. He rejects any notion that people can be represented fully by any single organisation, especially the state. There is not a universal sovereign in society because individuals cannot be represented comprehensively by any single form of association. Over time the democratic ideal has been lost in an inaccurate theory of representation, one that holds a person can *re*-present another absolutely. The accurate principle, that only particular functions and purposes which citizens have in common are capable of proper representation, is not nearly as broad. So the conditions that produce either effective representation or misrepresentation are that with the former, representation is 'specific and functional', and with the latter, it is 'general and inclusive'. Misrepresentation occurs when the initial reasons for granting representation lose their precision and distinctiveness. It is because the state sees itself as omnipresent and because parliament is premised on the absurdity of undifferentiated representation that, for the guild socialists, it is a farce. Serving as a remedial, the concept of function is the real principle of democracy, and should consequently be society's main differentiating criterion. In the sense that citizens have many different aspects to their personalities, they form an array of different associations. No particular interest can express the individual as a whole, so it must be structurally possible to provide for multiple interests. It follows that as there is no single general concept of citizenship, a system of interconnecting associations to satisfy specific purposes, each one demarcating the function of the association, is essential. Sovereignty exists only in the interaction between the various associations. Even then, communal sovereignty is incomplete because none of the groups can perfectly represent the totality of the community. As the state holds no claim to superior obligations, it loses its omnipotence. Any notion of state sovereignty is, therefore, inconsistent with the key defining principle upon which guild socialism, and by implication associational anarchism, rests (Cole, 1914: 154, 1972: 7–15, 1920a: 47–54; Wright, 1979: 58–60). The next step is to indicate what the functional principle entails in terms of organisational demarcation, beginning with the sphere of production.

The guild idea

The word 'guild' is borrowed from the dominant productive organisation of the Middle Ages, the 'gild'. The idea is not to literally restore the material conditions of mediaeval production but to reinvigorate the key principles that regulated their organisation. In particular are security of employment, faithful communal service, mutual aid and a high value for the skilled crafts. The mediaeval gilds did not always meet these demands. Cole, though, is not so much concerned with their actual achievement as with the general spirit which animated them. This is a communal morale that can appeal to "the finest human motives" (1920b: 42–6). A guild is a self-governing association which assumes responsibility for conducting its own internal procedures. It consists of all the people working within a given manufacturing or service industry and can hence be seen as a technological, homogeneous corporate body. The railway guild for example will include managers, porters, technicians, engine cleaners, signal personnel, etc. It is assigned by the community the objective of running an efficient railway. So long as it fulfils this task, its internal arrangements like choosing its officers and its methods of administration will remain its own business. There is no need to specify the exact number of guilds or draw distinct lines of demarcation between them. As Cole points out, railway and road transport may be run by distinct guilds, or by one guild with internal divisions. These are matters of convenience, rather than principle. The point to keep in mind is that every guild, in accordance with the functional principle, equates with and expresses a defined and coherent group of services (Cole, 1920b: 46–7).

For democracy to be real, every member of the guild must exercise it directly. The freedom of the small unit is therefore vital. The guild factories are the principal component of industrial democracy. With the workplaces mostly conducting their own affairs, the larger guild organisations will, in constant dialogue with the consumer councils, coordinate production to match supply with demand, provide raw materials, monitor the social relations of production and represent the guild in its external communal relations, such as other guilds and consumer bodies. The district committees will represent the various cooperatives and different classes of workers, and the national committee will represent the district and sectional interests. So the guilds are structured with organisational complexity, but their functional demarcation suggests they cannot be considered mini-sovereign statelets. They will be coordinated through the Industrial Guilds Congress (IGC), which is the ultimate representative confederation on the productive side. It is intended to act as the guild legislature, and on solely guild matters adjudicate in its capacity as a final court of appeal. It will also interpret the core principles of guild practice, and it will determine the basic pay for the different grades of workers in and between the guilds. Like the guilds, the IGC would have councils at the local and regional levels (Cole, 1972: 60–5, 1920b: 43–54, 59–62, 69–73).

This, in fairly succinct terms, is the basis of the guilds in Cole's libertarian socialism. Although the internal structures of associational anarchism's guilds are in many respects based upon their lead, certain revisions have been made. Cole sees the organisation of the guilds as being elastic enough to allow a variety of factories. In associational anarchism, this translates into a decentralised system of quasi-autonomous cooperatives existing within the same industry and in the same locality, by which I mean towns or, in rural areas, townships. In any given province, there could be any number of cooperatives. Let us say in Brighton the upholstery guild has five separate cooperatives. Together, they constitute this particular guild at the local level. The larger guild structures will continue to provide inter-cooperative linkage. It is these internal relations *within* associational anarchism's guilds that differ in certain respects from what Cole had in mind. They are now set within a non-capitalist market system, where they are regulated in distinct ways by distinct bodies. Sections two and three of this chapter explain these qualifications in more detail. The function of guild legislation has also been substantially reviewed; these and other innovations in jurisprudence are discussed in Chapter 5. We now turn to a sphere of equal importance, consumption.

Consumer councils and the civic services

In Cole's guild socialism, workplace relations are not the only social bond. In complementary terms, the consumptive sphere will also serve an integrative function. He sees consumption as possessing a maxim of differentiation analogous to, yet distinct from, production. The division is again not one of individuals; in accordance with the functional principle, it is between interests. He divides consumption into two main divisions, firstly, the household that includes individual choice, which he calls "personal and domestic consumption". The second is where use is undifferentiated and supplied in mass, which he terms "collective consumption". Separate organisations are needed to formally organise these demarcated interests, and Cole names them the "cooperative council" and the "collective utilities council" respectively. Their function is first to safeguard consumer concerns like the quantity and quality of production, the prices charged and the variety of need, and second to protect consumers from producers. To be genuinely democratic, it is essential that, like the guilds, these organisations are decentralised and local (Cole, 1920b: 79–92). Self-government must also apply to civic services. Cole sees the need for an education guild, a health guild and a guild for every non-economic civic service such as drama, music, medicine and sanitation. Along with the consumer councils, every locality needs a council to represent citizens' general interests in education and health. He accordingly calls these bodies the "cultural councils" and the "health councils". Their role is to articulate the civic point of view and cooperate with the relevant guilds to ensure supply meets demand. In choosing their consumer and civic council representatives, citizens will vote by way of wards within the town, or in rural areas the cluster of villages that make up a township (Cole, 1920b: 101–10, 123–6).

Following Cole, associational anarchism retains all these structures. A system of decentralised national guilds is, along with the consumer councils, the most central organisation. Importantly, there are additional tasks the latter will assume responsibility for that, given their high priority, are not merely supplementary. In particular, they will encourage economic agents to consume in conformity with the desires of their higher-selves. This prime objective is an inherent feature of freedom as Marxian-autonomy and will be mentioned frequently as the forthcoming chapters unfold.

The commune system

The other political bodies adopted from Cole's guild socialism will be the local, regional and national communes. Section two of this chapter will explain the modifications associational anarchist theory makes to both their powers and their role; here Cole's rationale, together with the most fundamental tasks he assigns them, are outlined. He critiques the doctrine of state sovereignty because, as noted above, its theory of undifferentiated representation distorts the functional principle of democracy. He also rejects the socialist collectivist belief, popular at the time in Fabian circles, that the state can adequately represent the interests of consumers. But he does visualise a role for a political agency of some sort, which cannot be historically continuous with the structure of the existing state. This is because the current political machinery is, in accordance with the Marxist critique, regarded as an "organ of class domination" and an "instrument of coercion". For Cole, this idea of the state, as external imposition, denies any possibility for self-government and freedom. Equally, in line with classical anarchism, he also rejects any recourse to a proletarian state, as it too would command excessive coercive power (1920b: 119–21).[1]

The coordinating body at the highest tier, the national commune, will consist of representatives from the industrial and civic national guilds, from the consumer and civic national councils and from the regional communes. A local commune would have some administrative tasks, but it is mainly a coordinative body. The guilds would manage their distinct services, and continuous cooperation with the consumer and civic councils would largely determine their product range. The communes will act as courts of appeal in disputes, and in this particular sense, they retain a sovereign power. But the functional organisations will, through mechanisms of consultation and negotiation, be the essential building blocks which together form a genuine self-governance. Administrative apparatus is, concurrently, diffused into these distinct yet interrelated spheres of democratic authority. Through these arrangements, government tasks are devolved to and carried out by the functional bodies. The commune will unite their communities by coordinating the producer, consumer and civic elements, which together constitute the totality. The private sphere is now one of cooperation and collective self-management. It is through the eradication of the central powers of the state and the enhancement of the decentralised powers of the various local guilds and councils that the doctrine of state sovereignty is transcended (Cole, 1972: 36–8, 1920a: 124–7, 1920b: 127–9, 35–41; Hirst, 1994: 103–4, 167–8).

Cole believes that the national commune will be a far less imposing body than the 'great leviathan' of today. Community work will be mostly local or regional, and any central task will fall to the various district organisations depending on their function:

> There would therefore be neither need nor opportunity for a centre round which a vast aggregation of bureaucratic and coercive machinery could grow up. The national co-ordinating machinery of Guild Society would be essentially unlike the present State, and would have few direct administrative functions. (Cole, 1920b: 136)

Here horizontal ties are reinforced, and any remaining vertical relationships are at the very least divided up (Cole, 1920b: 136–7; Vernon, 1980: xxxv).

It must be acknowledged though that despite his commitment to libertarian decentralisation, the extent and magnitude of the powers his commune system will need in order to coordinate effectively ensures it would be a formidable body politic. Its essential tasks are mainly financial, a court of appeal, to rule on functional demarcation and to control coercive machinery such as a police force; Cole expresses a desire for this last task to be self-governed locally by neighbourhood wards (1920b: 124–9).

Of these main tasks, two are worth highlighting. The first is financial, which involves the allocation of resources, the provision of capital and the regulation of incomes and prices. The second is constitutional law and coercive power (Cole, 1920b: 139–40). In terms of the supply of essential items, the commune will monitor any surplus, or bear any losses. It will also distinguish consumable goods (ultimate products) from capital items (intermediate, used for further production). This task cannot fall to the functional bodies themselves, because if more funds are granted to one then there will be less to spend on the others. Cole suggests every guild will prepare a budget, which, having been mediated through negotiation with the consumer or civic councils, will be presented to the commune which will bring them into harmony. It will then finally ratify the complete budget. In addition, it will also regulate the allocation of communal labour-power and the provision of capital. It will tax at source, from the combined labour of the guilds, and the surplus of any guild will go to the commune for re-allocation. Credit will also be controlled by the commune, and the guilds will only operate within these limits. The commune will therefore control the overall banking system (Cole, 1920b: 143–8). It will also pass constitutional laws to determine functional demarcation. Cole calls the national commune "the Constituent Assembly and the constitutional legislature of Guild democracy". But whether laws should be shaped in a 'formal written constitution' is a question he leaves open. The judicial system will be subordinate to the commune. The legal profession will be formed into a self-governing legal guild, and judges will be appointed from their ranks by the commune. The commune's interpretation of the laws it passes, which are limited to constitutional questions, will also be binding upon the judges. The functional bodies will have their own legislatures, but they can only operate within the boundaries conferred by the commune. Their use of coercive power must also be ratified by the commune (Cole, 1920b: 149–50).

These then are the tasks Cole ascribes to the communes. As the following passage will now indicate, through the addition of a democratic approach to investment planning, together with the introduction of a plural market system, associational anarchist theory heavily revises both the scope and the extent of their powers. It does this whilst, simultaneously, retaining the general form of guild socialism's functional devolution.

An unconventional plan–market synthesis

There are three sub-sections to this second section of the chapter. The first, 'Participatory planning', indicates how prices will be determined through an inclusive method. The second, 'Democratic investment planning', introduces David Schweickart's ingenious approach to the planning of new investment. In order to assimilate his scheme into the guild system, it will be subject to a thorough functional demarcation. The third sub-section, 'Recast markets', indicates how a market-exchange sector will be regulated by appropriate bodies in civil society.

Participatory planning

The fixing of prices will be determined by the guilds in conjunction with the corresponding consumers' council. For explanatory purposes, Cole considers the example of a single item, milk. The distributive guild will deliver the milk brought from the agricultural guild. The consumers have the cooperative council to deal with the milk question. The distributive guild will combine the amount it gives to the agricultural guild with its own distribution costs, and will then propose a price to the cooperative council. If they concur, this becomes the selling price. If not, negotiations between all three bodies continue until an agreement is reached. Only in the rare case of impasse is the commune asked to adjudicate. In one of these ways, through consultation and deliberation, Cole is sure a just price will emerge (1920b: 88, 141–2, 1920c: 1). Associational anarchism adopts this approach to price fixing. It will not, though, apply to the entire economy, but only to the goods and services required to satisfy basic physiological needs. So whilst market exchange will continue to have a role in relation to personal tastes, in the case of catering to essential needs, participatory planning will be the first priority. It can now be shown how the products that will be sold below their natural prices, i.e. the cost of their production, will be subsidised. Roger McCain clarifies the issue neatly:

> The determination of prices may lead to operating cross-subsidies...This involves a system of direct lump-sum transfers among the guilds, to cover the costs of production of some goods for sale below their 'natural' prices. These transfers are decided like other economic magnitudes under guild socialism – by direct negotiations among the guilds with arbitration by the next, more inclusive body in the case of impasse. (2001: B4)

Where there is occasion for operating cross-subsidies, the Industrial Guilds Congress will tax at source and draw the agreed amount from the labour-power of the guild cooperatives. This determination of prices is the first and most fundamental aspect of associational anarchism's social planning. It is not, though, the full story. To complete the picture, a more detailed account of investment planning is needed.

Democratic investment planning

David Schweickart is a market socialist whose model of 'economic democracy' (ED) prioritises worker self-management. Although cooperatives will compete, competition occurs against the backdrop of a democratic investment plan. This constitutes a second dimension, which is to complement workplace democracy. In ED, the totality of productive assets is publicly owned, with each firm paying a tax for their use. *New* investment is financed externally, through a national investment fund that is bankrolled by the capital asset tax. "Economically this tax functions as an interest rate on capital ... The proceeds of the capital-assets tax constitute society's investment fund, all of which are ploughed back into the economy" (Schweickart, 1998a: 17). The entire capital assets are regarded as collective property, although they are utilised by the various workforces that control them. There is no money market that unites private savers and private investors. The capital assets tax generates finance for new investment, funds that are dispersed through democratic channels. It is important to emphasise that it is not the entire economy that is planned. It is only new investment, which is investment that is not financed through depreciation set-asides. With respect to capital improvements, firms are free to spend their reserves in any way they like. This spending is considered ongoing investment and is distinct from the bank-financed new investment (Schweickart, 1993: 68, 71–4, 1998a: 16).

Schweickart states that social control over the supply of decentralised investment funds will be realised by interconnected plans and banks. Decisions about which projects to favour will be taken democratically at three general levels by elected legislatures. Open hearings will occur at each tier where expert and popular opinions can be shared. To begin with, the national legislature will determine how much to set aside for national projects (pollution control, sanitation, transport maintenance, etc.). It can also mandate the encouragement of certain types of projects by making suitable funding available. The rest is distributed to the regions on a per-capita basis. If a certain region has 8 per cent of the national population, then it receives 8 per cent of the investment fund. Here capital follows people, rather than the other way around. Regional legislatures will, for their part, make the decisions about where to channel public capital and which particular projects to encourage, only now obviously on a regional basis. The regional authorities will receive these sums and the remainder will go to local committees. The latter will then decide how much is to go into local public investment and, secondly, how much is needed to finance their own encouragement grants. Finally, communities will allocate funds to the banks in their localities. Every bank will get a portion of the investment fund received by the community. The exact amount will depend on how many firms are affiliated with it and on its record of making sensible grants in the past. Each enterprise within its area chooses a bank to affiliate too.[2] The selected bank will not only render the usual services of holding the firm's sales income and providing it with working capital, but it will also retain its depreciation reserves. Banks are free to make grants (note grants, not loans) as they please, charging a basic use tax in the majority of cases, although this rate may be reduced for promotional projects. For their criteria, they will use a standard of "projected profitability and employment creation". It is to these banks that enterprises will appeal for new investment capital (Schweickart, 1993: 74–6; Howard, 2000: 15).

This then is the bases of Schweickart's proposals. The market would still set prices, but in contrast to capitalism, the course of investment is not under the command of impersonal market forces. The manner in which funds are returned to communities is democratically planned. Workers, acting as citizens, can help determine the formation of the investment fund, and in this sense participate in directing the economy. There is no dichotomy between owners and non-owners of wealth stemming from property ownership. Whilst a given firm could yield a higher profit than others, it is distributed internally amongst all associates. As profits cannot be converted into capital wealth, firms cannot make money just by having it. With regards to political equality, individuals will have neither too much nor too little to be in either a dominant or subservient position (Schweickart, 1998a: 16–18, 1998b: 127, 1998c: 171; Howard, 2000: 14, 107, 156). Through a discussion on the use of an original market mechanism, with regards to consumption goods rather than labour and capital, monitored by functional bodies operating in a democratised civil society and not through an intervening state, the exposition that now follows will indicate how Schweickart's schema will be assimilated into the guild system.

Recast markets

What role does a capitalist class or capital, understood in the Marxian sense of value in motion, have in associational anarchism's political economy? The short answer is none. The means of wealth does not, unlike privately generated capital, move geographically to where it can secure the highest returns. The investment fund is mandated to return public capital to the communities where it initially originated. Capitalists are no longer indispensable. In democratic investment planning:

> there is no 'privileged class' ... i.e., a stable class of people with more power than the combined power of the elected officials ... there are no capitalists, nor is there any other set of non-elected officials who possess anything like the power of the capitalist class under capitalism. (Schweickart, 1998b: 127)

Of equal importance, neither is there any significant role for capital. As Chapter 1 explained, capital is not merely wealth, it is wealth invested in the hope of securing greater wealth. This inherent expansionary tendency guarantees that wealth, as it becomes obsessed with its own growth, will be self-centred. Recall that with democratic investment planning, as new investment is funded by the capital assets tax-generated investment pool, capital as self-expanding value will not exist. Although there are capital assets, the material means of production under the control of each cooperative, there is not the kind of capital which defines capitalist societies (Schweickart, 1998a: 19–20, 1998c: 169–70). Due to the brute demands of competitive accumulation, capitalists may be compelled to reinvest their profits in order to increase the value of capital, but the guild cooperatives are not subject to the same imperative to expand. Their goal is not to turn profit into capital, with its incessant drive to accumulate, but to secure the income of all members. It will be instructive at this point to explain the processes through which a low level of competition will be monitored.

In Cole's guild scheme, extra profits simply return to the local commune, which will facilitate further deliberations about future allocation and reinvestment, while in Schweickart's scheme, they are disseminated internally throughout the cooperative's workforce. As with the guilds, Schweickart's workers control their firms; they do not own them. But unlike the guilds, the worker-governed enterprises will be in open competition. It is on this question, the role of a competitive ethic, that a compromise between the positions of Cole and Schweickart can be sought. My contention is that initiating a restricted role for competition will certainly reconfigure the interrelations between the key anarchist values of equality, solidarity and reciprocity, but they will not be seriously jeopardised. Firstly, competition *between* the guilds will for the most part be non-existent. The various guilds are in service to the community; they are not competing with regard to their respective functions. How then might a measured degree of competition be monitored? The answer lies in *intra-guild* competition. Each guild will be responsible for the efficient running of a particular industry or service, and they all break down into quasi-autonomous cooperatives existing within the same locality, by which I mean towns and townships. Each individual guild will be responsible for overseeing competition within its jurisdiction. After all lump-sum transfers have been calculated, the guilds will retain their profits, and the distribution to their affiliated cooperatives will include a criterion of proficiency. So in contrast to Cole's guilds, the guilds in associational anarchism will regulate financial returns to their associated cooperatives. Cole is sceptical about profit being the only incentive to incite standards of efficiency – and, given the ethical critique that capitalism nurtures gluttony and greed, with much justification. But in a cooperative environment which embodies an inclusive social ownership of productive assets, a transparently regulated profit motive that aims to reward effort can provide a stimulus to innovate, without threatening community and altruistic values.

There are good reasons to believe the guilds can sustain this balancing act. As the Mondragon system – which is by far the most intriguing and intricate attempt to develop a cooperative economy – has formalised channels for inter-cooperative linkage, it can be cited in support of this claim. Briefly, the Mondragon cooperative system is based in the Basque Provinces of Spain and was founded in 1956. There are now approximately 22,000 workers in over 160 cooperatives, which divide roughly into seven main types: industrial, agriculture, service-sector, educational, retail, housing, bank and social insurance. The product range consists of kitchen appliances, furniture, electrical components, machine tools, bicycles and such. At the collective level, the cooperatives with similar productive technologies form part of inter-cooperative federations where they unite in what is known as 'cooperative groups', and where they subscribe to a 'contract of association' which determines cooperative structure and policy. In 1959 the first branch office of a credit cooperative bank, the Caja Laboral Popular (CLP), opened (in borrowed office space). By the late 1980s, the CLP had 1,200 staff working in 180 branches with a total of 300,000 deposit accounts; its total assets were $2.9 billion. In order to integrate the cooperatives and cooperative groups more tightly, the Congress of Mondragon Cooperatives was established in 1984. Its governing council consists of representatives from each cooperative group; every cooperative also has representation in Congress. The Congress officials quickly established a system in which the cooperatives, producing for the same market, operate closely together in order to exploit economies of scale. This implies that every cooperative depends, to some extent, on the others, and it ensures all cooperatives contribute to the complex in its entirety (Morrison, 1997: 8, 13, 19, 51, 85–6; Bradley & Gelb, 1983: 13; Thomas & Logan, 1982: 92, 117, 178, 181; Whyte & Whyte, 1991: 201–3, 236; Greenwood & Santos, 1992: 76).

The outcome is Mondragon's self-managing cooperatives collaborate within their respective industries, where they collect and share information on markets, finance and research. Hilary Wainwright stresses these arrangements "mitigate against the emergence of economic inequality and hence antagonistic competition, atomization of decision making, secrecy and economic opacity" (1994: 175). The federations of cooperatives (for associational anarchism read guilds) mirror the organisational forms of the individual cooperatives from which they are comprised.[3] Their social mechanisms seek to self-consciously preserve a balance between the personal needs of cooperatives and the wider goals of the community. Market success is important, but it does not subordinate the democratic ideal at the macro level. For inter-cooperation to have any substance, certain conditions must hold. Personnel must be transferrable, the appropriation of surplus must be subject to democratic adjudication and, crucially, competition must be regulated stringently (Wainwright, 1994: 175; Thomas & Logan, 1982: 38).[4] In keeping with the fine achievement of the Mondragon experience, the guilds are ideally suited to serve these functions.

Although the guild cooperatives will be operating within the same market, they will be integrated through relations of reciprocal benefit. In order to attract consumers and to prompt technological innovations, free competition will exist, only now it will be between equals. The local and where necessary regional committees within each guild, who are constituted through representatives from each affiliated cooperative, are responsible for monitoring relations within their particular industry. They may ensure advice flows to every locality equally, that material on markets and research is shared and that cooperatives adhere to a code of open books. In other words, an egalitarian dissemination of information will lessen the opportunity for the more successful cooperatives to exploit their market position and exert a disproportional influence upon future rounds of market transactions. This tendency will be further enhanced through policies of income equality and then differentials. My suggestion is that firstly, the overall incomes for all manufacturing industries remain consistently the same. The Industrial Guilds Congress (IGC) will set the basic salaries for all cooperatives, both within and between the guilds, in line with a 6:1 skills ratio. This is adopted from the Mondragon complex, where experience has shown that quality management has been attracted without sacrificing cooperative values. Remuneration for varying levels of skills within the cooperatives will also be differentiated, but they will fall within this range. Secondly, within every industry, individual cooperatives will no doubt produce with varying degrees of efficiency. Here it will be expedient to establish a supplementary dividend policy, which will be disseminated internally within each cooperative in line with rates of profit, the scale of which will again be uniform across all the guilds. This would be calculated periodically, annually perhaps, and will, like all other arrangements in associational anarchism, be subject to ongoing democratic adjudication.[5]

Clarifying the way in which Schweickart's model of democratic investment planning has been incorporated into associational anarchism's mode of production is a useful way to close this section. In Schweickart's scheme, at the highest tier, the state disseminates capital, generated through the capital assets tax; in associational anarchism, this task falls to the guild system. The elected investment fund legislatures will be integral to the IGC at the national, regional and local levels. The IGC will first determine the funds required at these three general levels for *public* investment – pollution control, sanitation, transport maintenance and such. But in terms of new investment for *productive* projects, the investment fund will be subject to a more defined functional demarcation at the local level. At this tier, funds from the regional IGC will now be dispersed through individual guilds. In the towns and townships cooperatives would, in accordance with Schweickart's suggestion, be affiliated with community banks. The difference is that they will be organised along guild lines. Community banks would therefore be guild banks, and the associated firms (guild cooperatives) would be of a similar industrial type.

In the manner in which information will circulate equally to every cooperative within a guild, supply can be arranged through extended use of networking and without recourse solely to market signals. The harmonising of productive plans and the exchange of knowledge between cooperatives, along with a quasi-egalitarian income policy, are intended to enhance cooperation. There will be no commercial secrecy between the cooperatives. Whilst they will compete for grants, the allocating criterion will be just as much 'social benefit conscious', in particular with novel innovations that seek to maximise job fulfilment, as it will be 'profit conscious'. An additional gain is that in the absence of capital, seen as self-expanding value, any remaining inequalities will be noncumulative. Hence, the value of mutual benefit within a guild neutralises in a large part a preoccupation that is irreversible in capitalist societies – the unceasing compulsion to compete belligerently in the desperate scramble to satisfy deliberately inflated consumer wants. These arrangements also overcome what I take to be one of the underlining drawbacks of Cole's guild socialism. If economic surpluses simply return to the communes, who will determine future allocation and reinvestment, then, it seems to me, major economic decision-making would quickly centralise. As the modifications introduced in this section have removed all administrative functions from the communes, they will do much to negate centralising tendencies. These measures will, I conclude, form the basis of genuine self-governance.

In sum, I have contended that the distribution of essential items cannot be determined predominantly through market forces. But markets in consumption goods can, upon suitable revisions, serve certain functions well and, importantly, in a decentralised direction. For the resulting plural market system to operate in accordance with anarchist values, it must be monitored by transparent bodies that are far closer to producers and consumers than the modern state. As Parts II and III of this book will argue, through this particular approach supply and demand curves can be coordinated efficiently without relying exclusively on the limited information provided by price signals, or the cumbersome and ultimately deficient calculations of state planners.

Humanised production

The two sub-sections in this final section of the chapter will define the main organisational forms through which labour may, realistically, be transformed into a skill-enhanced and aesthetic affirmation of life. Establishing de-alienating conditions universally is essential to what I have called the functionally demarcated path to a left-libertarian higher-self.

A paradigmatic guild cooperative

As noted above, the Mondragon experience still provides the most sophisticated example of a successful cooperative complex. In particular, the guiding principles of their cooperatives mirror the anarchist values of horizontalism (anti-hierarchies) and decentralisation. Centralisation increases the likelihood that organisational structures would succumb to oligarchic control. The growth of administrative apparatus progressively threatens the cooperative spirit in direct proportion to the decline of face-to-face intimacy. Bureaucratisation has, however, been avoided and self-management sustained in the Mondragon system through a decentralised strategy. Rather than form large centralised economic units with satellite departments, autonomous cooperatives are associated into groups. As soon as developing cooperatives reach a certain size, they divide into two, rather than remain as one large organisation. The Mondragon planners prefer cooperatives to be no more than 350–500 people. If they exceed this limit, the democratic process becomes obstructed, as large numbers jeopardise meaningful participation. At the same time, experience has shown that 500 is large enough to accommodate industrial realities (Thomas & Logan, 1982: 28–9; Morrison, 1997: 76, 81, 127). Unsurprisingly, Mondragon's size restriction has been much admired. "The small size of each particular Mondragon enterprise is no doubt one of the reasons for the harmony and constructive enthusiasm that impress most of those who visit the place" (Clayre, 1980: 172). For much the same reason, associational anarchism will incorporate these decentralised features into its political economy.

Likewise, it is the internal design of a prototypical Mondragon cooperative that will be adopted in the guild cooperatives. Very briefly, the sovereign body is the general assembly, which elects the Control Board. For their part, the latter appoints management who oversee the accounts/finance, production, marketing and personnel departments. There are three other important internal bodies: firstly, the Management Council, which is responsible to the Management and Control Boards; secondly, the Social Council, a body elected by all members via their work sections, which monitors the Management and Control Boards; thirdly, the Watchdog Council, which provides the ultimate security for the smooth running of the cooperative (Morrison, 1997: 76, 81–2, 127; Thomas & Logan, 1982: 26–9, 40; Clayre, 1980: 172). The primary interest of the governing councils is to represent members in their capacities as *co-owners*, while the social councils are chiefly concerned to represent them as *co-workers*. These multiple structures serve a double purpose. As co-owners, cooperators have interests in the long-term survival of their cooperatives; as co-workers, their concerns are based on income and congenial working conditions (Whyte & Whyte, 1991: 230). Drawing from Mondragon's initiative, it will be the responsibility of the social councils in the guild cooperatives to design and sustain creative conditions in the workplace.[6] What then will this involve?

De-alienated labour

With the capitalist technical division of labour, insular workers commonly only produce fragments of the final product, and often just one tiny fragment at that. Manufacture isolates different stages of production, which often requires only one very basic technique. All other potential skills remain dormant. Providing the necessary corrective, a de-alienated mode of production prioritises what is essential for a human life to reach its full potential, the development of the whole range of physical and intellectual capabilities. In a system of integrated labour, workers must organise labour processes themselves, and it is crucial that they recognise the finished product as the result of their collective activity. For work to become engaging and meaningful, the monotonous drudgery of the traditional conveyor-belt assembly line needs to be broken down and remoulded into teams of workers entrusted to complete the entire task. Here job interchangeability replaces an uncompromising and highly defined division of labour. As all groups now have to master a range of tasks, every cooperator assumes responsibility for a varied and complex set of operations. This enables multi-skilled workers to grasp the real significance of their work, giving them a sense of how they contribute to the collective process (Gorz, 1988: 32, 40, 1999: 32–3; Horvat, 1982: 89–90, 433–6; Kropotkin, 2018: 7–10). At the theoretical level, there is the appealing scheme of 'balanced job complexes' proposed by Michael Albert and Robin Hahnel.

They argue that the opportunity to develop skills in decision-making must be egalitarian. When work is mundane and uninspiring, self-esteem is depressed; when work is enticing and stimulating, self-esteem is enhanced. This is why they advocate a system of multi-workloads for each individual cooperator. As its name suggests, this procedure refers to a workplace democracy in which every member enjoys a job complex constituted through "comparably fulfilling responsibilities". Work duties are thoughtfully combined so that diverse job complexes are equally empowering. Rather than organise work tasks into the same levels as wage-labour frequently does (the organisation of jobs with similar qualitative features into homogeneous categories), they are combined into job complexes which have an equal mixture of responsibilities. One person's multiplex may include extremes of both exciting and tedious tasks, while others may be more uniform. But in all cases, it would not be possible for an individual's workload to include only one end of the continuum. Through comparable circumstances, everyone's work has the same qualitative impact, thus moving towards equitable decision-making (Albert & Hahnel, 1991: 19–21). It seems probable that a general socio-technical competence is more likely to emerge when every member of a cooperative is entrusted with comparably fulfilling responsibilities. As balanced job complexes are intended to disseminate all kinds of knowledge widely, designers will have a greater understanding of the social nature of the work, while workers will have a deeper insight into its technical aspects. The internal structures of the guild cooperatives will therefore allocate work along these general lines.

In some regards, though, they will differ from the strict egalitarianism proposed in Albert and Hahnel's scheme. In order to see why, consider very briefly the questions raised by the prominent market socialist Michael M. Howard. He finds their approach admirable, but there is a conceptual difficulty in "how to compare incommensurable qualities like dangerousness and pleasantness" (2000: 103). There will be much room for honest contentions around what should count as reasonable and fair. Ultimately, "someone has to pass judgement on the equivalence of different job complexes" (Howard, 2000: 103). In addition, Howard also wonders where the motive to contrive novel ideas would come from. Albert and Hahnel recognise that initially some material incentives to spur innovations would be provided by "job-balancing committees". Howard's concern here is that such committees "have enormous discretion over very complicated issues concerning the comparability of different sorts of work and take much of the freedom of job design out of the hands of those engaged in the work" (2000: 104). In response, integrating balanced job complexes into the guild system will require certain revisions that, I would say, can go some way towards meeting Howard's concerns. Two key interrelating points can be made here. Firstly, the basic frameworks of job apportionment will be carried out by the local guild bodies, which are constituted through representatives from all affiliated cooperatives, and which will assume the role of job-balancing committees. It is not unrealistic to suppose they can draw up rough guidelines through which many tasks can be placed within the broad desired and undesired categories.[7] The more precise details could then be left to each cooperative to arrange through internal democratic deliberation. There may be some grey areas in terms of what specific jobs fall into which of the two general categories, but other cases are clear enough. In any given workplace, whilst it may be difficult to identify a definitive common basis to serve as a standard measurement of qualitative comparison, each worker will know instantly where the extremes are; that is, which particular tasks they find the most, and the least, stimulating and rewarding. This leads to the second point. Recall that the cooperatives of each guild will establish a 6:1 ratio of income differentials, within which the salaries of workers with distinct levels of skill and training will vary accordingly. As such, the allocation of work tasks may not always be as equal as they are in Albert and Hahnel's scheme. In order to preserve their autonomy, every cooperative will self-determine in more detail the particular configurations of their job complexes. Perhaps a given cooperative will decide that the members with highly specialist skills should be left with more time to innovate. Yet even here, the duller tasks established by the guild job-balancing committee will still be circulated inclusively. In terms of accounting hours, it may no longer be on a purely equal basis, but everyone, including the highly skilled, will take a stint with the least pleasant tasks. This approach to breaking down rigid divisions of labour can go some way towards balancing the unequal influence of skill levels while respecting income grades. What really matters then is not strict egalitarianism in workloads and financial rewards, but that all associates have ample opportunity to develop their skills. In this way, no single individual will be denied access to self-actualising work.

This prefigures a more substantial role for the social councils. As deliberative forums, they provide the space through which to evaluate experiments in work design. These bodies can, as mentioned, also deal positively with the least attractive tasks. Noam Chomsky believes research should be aimed towards redesigning technology in order to meet the needs of producers, rather than forcing them into technical arrangements that only serve capitalist priorities. With advances in technology, it is increasingly possible that much unpleasant work can be automated. Within an enlightened industry, many of the boring tasks can be consigned to sophisticated machinery, leaving workers free to explore more intriguing projects (Chomsky, 2005: 136, 143–4). Likewise, for Kieran Allen, an escalation in the development of the forces of production has, in the appropriate context, little to do with higher output of GDP, but much more to do with the reduction of working time and an increase in the value of fulfilling labour (2011: 196–7). In terms of how to institutionalise the latter, given that the guild cooperatives have some autonomy over the precise ways in which they arrange their balanced job complexes, those that have done the most to enhance self-actualising work can, in light of the social benefit criteria of the grant scheme explained in the second section of this chapter, make the strongest claims to the guild banks for new investment funding. It is then through these methods that associational anarchism replaces the involuntary servitude of wage-labour with enrichment projects, where technological imperatives fall within the range established by social objectives. Only then can workers produce in ways that satisfy the creative impulses inherent in their being.

In complimentary terms, consumption will also be political and ethical. The *raison d'etre* of the consumer councils, who will operate collaboratively with the guilds, is instrumental here. Crucially, their social research can identify unmet demand, and they provide a forum within which consumers may air their grievances; in addition, through their advisory capacities, they will be a valuable social force for guiding consumer choice. This applies particularly to the cooperative consumer councils, who will serve extra-market and market-regulating roles at the local level. As the forthcoming chapters unfold, these two interrelating objectives will be referred to frequently; this is especially so in Chapter 7, where they are discussed at length. For now, suffice it to say that the general idea is consumers will soon come to realise they can survive without the mountains of needless trash capitalist production continues to churn out. Rather than purchase solely on the bases of fashion trends or designer labels, conscious consumers will be more concerned with questions regarding the material conditions through which goods were produced, together with the ways in which productive technologies impact the natural world; it is this kind of reflective behaviour that I have termed the consumptive higher-self. Here there will be little room for retail ceremonies or the ritualisation of town-centre shopping complexes as a substitute for the worship of religious deities.[8]

Conclusion

This chapter has indicated how the pluralist mediation of state and civil society developed in this book is predicated upon new ways of combining participatory planning with non-capitalist markets. In contrast to liberal and statist societies, associational anarchism harbours a self-governing civil society with decentralised coordinating bodies. Government functions are delineated and entrusted to the self-managing functional agencies for their administration. Through these measures, an unyielding central bureaucracy is averted, and the doctrine of state sovereignty is simultaneously repudiated. In this unusual approach to merging planning with markets, as the direction of the democratised economy is determined through open dialogue between organised production and organised consumption, the coordination of supply with demand is, as far as it can be, an inclusive and transparent process. I have also indicated tacitly how the market imperatives that give rise to bourgeois values will be negated. Competition, together with its inevitable companion, overly zealous advertisements, will not take the same form they do in market forces economies. The functional bodies will instigate schemes of networking through which to disseminate information, supplied by the two consumer councils, equally to every cooperative within each guild. The idea is that commodities will no longer be the centrepiece of economic life, and their production and distribution will only occur through the parameters established by the social method of pluralist planning. These revitalised themes are drawn from the functional mode of democracy originally articulated by Cole. On the condition that his commune system is revised in the direction explained above, and its economic functions relocated to a humanised plural-market system, they enable an anarchist reading of his guild socialist writings.

Notes

1 Cole does, however, picture a role for a transitional period of public ownership in heavy industries with considerable fixed capital. This temporary period of state management must, he adds, coexist with democratic control within the workplace (1920b: 203–6).

2 Community banks will have a cooperative nature. Their governing councils will be made up of representatives from their own work forces, from the community planning agency and from the firms affiliated to it (Schweickart, 1993: 75).

3 For a fuller exposition of the democratic structures within the Mondragon complex, see Wyatt (2011). For a briefer account, see section three of this chapter.

74 *A new genre of social anarchism*

4 In defending his model of associational socialism, which introduces powerful anti-monopoly measures in order to avoid huge concentrations of authoritarian power, Paul Hirst makes exactly the same point. His scheme "would accept market exchange but seek to encourage cooperation, mutuality, reciprocity and charity. In the right framework cooperation can compete effectively with materialistic individualism" (1990: 101).

5 Chapter 10 will explain that these particular proposals are nearer to anarcho-collectivism than anarcho-communism.

6 On a sober point, Sharryn Kasmir found that the social councils were commonly held by cooperative workers to be ineffective, and that participation in them was generally low (1996: 133–41, 161–3, 195 *cited in* Howard, 2000: 128, 145). Perhaps on a more optimistic note, her suggestion that cooperators may turn to a 'syndicalisation' of the cooperatives in order to build new democratic organs within a wider integrative social context is, I would say, pretty much what the guild system provides. For Cole's revision of syndicalism, which strongly informs the organisational contours of associational anarchism, see section one of Chapter 6.

7 These guidelines will always be subject to review upon bottom-up feedback from the affiliated cooperatives. This will form part of the committee's implementation of the general will of the local guild. Section one of Chapter 5 explains what this means in more detail.

8 The terms in this last line are adapted from Roy Morrison (1997: 108).

4

Bridging the Marxist–anarchist divide

For the anarchist, freedom is not an abstract philosophical concept, but the vital concrete possibility for every human being to bring to full development all the powers, capacities, and talents with which nature has endowed him, and turn them to social account. (Chomsky, 1970: vii)

Now that the political economy of associational anarchism has been laid out in full, it will be helpful to complete this first part of the book by bringing together in a few summary paragraphs the new forms of its hybrid constitution. This is the task of section one, 'Functional democracy reconfigured', the kernel of which is democratic pluralism. Section two, 'The triadic relation, advanced selfhood and self-actualising forms of labour', confirms the ways in which the institutional arrangements within and between the guilds and consumer councils complement the twentieth-century anarchist notion of developed selfhood.

Functional democracy reconfigured

The content of associational anarchism's essential maxims – in particular the new forms of local decision-making, self-governance, egalitarian access to productive resources and the universalisation of de-alienated labour – are very much anarchist in essence. That said, certain social anarchist tenets have been modified. There are now some roles for a body-politic, an ethic of representation, hierarchical structures, legislation and centralisation, together with a weakened commitment to strict economic equality of outcome. Firstly, and perhaps most significantly, there is an ultra-minimum arbitration function in the form of local, regional and national communes. Their authority is, however, restricted to nothing more than adjudication in cases of impasse between the functional bodies brought before them; with no powers of arbitrary intervention, the substance of sovereignty has been hollowed out and radically redefined. In place of the modern state, then, stands a more democratic and transparent court of appeal. Politics is now relocated within the institutions of civil society, which is the summation of voluntary differentiated associations. Here there is recourse to representative structures, but in sharp contrast to undifferentiated parliamentarianism, they are broken down into distinct yet interrelating formations within a direct democracy. Crucially, the elected bodies within all interacting components will be accountably held,[1] and pluralist boundaries suggest there will be no monopolies of knowledge or power that override the organisational detachments of demarcated spheres. Consequently, although there will be networks of smaller and less imposing hierarchies, they will be set within a wider context of horizontalism at the local community level, where they will be neither rigid nor oligarchic. There is also a place for a system of direct self-legislation. Chapter 5 will explain how popular sovereignty in the form of guild jurisprudence can operate in a reframed social anarchist configuration. Then there is a modification of the anarchist emphasis on decentralisation. In the model of democratic investment planning assimilated into the guild system, there is for practical reasons some central administration. But as I argue in Chapter 6, is it tightly curtailed, vertically divided and fairly innocuous. These, in brief, are the forms through which associational anarchism's re-politicised civil society repudiates any notion of a sovereign state. The guilds and consumer councils are, as will now be evident, the democratic institutions that bring politics closer to the hearts and minds of local groups of citizens.

For many years now, arguments within anti-capitalist circles have raged about how best to manage the economy, the most tenacious of which is whether a centrally planned or a market economy or a combination of the two can realise socialist goals. In picturing an atypical mixed-economy, associational anarchism offers an alternative approach to the financing of industries and services. Its key contention is that planning needs to be social rather than central. In order to incorporate the prime anarchist values of egalitarianism, anti-authoritarianism, mutual aid and self-governance, decision-making must be democratic, participatory and transparent. Social planning through consultation and negotiation is, I argue, realised more effectively through a system of interrelating demarcated organisations operating in a non-statist context. As Chapter 3 explained, the functional agencies in civil society will determine the price of all essential items, and they will democratically organise investment plans. Planning is not then extended to the more intricate details of production and consumption in the towns and townships. Whilst it is true that the latter is an idea adapted from the market socialist literature, it is not in contradiction to my claim that the argument of this book is developed from a social anarchist perspective.[2] Through a thorough functional demarcation, Schweickart's scheme is relocated firmly within an anarchised pluralism, where it now forms a strong ideological and organisational lineage to the key ideals of nineteenth-century class-struggle anarchism.

In order to minimise the powers of the commune to the absolute minimum, a subordinated role for a market mechanism of some kind had to be admitted. This is mainly in relation to consumption goods, and not labour (or at least wage-labour as a commodity form) and capital. Yet even here, market distribution is only applicable to a social anarchist political economy if certain conditions hold. The mild guild market system, regulated horizontally through the networks of public agencies – rather than through hard markets forces, plutocrats or intervening states – is constituted through a pluralised egalitarian control over the means of production, where there is neither a capitalist class nor a dominant role for capital, understood as obsessive self-expansion. This comes with the recognition that there will be no strict equality of outcome. But as huge concentrations and centralisations of capital and wealth cannot accumulate, at least not to the extent that class divides form, equality of opportunity is more sustainable than it is in systems of untrammelled markets, which, as Chapter 7 will argue, guarantee monopoly rule. On this point, there are two important tasks of the local guild committees that are worth recalling. They will ensure that none of the affiliated cooperatives transgresses the 500 principle – this way there will be no inequalities of power that come with numerical advantage – and also that no cooperative will be forced to sacrifice its democratic structures in the pursuit of commercial gain. Through these arrangements, a soft competitive ethic can serve its purpose without impinging upon the internal design of the guild cooperatives. Rather than the guild-regulated markets exerting constraints on workplace humanisation then, it will be the other way around.

The triadic relation, advanced selfhood and self-actualising forms of labour

The associational anarchist conception of freedom is a particular amalgamation of certain ideas from the self-determination and self-realisation traditions, together with a revised account of non-coercion. It will now be clear that it does this through a Marxist-humanist conception of the idealist higher-self, framed within the triadic relation and located within a reinvigorated and anarchised guild socialism. Defining succinctly how these decentralised structures of mutual aid continue the traditional anarchist project of developed selfhood will be a suitable way to bring this first part of the book to a close.

Both Marx and Kropotkin loathed the monotonous toil of wage-labour. The former expressed his concerns vividly in *The Economic and Philosophical Manuscripts* of 1844. In much the same way, Kropotkin pointed to the callous and impoverishing effects of minute divisions of labour, and how this "brutalising atmosphere" destroyed any "love of work" and "capacity for invention" (n.d.: 15, 153–5). In seeking alternative forms of labour, freedom as Marxian-autonomy prioritises the superior creative capacities inherent in all individuals, understood as ensembles of cooperative social relations. Section three of Chapter 3 indicated what exactly the move beyond alienation and into a fulfilling and skill-enhancing mode of labour will involve in organisational terms. A key aspect of the associational anarchist higher-self, de-alienation, is chiefly the new forms of deliberation within the democratised workplace, as characterised by the Mondragon model, and the design of balanced job complexes, where intricate procedures will not be broken down into their most basic components. Here technical processes serve to maximise human capacities. Where mundane and highly repetitive tasks cannot be fully eradicated, they will be divided up and allocated equally to all cooperatives that together make up a particular guild in any given town or township. In this way, there is room to include in the workload of every individual cooperator aspects of the more rewarding and satisfying tasks. This elevation of the value of creativity is very much the one shared by the young Marx, and it is equally in line with Kropotkin's vision of anarcho-communist production, where fully rounded individuals are trained to turn their hands and brains to both manual and mental work (Turcato, 2019: 239).

This triadic conception embraces the wider anarchist notion of advanced selfhood, where individual uniqueness is expressed within integrating relations that benefit all parties. To very briefly reiterate, key twentieth-century anarchist thinkers developed theories of freedom which "employed both a negative conception of liberty as a lack of external imposition on the decisions of individuals, and also a positive conception of liberty which rested on a concept of autonomy or self-mastery" (Honeywell, 2014: 130). In their work, individual autonomy is coupled with self-governance, so that personal growth is interlinked with social responsibility. This model of freedom rests upon the participatory, self-expanding and self-governing components of selfhood. Treading firmly in their footsteps, Parts II and III of this book will illustrate the ways in which freedom as Marxian-autonomy also espouses the self-realising ideals of positive approaches, and, in complementary terms, a "negative sensitivity" to the external intrusions upon the choices and actions of independent individual agents (Honeywell, 2014: 130–4). For present purposes, it is enough to say that as people need more creativity in their lives, not simply more commodities, work must be far more than a mere means to other ends. Labour can be considered a rewarding experience when it is not routinely avoided in conditions that have already satisfied material needs. For Andre Gorz, the key question is basically whether a person's work enriches or impoverishes their being (1988: 80). Fulfilling the demands of the former universally is a fiendishly difficult task, but through the institutional arrangements summarised in this chapter, significant steps can be taken in that direction. A key contention of this book is, then, that our new genre of class-struggle anarchism provides the atypical non-authoritarian means through which to transform labour beyond the menial tasks of alienating work and into a multi-skilled and aesthetic life-confirming experience. This, the associational anarchist contribution to the wider anarchist conception of advanced selfhood, may be regarded as a left-libertarian higher-self.

Conclusion

Honeywell's neat exposition of the five main anarchist figures illustrates why they associated the onslaught of economic and political authoritarianism with the crushing of vigorous individuality and thereby the opportunity for self-governing communities. Hierarchical systems of mass representation and the centralisation of economic and political power encroach upon freedom, understood as the individually and socially embodied self (Honeywell, 2014: 130–4). The necessary corrective must encourage self-management through anti-authoritarianism, egalitarianism and decentralisation, together with a re-empowerment of personal initiative and social conscientiousness at the local community level. This, I suggest, can be arranged through the institutionalisation of continuous dialogue between democratic associations of producers and organised consumers. The associational anarchist plural democracy is the practical application of the key ideals of class-struggle anarchism, and it is the libertarian edge of democratic Marxism. The seven evaluative chapters that now follow will develop this argument.

Notes

1 There is an array of empirical evidence on workplace democracies to substantiate this claim; see Wyatt (2011).
2 The same applies to Chapter 8's engagement with the work of the market socialist Michael W. Howard.

Part II

Libertarian politics: social coordination through functional decentralisation

Co-ordination becomes increasingly vital, and there appear only to be two ways in which it can be achieved: by the market (each enterprise sells its products to the next and regulates its output by considerations of profit) and central planning (a central agency instructs each enterprise to produce a certain output using given inputs). No anarchist has devised a plausible third alternative. (Miller, 1984: 171–2)

Having now thoroughly established the associational anarchist conception of liberty, and following this having provided an account of social anarchism and a full exposition of its associational mode, the forthcoming chapters will in effect draw these two together. To briefly reiterate, one of the central claims of this book is that both self-determination and self-actualisation must occur equally in the democratised spheres of production and consumption, within which agents will gladly produce and consume with the rationality and morality of their higher selves. Simultaneously, sets of negative freedoms have either been reframed or fully retained. So although freedom *from* must take its place within a conceptual framework that is comprised in the main by a particular freedom *to do/become*, it nevertheless forms an integral element of this book's configuration of freedom. One of the questions addressed in the chapters that follow is, then, whether communities constituted through functional groupings can self-manage and ascend into the communal higher-self while simultaneously paying sufficient regard to a domain within which the individual is sovereign. I will contend forcefully that they do. But my argument goes a step further; it claims that the latter domain, which in principle is essential to any society that values subjective freedom, can only be fully protected if it is set within the former kind of community.

In defending this proposition, this second part of the book can be read as an attempt to vindicate the specific anti-statist arguments explained in Chapter 2. The modern liberal state is invested with certain powers that are said to be essential to effective coordination, and to the maintenance of social order. As we have seen, it is these kinds of claims that anarchists dispute. Yet we go much further; from our perspective the state is treated as a parasitic body that will go to any lengths, often with extremes of violence, to pursue its own capitalist-centred ends. For anarchists, the state is an unnecessary evil. In disputing this position, David Harvey recognises that anarchists are fiercely anti-capitalist, but he adds their effectiveness is limited due to an unwillingness, or inability, to create commanding organisational forms robust enough to mount a serious challenge to the existing system. He therefore argues that post-capitalist society can only be realised through the seizure of state power. So although this would mean radically transforming the structures of the modern state, he nevertheless recognises the need for a state of some kind. As local social movements are unsuited to this task of reworking the state–finance nexus, he concludes the anti-capitalist revolutionary movement cannot afford to ignore the state (Harvey, 2010: 254–6). David Pepper makes a similar point:

> to achieve a globally coordinated egalitarian production and distribution of goods and resources, with utmost ecological care, peace and social justice – to do this anarchistically on the basis of loose, spontaneous, direct democracy (even majority, let alone consensual) among millions of substantially autonomous communes, coops, city regions and bioregions – this stretches credibility. (1993: 227)

He therefore recognises the need for a state-like institution, which in form would be a 'Rousseauesque' benign state, to operate mainly at the local level (Pepper, 1993: 227).

So the question is: how may the politic–finance nexus be reworked in the absence of a state of some form? How, that is, may an egalitarian production and distribution of products and services be successfully coordinated through genuinely self-governing means? Associational anarchism answers these challenging questions by placing coordinative and distributive functions in the hands of re-politicised functional organisations in civil society, through a democratisation of investment planning, and by proposing a decentralised commune system to serve only as a court of arbitration. It is this scheme that is defended in the following three chapters that make up this second part of the book. Together they reject the dual need for a centralised state and a market forces economy, and in doing so they offer a rebuttal of David Miller's claim that no anarchist has ever offered a 'plausible third alternative'. Chapter 5, 'Legal authority beyond state imposition', discusses the alternative structures that will take the place of state agencies at the local community level. Chapter 6, 'Free federation', addresses the important theme of federal coordination. In doing so, associational anarchism's newly formed functional federation is filled out in finer detail. Chapter 7, 'The organisational contours of an unorthodox mixed-economy', is where the dialogue with Hayek begins. I firstly reject his defence of capitalist society, then secondly I go on to defend the alternative structures for decentralisation and horizontal networking theorised in this book. These three chapters lead to the definitive conclusion that a state of some kind is not, in contrast to the concerns of Harvey and Pepper, essential to the imperatives of social order.

5

Legal authority beyond state imposition

A basic distinction is drawn, usually implicitly in anarchist thinking between hierarchical power and exploitation, which exercises force and coercion to perpetuate a basically unjust and inequitable society, and legitimate coercive power, derived from collective and democratic decision making used to create and sustain a libertarian and socialist order. (Schmidt & Van der Walt, 2009: 67)

Hitherto, I have suggested that Cole's guild socialism sits, with suitable revisions, comfortably in the social anarchist tradition. This chapter begins the evaluation by addressing the conceptual schema of associational anarchism's legal framework, which may be thought of as non-parliamentary jurisprudence. Very briefly, anarchism points to the possibility of life beyond the law, of a social order held together by a cooperation that, where necessary, may be legitimately coerced for the reasons captured in the above quote from Schmidt and Van der Walt. The anarchist renunciation of legal authority rests on two key interrelated claims. Firstly, laws are restrictive in the sense that people are prohibited from acting in certain ways, and secondly, as laws are based on fraud and violence, they have no legitimate authority. Anarchists reject the state then as they regard it above all as a legal association. Further, as we saw in Chapter 2, the classical anarchist analysis points to the state as a set of institutions all of which support class privilege. In an anarchist society class divides will not survive, so neither will the modern state in its current form. Social life will assume self-regulating forms as there will be general agreement about the importance of voluntary moral rules. The basic idea is that for the most part codes of conduct will not be broken as people will naturally seek to avoid informal punishment and to gain just recognition and reward. Nevertheless, anarchism still needs some form of coercive power to prevent violations of individual freedom. In general, it has been suggested that minor infringements can be left to public pressure, with more serious cases solved through trials, compensation, isolation and ultimately expulsion (Schmidt & Van der Walt, 2009: 9, 15–17, 19–21, 70–1; Newman, 2012: 310; Miller, 1984: 173–4).

In the two sections of this chapter, some important qualifications to these claims are made. In the first section, 'Guild jurisprudence', I will argue that as long as laws are determined inclusively through non-parliamentary means, and on the provision that they are not enforced by the coercive institutions of the state, an anarchist legal order can be coherently theorised. Section two, 'Social order through voluntary cooperation', then indicates how interpersonal conflicts beyond the sphere of production may be settled consistently without recourse to a centrally administered judiciary. At this point, the accounts of natural, or customary, law theorised by Bakunin and Kropotkin are developed along associational anarchist lines. There are obviously many complex issues involved in any account of informal methods of social control. Here the organisational contours can only be traced in outline form and are, as with everything else, subject to revision upon further analysis.

Guild jurisprudence

There are two sub-sections to this first section of the chapter, which together stipulate the conditions through which the guilds will self-legislate within their own jurisdiction at the local level. My suggestion is that legal decision-making should assume the mode of general will deliberations. The idea is that individual cooperators will determine the legal rules they themselves agree to comply with in their productive lives. This implies that laws are made only by those who have obligations to obey them, through a process that establishes solid bonds within each guild.

Direct democracy in the guilds

> The problem is to find a form of association which will defend and protect with the whole common force the person and goods of each associate, and in which each, while uniting himself with all, may still obey himself alone, and remain as free as before. (Rousseau, 2005: 8)

The argument that now follows will in one sense reject yet in another sense endorse this famous line from the canon of modern political thought. It does this by radically redefining both the "form of association" and the political setting within which it is centred. The first task is to explain the rationale for, and the methods through which, each guild at the town level will pass its own legislation. My thesis draws substantially from Cole's adaption of Rousseau's treatise on the general will. In his guild socialist writings, Cole attempts to integrate particular and general wills within the same community. He develops the argument that a whole network of lesser general wills exists, and as they need not pose a threat to the general will at large, levels of organised will may exist in harmony (Cole, 1914: 151, 156; Vernon, 1980: xxvi–xviii, xxx–xxxi). I will agree with Cole's critique that as the many associate wills, all of which are essential to the "fullest possible expression" of the general will (1914a: 156), cannot possibly be accounted for by a singular political body, Rousseau was mistaken to associate the general will with a sovereign body politic. But, I will add, Rousseau's statement that democracy is only really democracy when it is direct and that votes should, after private reflection, be cast in accordance with what one supposes to be morally right for the common good, can and should be revised along associational anarchist lines. In this way, his imputed totalitarian democracy can be remodelled as a libertarian democracy. And if legal decision-making follows these specific guidelines, it will be compatible with the key principles of social anarchism. Let us start with Cole's argument that left-libertarianism must offer a viable alternative to the doctrine of state sovereignty.

He begins by engaging with Rousseau's theory of associative and general wills. Rousseau recognised that social life is the expression of organised will. His conception of the general will, and its affiliation with a political authority, is the key to understanding his social contract. For Rousseau, although an associational will may for its members be general, it is individual in relation to the state. Due to a concern that associations may conspire against the general public, he thought they should always be subordinate to the body politic, which consequently becomes sovereign (1998: Book 2: 3–4). For this reason, he regarded the state as the most general and qualitatively distinct form of association, which exceeds morally the array of smaller associations within its domain. But for pluralist thinkers like Cole, smaller associations are not necessarily selfish, and providing none are in a position to disadvantage the others, they may express the common good; in this sense, they embody in part the general will. As such, when society is regarded as a network of interdependent functions, all of which point to the same general end, the state loses its eminent position as the supreme representative of the common good. It follows that any obligation to the state cannot account for all other social obligations, and therefore it cannot legitimately claim omnipotence. In sum, Cole argues that, contra Rousseau, as the general will cannot express itself completely in any singular piece of social machinery, an organised body of any kind can only partially express it. "With Society, the complex of organised associations, rests the final more or less determinate Sovereignty. We cannot carry Sovereignty lower without handing it over to a body of which the function is partial instead of general" (Cole, 1914: 157). For Cole this was Rousseau's error; he placed in a political association that which can only reside in the whole of society (Cole, 1914: 140–4, 151–9, 1920a: 132; Vernon, 1980: xvi–xxi).[1]

Cole's critical appraisal of Rousseau suggests the need to revise the latter's concept of the general will along an anarcho-pluralist path. The first point is that in a direct democracy, where participants deliberate and then vote on a particular law, they are obliged to abide by it. In this way, they jointly determine the content of their collective obligations. In this kind of context, it is not a distant entity like the state that demands obligation; it is owed to one's fellow cooperators. In discussing the 'anarchist contract', Robert Graham points out that legal rules may still govern the internal affairs of the organisation, but as they are legislated on a collective basis, coopera-tors remain superior to them and can amend or ultimately reject them. As a collective body, the associated citizens constitute a political authority of sorts, "but their authority is based on horizontal relationships of obliga-tion between themselves, rather than on the vertical relationship existing between the individual and the state" (Graham, 1996: 78). So instead of pledging obedience to the state in exchange for protection, citizens enter into reciprocal relations founded upon voluntary choice. This is because contracts are always subject to revision at the inter-subjective level, and parties remain free to dissociate on their own judgement. For Graham then, there is no anarchist contradiction between direct forms of democracy and free agreement. "While this may commit the anarchists to some sort of political authority, it is not the same kind of authority as that claimed by the state" (1996: 78–9; 77–9).

In congruity with Graham's reasoning, associational anarchism organises legal decision-making along these lines. Invoking Cole's contention that sov-ereignty cannot rest with the state, I would only add that the direct democ-racy in the guilds at the local level should take the form of a Rousseauian general will deliberation. The general will on any given matter equates with the common good. As it captures what is equally best for everyone, it can be thought of as the general interest. After the deliberations, when it comes to the actual act of voting, citizens are asked to consider the matter at hand from a wider perspective. So the general will is more than the aggregate of private interests, which is only the will of all. Private or particular will refers to the interests of atomised individuals. The general will equates with the interests of individuals seen as integral parts of a wider collective. This is to say that the private will relates to what is in the best interests of each indi-vidual seen in isolation from the community, whereas the general will relates to what is in the best interests of each individual seen as an indivisible part of their community. It is important to stress that in general-will voting, a citizen is asked to consult solely her own moral conscience. Only in this way can individuals serve the public by revealing what is in the common good, which is the opinion that receives the most votes. As Mark Cladis explains, the 'will' is one of individual moral autonomy, and the 'general' is the public dimension of the willing (2007: 198). It follows that the general will is not a mysterious property of an abstract metaphysical entity. It is purely the will of individuals, morally driven and with an overriding concern for the collective.[2] The private and general wills of individuals may differ in their interests and their aims, and there is an internal battle within every individual that divides their judgements,[3] but they both belong to human beings and only to human beings (Rousseau, 1998: Book 1: 10, Book 2: 3, Book 4: 4; Levine, 2002: 72–3; Wokler, 2001: 86–7).

As general will deliberations are impartial, which means options are evaluated from the position of generality, they are agent-neutral. All participating parties can see them equally as their own. This may be termed 'disinterested' voting, as the casting of a vote is not decided by one's private interest. So for Rousseau, when citizens vote their choices are not premised upon *preferences*, the combination of which would only be the summation of private wills; they represent *judgements* about what is held to be in the general interest. In a *de jure* political system then, individuals are both citizens and subjects – they determine the laws that they then obey, and in doing so they only impose on others what they submit to themselves. Clearly, everyone respects the same conditions. Here individuals are only subject to the "constant, unalterable and pure" general will, which is established through their own legislation, and through which they obtain civil freedom (Rousseau, 1998: Book 4: 2–4; Levine, 2002: 75, 78, 84–5; Hampsher-Monk, 1992: 183–5). As I will shortly indicate, once this reasoning is applied to a system of workplace decision-making, rather than an authoritarian political body, it gathers a libertarian momentum. As mentioned, the general will can never be expressed fully in any one body, no matter how formidable it may appear. It is within the interlocking web of intermediate associations that sovereignty rests, and even here it is always only partial. To return to the opening quote from Rousseau, only in the guild system, each with its own lesser general will, which, simultaneously, is effectively a fractional expression of the general will at large, can cooperators unite whilst remaining "as free as before".

The general will in the guilds

The next task is to explain what forms decision-making will take in terms of content. In his discussion on anarchist organisation, Howard J. Ehrlich distinguishes long-term decisions, which are concerned with aims and policies, from administrative decisions, which are routine and chiefly concerned with the daily running of the organisation. The former are *strategic* decisions, and the latter are *tactical* decisions (Ehrlich, 1996: 63). When this reasoning is applied to guild self-legislation, it is only strategic decision-making that should be approached from the perspective of the general will. As tactical decisions are likely to differ from workplace to workplace, each cooperative will innovate its own arrangements; one imagines consensus decision-making will have some role here. So in the first place, individual guild cooperatives will make their own *tactical* decisions. Then the guilds at the local level, each one consisting of all the affiliated cooperatives within their own particular industry, will make the *strategic* decisions. In the sense that individual cooperators are at liberty to leave their cooperative, they are under no formal obligation. This means that the freedom of the individual is not threatened in the two senses that (a) they themselves determine the legal rules of their guild and (b) they are free to dissociate on their own accord, thus ending the jurisdiction of their current guild.

This approach to economic democracy allows a more sympathetic reading of Rousseau's political thought for four main reasons. As indicated above, he believes there is a general will on each issue, and through the appropriate deliberations, it can be discovered. One of the standard critiques of his legislating assemblies questions how it can be guaranteed that citizens will arrive at the general will, rather than the will of all. Rousseau's solution is to arrange the societal institutions that mould popular opinion in a way that engenders public-spirited and righteous citizens, as a virtuous citizenry is a precondition for freedom as autonomy. Associational anarchism seeks a distinct route to the development of a moralistic and conscientious mode of thinking. It is the felicity provided by self-actualising forms of labour that provide the prerequisite function Rousseau ascribes to civic religion. The idea is that life within a guild cooperative will instil in its members an obligation to the common good. At the local level, the chances for a serious conflict to exist between the general and particular wills within each single cooperator are, in the normal course of events, lessened. Fundamentally, everyone wants the same thing, a fulfilling and successful working environment within each cooperative, and an efficient guild at the wider local level. In a democratic workplace, it is very likely that the general will of each cooperator will be of a similar strength to their particular wills, and where there is a conflict of wills, it is less likely that individuals will be mistaken on what the general will is, as they will be voting on matters they experience daily and therefore understand intimately. So rather than turn to a civic religion to precipitate social solidarity, the essential high-mindedness is engendered through the participatory forms inherent within each local guild.

The second reason is in relation to the value of smallness. Rousseau was fully aware that the ideal of freedom as obedience to self-made laws is compromised by the scale of size:

Suppose the State is composed of ten thousand citizens. The Sovereign can only be considered collectively and as a body; but each member, as being a subject, is regarded as an individual: thus the Sovereign is to the subject as ten thousand to one, i.e., each member of the State has as his share only a ten-thousandth part of the sovereign authority, although he is wholly under its control. If the people numbers a hundred thousand, the condition of the subject undergoes no change, and each equally is under the whole authority of the laws, while his vote, being reduced to a hundred-thousandth part, has ten times less influence in drawing them up ... From this it follows that, the larger the State, the less the liberty. (1998: Book 3: 3)

In other words, the larger the state in numerical terms, the more disproportionate the relation within oneself between prescribing a law (in the capacity of sovereign) and obeying it (in the capacity of subject). This is one of the main reasons why he favoured small city-states (Rousseau, 1998: Book 3: 3; Hampsher-Monk, 1992: 186). But as section one of Chapter 3 explained, even within self-governing communities of modest proportions, there are major problems with undifferentiated decision-making. As the necessary corrective, functional demarcation not only establishes smaller electorates but also has the additional benefit of narrowing the range of issues that direct democrats will be asked to consider. To reiterate, experience has shown that when the membership of the productive unit does not exceed 500, internal democratic procedures are not frustrated; hence the restriction of every guild cooperative to this limit. Whilst each guild member will participate only in tactical decision-making within their cooperative, it is the same individuals who will also determine the general will of their whole guild at the town level. So even though the local guilds will be fairly large entities as they are constituted through affiliated cooperatives, as they are comprised of experienced participatory democrats, and as there is a relative diminutiveness in the scope of decision-making, the disproportionate problem is to a significant extent weakened.

In the third place, there are the egalitarian social relations within the guilds and how they correlate with Rousseauian moral autonomy. For Rousseau, an individual's general interest is the interest she has as a citizen. It is only this interest that should be consulted when considering any case with a political consequence. This implies that the general will cannot be imposed upon subjects by an external body; it must be sensed introspectively by each individual. Rather than simply echo uncritically the opinions of one's immediate associates, Rousseau thought citizens should make every attempt to think for themselves and formulate their views alone. In this way, their personal judgements would not be altered by particular group interests or the opinion of others. So in their role as a citizen, every individual should act autonomously by considering, solely, her own general will. He added that as the independent opinion of each separate citizen is just as valid as anyone else's, a genuine democracy requires a degree of economic equality (Rousseau, 1998: Book 2: 4, 20; Wokler, 2001: 87; Hampsher-Monk, 1992: 187). The local guilds will embody this reasoning in practical terms. Along with a quasi-equal income policy, there is the harmonised amalgamation of responsibilities arranged through balanced job complexes, which are intended to empower the ability of each cooperator to participate meaningfully in decision-making. As the autonomy of each valued member will not be impaired by internal relations of domination and subordination, the introspective judgements formed solely through one's own volition can evolve more profoundly.

Lastly, each cooperative will elect the members of the town committees who will assume responsibility for implementing the general will in their respective guilds. The personnel of these bodies will be part-time, temporary and continually rotated, and they will also form the first level of wider federal structures.[4] Positively speaking, when representatives are elected from direct democratic constituencies, especially a full-time association like a guild cooperative, it is less difficult to hold decision-making accountable. This is because if real democratic relations are experienced intimately in a day-to-day forum, they become subjectively ingrained, so to speak. In effect, the practice of actually living democracy on a daily basis will tend to imprint deeply upon each cooperator. There is an array of empirical data to substantiate this claim.[5] In these conditions, representatives will exist within a participatory climate of well-informed voters. This will do much to ensure the cooperatives and local-level committees act closely together and in congruity.

These, then, are the four key ways – identification, size, autonomy and implementation – in which the direct democratic forms in the guilds may be ameliorated by steering them along a neo-Rousseauian path. Restricting the size of functional electorates and effectively limiting the ambit of their decision-making provides a sound foundation for participatory politics to take root. These arrangements not only cast serious doubt upon Rousseau's totalitarian critics but also show how he can be revised in line with anarcho-constitutionalism. In the realm of freedom there is no correct answer to the question 'what should the whole community do?' But there is one in a technological, homogeneous organisation like a guild. Following Rousseau, my contention is that in every guild at the local level, (a) there is a general will on every separate issue, a will that is not reducible to the aggregate of private wills, (b) it can be identified through the agency of volitional cooperators, (c) resulting laws will not be oppressive as it would make no sense for any single cooperator to submit to a self-imposed restriction beyond what is required to attain the general will, and (d) following on directly from (c), all proposals must meet with general approval.[6] It therefore seems appropriate for associates of all affiliated cooperatives, acting as integral parts of the whole, to place themselves under the supreme direction of the general will of their local guild. For these reasons, it is a typical guild cooperator who fits the mould of Rousseau's ideal citizen as an independent civic-minded individual capable of autonomous deliberation, and one who fully abides by the common good.

Conclusion

I have argued that the above aspects of Rousseau's social contract are, when suitably reviewed, a worthy addition to the direct democracy of the associational mode of anarchism. As we have seen, the idea that autonomy equates with self-rule involves the Rousseauian claim that people can remain free as long as the laws which determine their behaviour are prescribed by themselves. On MacCallum's triadic relation, citizens ('X') are free from domination ('Y') to legislate their own laws ('Z'). In fact, Rousseau was a forerunner for both the republican and the idealist traditions – people are free only when they live by their own self-made laws, and when their lives are guided by the general will they gain moral liberty. This enables them to transcend base desires which are inimical to their real nature. Indeed, the impulse of appetite amounts to slavery, whereas action that accords with the general will has a more intimate liberty. It is in this sense that Rousseau's social contract claims to reconcile authority with autonomy (Rousseau, 1998: 19; Swift, 2001: 64–6; Miller, 1991: 2–6). Much of this is, subject to the above revisions, in accord with freedom as Marxian-autonomy. Alex Prichard recognises that from the canon of modern political philosophy, Rousseau has probably had the most profound influence upon the progression of anarchist thought (Prichard, 2019: 74). As C.A. McKinley observes, Rousseau identified all government institutions as oppressive, purposefully designed to maintain the privileged property rights of the wealthy – a critique that, as Chapter 2 explained, is central to anarchist discourse (McKinley, 2019: 309–10). Likewise, given Rousseau's original insights into popular democracy and sovereignty, Peter Marshall also sees him as a key figure in the anarchist tradition (2008: 128). Rousseau's final authoritarian and statist democracy can only be rejected from the anarchist perspective. But his insistence that in a genuine democracy legislative power should rest with the people and that for collective participation to be effective it must occur on a small scale and be set within a largely egalitarian economy offers, from the associational anarchist point of view, a solid premise upon which to build real democratic structures.

Social order through voluntary cooperation

Now that the direct democracy in the local guilds has been defined, this second section of the chapter will outline the methods through which a non-statist legal order can be devised at the town level with regard to life beyond the productive sphere. There are two sub-sections through which this is done. The first, 'Michael Bakunin, Peter Kropotkin and customary law', introduces their accounts of natural law, their critiques of state law and their proposed solutions. They both thought that as most crimes are acts against property, when private property relations change, and where all basic needs are abundantly fulfilled, crime rates will drop. But they also recognised that some crimes are bound to remain, especially in the early stages of post-capitalist society. The second sub-section, 'The justice councils', outlines and discusses how associational anarchism addresses this problem.

Michael Bakunin, Peter Kropotkin and customary law

> Anti-social acts need not be feared in a society of equals, in the midst of a free people, all of whom have acquired a healthy education and the habit of mutually aiding one another. The greater numbers of these acts will no longer have any *raison d'etre*. The others will be nipped in the bud. (Kropotkin, 1970: 235)

To reiterate, anarchism seeks to move beyond the main sources of power in capitalist society which stem from class privilege. Law and capital are seen as twin brother and sister, who advance hand-in-hand. Laws strengthen the organisation of government, which in turn maintains the economic conditions through which capital monopolises wealth. So the modern legal code expedites the exploitation of labour by capital through property law (Kropotkin, 1970: 207, 210–11). Anarchism therefore calls for the abrogation of laws and the mechanisms that impose them, whilst retaining the set of recognised social customs and mutual agreements that are naturally spontaneous and without which society cannot exist. Bakunin contrasts his concept of 'natural society' with statist 'artificial society'. The former is regulated through the shared habits and feelings that propagate the species, together with the traditions, morals and norms generated in the dynamics of daily life. These kinds of laws are inherent in nature, rather than the product of the arbitrary will of an authoritarian minority (Bakunin, 1973: 226–7; Dolgoff, 1973: 6–7). In a similar vein, Kropotkin calls the historical development of sociable habits 'customary law'. These real laws people live by are the unwritten customs which antedate formal written laws. A continuingly evolving 'fugitive equilibrium' of various forces, and not forms that are crystallised and immobilised through codified law, is the natural harmony. Only if people see each other as equals can they embrace the moral law "Do not to others what you would not have done to yourself" (Kropotkin, 1970: 176, see also 123–4, 149–50, 157–8, 174–6, 181, n.d.: 86–7, 90; Baldwin, 1970: 114).

Kropotkin adds, however, that a very different set of desires, and so therefore contrasting social customs and habits, has also evolved. These include the urge to dominate others and to seize the products of their labour. The ruling minority perpetuate customs that serve only their own interests. The larger part of bourgeoisie law is, as mentioned, to protect private property and the accumulation of personal wealth. The goal of the modern legal system is therefore to maintain the subordination of the workforce so that capital can continue to maximise profit. But if codified laws were presented in this light, they would not be generally obeyed. So legislators confounded the two opposing currents of social customs; they coupled together "the maxims which represent principles of morality and social union wrought out as a result of life in common, and the mandates which are meant to ensure external existence to inequality" (Kropotkin, 1970: 205). Essential customs, the acceptance of which needs no law, are cleverly coded so they intermingle with the usages enforced by the ruling class, which are injurious to the majority and are enforced solely through fear of punishment. Kropotkin calls this the "double character of law" (1970: 203–6). With regard to the treatment of offenders, he believes that prevention is the best cure. The majority of cases brought to court are caused by disorganisation in the production and dissemination of wealth, and not, despite its malleability, through any perversities in human nature. Only in a system of rampant inequality and poverty are the police force and the judiciary necessary. Grinding poverty demoralises people, especially when overt luxury is flaunted shamelessly in close proximity. The inflated desire to exhibit wealth within a money-obsessed cult encourages the relentless pursuit of profit at the expense of others, which can only be offset by finding ways to develop the superior faculties of people's minds and hearts (Kropotkin, 1970: 71–3, 230–5). The best corrections to the personal diseases that lead to crime are fraternity, sympathy and liberty. So law-making must be abolished through the socialisation of property, and social control left to custom and education. In a caring community, disputes would be settled straightforwardly by arbitrators (1970: 212–19).

My proposition is that the guild system of self-legislation provides the background setting through which to check the desires and customs that give rise to the double character of law Kropotkin identified. As this inclusive approach to legality is situated within a democratised and egalitarian economy, guild laws and their knock-on effects at the wider local community level will avert any tendency likely to engender the privileged interests of dominant minorities. In these conditions, a fugitive equilibrium may evolve more naturally. The task now is to discuss the methods of selecting Kropotkin's arbitrators and the form they will assume.

The justice councils

As we have just seen, it is through new egalitarian social conditions and the force of non-political sanctions that crime – taken generally as anti-social behaviours that violate individual freedom – is neutralised in a social anarchist community. This social order is, however, not really without authority, as non-conformists still face sanctions. Impromptu social influence may be a non-compulsory form of authority, and it may be exercised collectively on geographical or functional bases, but there is no doubt its consequences can be overwhelming. It seems likely that informal sanctions, exercised by way of the majority showing little inclination to befriend criminals, will usually result in the latter moving on. This implies that interpersonal systems of enforcing social control through the weight of popular opinion are problematic, a point fully acknowledged by Bakunin. He agrees that whilst peer pressure is not imposed through threats of judicial punishment, and it may be more imperceptible, it can be just as insidious and pervasive. Impressions and events are transmitted informally, where they are modified and mutually complemented. The resulting collective conscience, which is embodied in every detail of life, forms an "intellectual and moral atmosphere". "It dominates men by customs, by mores, by the mass of prejudices, by the habits of daily life, all of which combine to form what is called public opinion" (Bakunin, 1973: 239). This exerts a strong hold over the people, "the pressure of society on the individual is so great that there is no character so strong, nor an intelligence so powerful as to be entirely immune to this despotic and irresistible influence" (1973: 241). So although public opinion serves the necessary social function of binding individuals and groups together, wherever it is contaminated by ignorance and prejudice, it can oppress just as ruthlessly as the most tyrannical state (1973: 239–42).[7] The danger is that social pressure through verbal reprimand, boycott and ostracism could exert excessive psychological pressure, which risks reducing citizens to docile and passive entities.[8] In the sense that certain activities would be effectively off limits, the range of choice will be limited by the vigilance of custom and tradition. So as moral coercion can reform conduct just as excessively as political coercion if not more so, it is potentially a serious threat to personal freedom (Miller, 1984: 55–7, 154–5; Marshall, 2008: 649–51).

It is because David Miller sees the adherence to voluntary moral codes as precarious that he reaches a non-anarchist conclusion. He stresses firstly that most people need a little pressure from those around them, and secondly that the moralising force will be more intense in tightly knit communities. This implies that the claim that most people will be socially responsible due to shared solidarity carries much force in a small village, less force in a larger town and even lesser force at the wider societal level. If this is the case then moral self-regulation can only secure social order in small communities. But even in a community harbouring a libertarian consciousness, a social control that abolishes formal law may rely excessively on coercive public opinion, thus engendering a loss of anonymity and individual freedom. April Carter thought likewise:

> It is true that a genuine and fairly stable community like a village may show more concern for individuals, and more tolerance of eccentricity, than a larger society governed by general codes and fashions; but its disapproval is also more overwhelming. (1971: 86)

So where does this leave the anarchist ideal that to be free people must be able to move away from given ways of life? Freedom conceived in these terms presupposes a diverse and flexible culture within which a miscellaneous assortment of lifestyles, all of whom express their own unique view of the good, will naturally attract those who share its outlook. But as moral regulation will be weaker in this kind of open society, it will, Miller concludes, require legal governance, in which case, there is no escaping the need for a detached system of control, one with a police force and impersonal courts (1984: 174–5, 183). As I will now show, associational anarchism's alternative social and legal codes can serve their purpose without falling back into the abyss of statehood.

A key hallmark of a genuinely free society is the extent of eccentricity and diversity it can offer. In order to sustain variety in lifestyles and difference in social forms, sentiments like private judgement and critical thought ought to come before social censorship (Marshall, 2008: 651). If anarchists reject laws because they inhibit the freedom of individuals, then, logically, we must also be concerned about the informal techniques of moral reproach that risk doing precisely the same. It may well be then that the discouragement of only minor offences should be left to congenial yet purposeful social pressure. So initially it seems legitimate to reinforce informally a shared common morality in a verbal context spontaneously. When public pressure is applied conscientiously, and within a limited context, it can as Kropotkin wished educate rather than oppress. But in the sense that social order should not equate with identicalness, interpersonal relations must be organised through more formal routine procedures, whereby the role of mutual censure is restricted. It is at this point that we can turn to the idea of justice councils, paying particular attention to how they will be organised without violating the central tenets of anarchism.

The first consideration is how the justice councils will be chosen in accordance with the egalitarian and self-governing forms of the local communities. The immediate issue is that there may already be enough direct elections from popular assemblies in the functional organisations. There comes a time when, due to the sheer volume of collective participation a direct democracy requires, it reaches a saturation point. There is, however, an alternative option. Brain Martin's concept of 'demarchy' involves the idea that in a genuine democracy constituted through functional groupings, members could be randomly selected, rather than elected (1996: 131–5). In his discussion on Cole's proposal that the sphere of consumption should be organised through a system of decentralised councils, the guild socialist sympathiser Roger McCain makes exactly the same point. He is worried about low voter turnout in the election of representatives to the consumer (and civil) councils. Like Martin, McCain believes a remedy may be found in the concept of 'randomocracy'. As its name suggests, randomocracy implies that personnel are not elected but chosen at random from appropriate lists (2001: 2). One of the strengths of the 'demarchy-randomocracy' strategy is that it gives everyone available an equal chance of being selected, without becoming overly bureaucratic. It can also calculate quickly and efficiently the correct ratios of categories like race and gender. For these reasons, the justice councils will be drawn by lot from their local communities.

Perhaps the most appropriate way of doing this is to build upon the foundation already provided by the cooperative and collective-utilities consumer councils and the cultural and health civic councils. These four councils are, geographically speaking, amongst the most permanent features of every local community. Particular guild cooperatives are invariably liable to come and go, depending on fluctuations in consumer demand. But as people obviously consume daily, the councils will remain constant. My suggestion is that all four councils periodically select, by lot, from drawn-up lists the personnel who together will form, on the customary part-time, temporary and 'continuing proportional rotatory' basis, the new council for a limited duration. Their main role will be to organise the various juries, who will then adjudicate autonomously. In the sense that there is barely any call for federal structures, the random selection of the justice councils will be a largely autonomous affair of each local community. Likewise, the application of the jury's verdicts will be the collective responsibility of the local inhabitants. If an enforcement agency is required, which initially seems probable, it too may be constituted in much the same way, i.e. its members would be temporary, part-time, regularly rotated and organised through the justice councils.[9] In all likelihood then most people would serve their local community in one of these ways at some point in their lives.

Reliance upon local juries to maintain social order complements the functional devolution of local communities. One would expect there will be fewer major discrepancies in the interstices outside the web of guild self-legislation. In his rejection of anarchism, Miller stresses that without general laws to determine future decisions, as each case is tried on its merits, on what grounds would uniformity emerge? It may be doubted whether plaintiffs could predict the criteria that will be used in their case should they file a lawsuit. A code of legal rights does at least provide this. "Law ... forms a nucleus around which less formal methods of settling disputes can cluster, but these other methods could not be expected to work in the same way in the absence of any authoritative guidelines to follow" (Miller, 1984: 178, 176–8). Although here he is referring to the ludicrously named anarcho-capitalist system of commercial arbitration agencies, similar reasoning may apply to associational anarchism's plural-codified sets of laws. The authoritative guidelines will stem from the guilds, whose laws will indeed act as the required nucleus, or rather nuclei, around which the juries can, via the justice councils, cluster. It is true that the guilds are obviously legislating in the sphere of production, and the justice councils are operating within the wider local community. But it is equally obvious that they share the same geographical ground. As the temporary and part-time members of the justice councils will also be members or affiliates of a guild, which will have similar arbitration councils to settle intra-guild disputes, interlocking directories may be set up through which to shadow, mentor or perhaps even exchange personnel. The finer arrangements can be left to time and place, and there will no doubt be many more intricate details than I have allowed for here, but the general idea is clear enough. Only within the backdrop of a functionally demarcated system of self-legislation, where spontaneous convergence on consistent bodies of rules is not hampered by unyielding class divides, can independent juries resolve disputes fairly on a case-by-case basis.

Conclusion

Having now provided an account of the organisational means through which to coordinate the three main extra-parliamentary methods a stable social order requires, it can now be seen how a fugitive equilibrium may evolve in a local community embodying a plural legal system. Most immediately, there is the egalitarian nature of the guild system, which denotes equal access to the material means of life, inclusive participation in workplace decision-making and, especially, the prime value of the creative and self-enhancing aspects of self-actualising labour. By the latter I mean the work of all cooperators is organised so that their social being is enhanced, rather than depleted. A mode of production that consciously seeks to universalise self-fulfilling labour provides a favourable social context for reducing crime rates. Invoking Kropotkin's reasoning, where everyone's workload is equally inspiring and rewarding, professional envy and jealousy will not serve as the same stimulus to crime as it does in class-divided societies, where the gulf between the haves and the have-nots is inevitably huge, and where the self-actualisation of the latter is seldom even a minor consideration. It follows that as there are not two conflicting streams of social customs and habits, there is no recourse to deceptively amalgamate the two contradicting sets of law identified by Kropotkin. In addition, if Bakunin is correct that no one is entirely immune from the ubiquitous collective consciousness, the 'moral atmosphere' of public opinion, then psychological pressure should be kept to a minimum. Otherwise, citizens would be reduced to tame and overly obedient beings. This, it seems to me, would be just as destructive to the fugitive equilibrium as the crystallising and immobilising consequences of formally written state law. So in order to protect variety and diversity in ways of life, social censorship can only play a lenient role. It will apply mainly to cases that threaten the liberty of others in minor ways. Other than this, the natural equilibrium of unwritten customs and sociable habits can continue to evolve through conventions that adjust and readjust continuously in line with the developments of a free community. In sum, the combination of a guild system of self-legislation, qualified verbal disapproval and the formality of the justice councils is more anarchist-friendly than when criminal acts are discouraged solely through social pressure that would at times need to be severe.

Notes

1 On a point of interest, rather than read Rousseau as a theorist of monistic unity, the pluralists argue it is more the eradication of privileged fractions that he had in mind. Rousseau treated organised will in these terms because at the time partial associations were bastions of privilege, in which case his contrast of the state with particular interests only reflects the conditions of pre-revolutionary France, where partial associations were hugely unequal (Vernon, 1980: xviii–xix). For an insightful appraisal of Cole's adaption of Rousseau, which contains a critique of the former's "essential ambiguity", see Richard Vernon (1980: xxi–xxxiv).

2 For Rousseau, when citizens deliberate about the common good they should temporarily withdraw into the recess of their own thinking. Yet as Cladis asks, what exactly is the object of their solo contemplation? "Is the general will an independent, pre-existent cognitive reality which citizens are asked to *discover*? Or is the general will a contingent, compiled representation that citizens *create*

by voting?" His answer is that *The Social Contract* contains both views (2007: 206).

3   As the second section of Chapter 6 will explain, the democratic planning of investment can ease this inner tension within every citizen.

4   Here I imitate directly the design of the voluntary organic units that form Chomsky's 'left-libertarian anarchism'. "[I]n a properly functioning advanced industrial society organised along libertarian lines ... executing decisions taken by representative bodies is a part-time job which should be rotated throughout the community and, furthermore, should be undertaken by people who at all times continue to be participants in their own direct activity" (2005: 138).

5   See Wyatt (2011).

6   The terms in (c) and (d) are adapted from Howard, who, on a point that may be of interest to anyone considering liberal critiques of the general will, notes that for Rousseau, there is a tie "between the negative liberty of the moderns and the positive liberty of the ancients, which he makes primary: In a well-ordered society, the (negative) freedom of each will be secured by the rationality and restraint of the general will" (2000: 35).

7   Bakunin is not alone in thinking this. In his discussion on the tyranny of the majority, J.S. Mill infers that social discipline, in the form of prevailing opinion and feeling, is often "more formidable than many kinds of political oppression, since, though not usually upheld by such extreme penalties, it leaves fewer means of escape, penetrating much more deeply into the details of life, and enslaving the soul itself" (1991: 8–9).

8   On the virtue of individual assertiveness as the counter-balance to docile obedience, Laurence Davis's summary of Ursula K. Le Guin's fictional novel *The Dispossessed* (1974) is illuminating (2019: 60–3).

9   This is in line with Cole's proposal that the wards within the towns and townships should "appoint and control" local constables (1920b: 129).

6

Free federation

The previous chapter discussed guild self-legislation at the town level. Turning now to the regional tier, the two sections of this chapter will discuss the forms federal coordination may assume. Section one, 'Freedom and federated networks', argues that the functional principle of representation will be a valuable addition to a social anarchist constitution. Section two, 'Radical republicanism', completes the exposition of associational anarchism's federal structures by indicating how the schema of democratised investment planning outlined in section two of Chapter 3 enables a general commitment to an accepted common good in the public sphere. At this point, the anarcho-republican perspective is introduced, and I show why its proposal that 'freedom as non-domination' must be recast in a non-statist constitution which moves beyond the institution of private property leads straight to associational anarchism.

Freedom and federated networks

There are two sub-sections to this first section of the chapter. The first, 'Michael Bakunin, Peter Kropotkin and G.D.H. Cole', outlines Bakunin and Kropotkin's proposals of a free federation, which are then juxtaposed with Cole's functional federation. Although all three thinkers are proposing remarkably similar systems of federal coordination, the idea itself throws up an awkward theoretical dilemma that stretches social anarchist theory. This is the claim that an anarchist federation contains an irresolvable strain between the demands of decentralisation and the redistribution of natural resources. The second sub-section, 'The undigested stone in social anarchist thought', argues that the guild system goes some way towards meeting this apparent contradiction, and even if it cannot resolve it in full, a loss of complete voluntarism can be justified by appealing to the key anarchist principle of mutual aid.

Michael Bakunin, Peter Kropotkin and G.D.H. Cole

Bakunin thought that the aspiration to be free exists within every individual. He refers to this psychological maxim, the "instinct of revolt", frequently. Inside everyone, there is "an inborn irresistible urge – the source of all free-dom – to rebel against any arbitrary measure, even if imposed in the name of liberty" (1973: 194). Elsewhere he calls this natural tendency the "spirit of revolt", or "goddess of revolt", which is the "mother of all liberty" and a powerful agent of human emancipation (1973: 283, 308; Avrich, 1973: xiv; Dolgoff, 1973: 5, 15). It follows that freedom involves a social recognition of oneself as a free being, which naturally extends to everyone else. Liberty cannot, therefore, be attained in equal measure where people are dispossessed of property. "One must live in a dream world to imagine that a worker, under the prevailing economic and social conditions, can really and effectively exercise political liberty" (Bakunin, 1973: 171). So although the drive to freedom is inherent in human nature, it emerges dialectically within historical and social settings and will only be fully attained in a society that embodies economic as well as political equality, without which liberty will be a "horrible and cruel deception". In order to obtain freedom then, the anarchist revolution must abolish class and privilege, together with "the radical dissolution of the centralized, aggressive, authoritarian state, includ-ing its military, bureaucratic, governmental, administrative, judicial, and legislative institutions" (Bakunin, 1973: 96, see also 76–8, 87, 96–9, 171–2, 237–8, 285, 295, 303; Prichard, 2019: 77).

As freedom must be organised, it cannot, Bakunin adds, be separated from workers' control or other self-managing local groups. These units can only function efficiently if they are coordinated. But social life cannot be organised from the "summit to the base". A network of free horizontalised federations preserving local autonomy is therefore the only feasible alterna-tive to the authoritarian state. Federations may form to address regional issues, in particular with inter-communal functions like transport and com-munications, together with the provision of essentials like clean water and energy. Networks of rotated delegates, mandated by local citizen bodies, would form the regional and national federations. Each administrative unit would coordinate with others across wider geographical and functional scales. They would interlink so that the members of one help administer the others. In this way, none can assume dominance. Significantly, general councils would be "trailing appendages", operating behind the spontane-ous actions of the localities. As they are self-determining and "consecrated by liberty", local communities may always secede, otherwise, the federa-tion would quickly assume centralised forms. But given their strong mutual attraction and common interests, especially in resolving disputes, the losses involved in withdrawal will usually outweigh the gains (Bakunin, 1973: 7–9, 77–8, 82–3, 99, 105; Prichard, 2019: 83; Dolgoff, 1973: 5–8; Pepper, 1993: 153, 159, 176–8).

Like Bakunin, Kropotkin equates freedom with solidarity, which does not imply the freedom to do anything. People can obviously never be free from taking the steps required to satisfy physiological needs. As soon as hunger drives them forward, they are no longer the 'care for nothing' frequently held up as the model-free person. In an economic sense, people are free when their means of existence are guaranteed – when, through equal access to material resources, they are not impelled to sell their muscles and brains in ways that lead to their exploitation. So freedom is not treated as something asserted against other people, it is regarded as a social product. Kropotkin did regard anarchism as individualistic, but this is in the sense that a truly democratic and egalitarian socialism would provide for the equal development of all. In this communist sociability, genuine individuality would replace 'misanthropic bourgeois individualism'. Again, like Bakunin, Kropotkin also visualised a freely federated system within which bodies of delegates would form networks of regional and national committees. He pointed to the lifeboat institution as an exemplar of a voluntary organisation which could function non-coercively on a large scale, and without any intervention from an external agency. Delegates would return from committee meetings not with a law, but with a proposition which may or may not be accepted. For Kropotkin, is it vital that communities are federated in this way so that membership can be exchanged or rotated. Small communities, even those with a 'punctilious morality', are not large families. People can inhabit the same locality only if they are not continuously enforced to encounter one another at every moment. He thought that small communities cannot last long in total isolation, and if one did, it would probably mean its members had forsaken their individuality (Kropotkin, 2009: 7, 9–10, n.d.: 34–5; Schmidt & Van der Walt, 2009: 9, 38, 47–52, 242; Dolgoff, 1973: 289). For both Bakunin and Kropotkin then, freedom can only be realised through these kinds of social contexts.[1] With their ideas on free federalism outlined, it can now be shown how Cole's sympathetic revision of revolutionary syndicalism resulted in a federal structure that is remarkably similar in its organisational detail.

The central tenet of syndicalism is the belief that a nexus of revolutionary unions, each one assuming democratic control over their respective industries, are the practical means through which to expropriate productive resources; hence initiating the move into a libertarian socialist society founded upon real self-management. The new egalitarian system of bottom-up control is envisaged in opposition to the modern state and capitalism, both of which are rigidly hierarchical and run by elites. Although some syndicalists went on to embrace the authoritarian right – Roberto Michels, for example, found his charismatic leader in Mussolini – syndicalism was a major component of anarchism from its very beginnings, the period of the First International, and its aims and principles were welcomed by most of the early anarchists. Thereafter, "[s]ydicalist unions were the largest formal organisations in the history of anarchism" (Van der Walt, 2019: 257, see also 249–53; Schmidt & Van der Walt, 2009: 134–6, 142, 190). Bakunin, a leading theorist of syndicalism, believed in a prefigurative sense that industrial unions not only could lead the way into revolutionary change but would also form the nucleus of post-capitalist society. A radically renewed federation of trade unions would bring production under the self-governance of the workers, who would assume responsibility for management tasks. But he thought society should not be controlled by unions alone. A free society can only be a pluralistic society, where various individual and social needs can be satisfied in a decentralised system of differentiated yet interrelating organisations (Bakunin, 1973: 308; Avrich, 1973: xxv; Van der Walt, 2019: 253–4; Dolgoff, 1973: 20). As we shall shortly see, in theorising his account of political pluralism, Cole came to the very same conclusion.

Syndicalism is also in congruence with anarcho-communism. As Van der Walt explains, Kropotkin was an exponent of syndicalism, while, generally speaking, syndicalism shared the anarcho-communist goal of a fully democratised stateless society (Van der Walt, 2019: 254). Indeed, Kropotkin argued that the state is a threat to liberty when the management of social organisation, in particular production and distribution, is assumed by its government. The solution can only be a 'higher form' of social organisation, arranged into a self-governance consisting of territorial and functional decentralisation. This calls for subdivision in spheres of action as well as the character of functions (Kropotkin, 1970: 50–2). In his discussion on the Paris Commune of 1871 (18 March to 28 May), Kropotkin emphasises further that on its own, territorial decentralisation is not enough. The Commune was short-lived because the people did not triumph economically (1970: 51–2, 163). There are striking similarities with Cole's functional devolution. Kropotkin referred to the medieval guild repetitively as an example of freely cooperating productive associations. These associations of mutual support maintained justice with a "humane, brotherly element". As each independent guild had its own self-jurisdiction and general assemblies, they generated "a full organic life which could only result from the integrity of the vital functions" (Kropotkin, 2014: 127). The craft guilds in particular placed great value on pleasant work, and manual labour was in general held in high regard. In this sense, the guilds answered to an "inrooted want of human nature" (2014: 112, 125–8). No wonder Cole declared just before his death that the works of Kropotkin and Morris inspired him far more than any state socialist (Cole, 1958: 7, 26).

Cole noted that whilst trade unionism is the mother of syndicalism, anarchism is its father (1972: 239, 243), and in this sense, syndicalism had taught the early guild socialists a great deal (1920b: 213).[2] In particular, syndicalism held sound theories with regard to economic democracy and honourable work. As it sought to satisfy workers' desire to control their means of production, it remains a vitalising force. He added though that syndicalism had rejected state sovereignty only to enthrone in its place the quasi-sovereign power of organised labour. This counter-absolutism is an exaggeration of an otherwise just demand:

> The workers ought to control the normal conduct of industry; but they ought not to regulate the price of commodities at will, to dictate to the consumer what he shall consume, or, in short, to exploit the community as the individual profiteer exploits it to-day. (1972: 38)

Cole's solution is to revise syndicalist theory along pluralist lines while retaining its central idea. As section one of Chapter 3 explained, in his mature guild socialist writings this involves chiefly a separation of functions between organised production and organised consumption. As the state has lost its exclusive right to legislate, there is no longer an "omnicompetent, omnivorous, omniscient, omnipresent Sovereign State" (Cole, 1920a: 11, 1972: 38, 249–51, 1920b: 213; Corina, 1972: xix).

Drawing from Cole's left-libertarian writings, associational anarchism's conceptual schema shares anarcho-syndicalism's primary emphasis on transcending class divides and workplace autocracy. The guild cooperatives will control their means of production, but other community bodies will, in the form of two consumer councils, monitor the items produced. The idea is that the local guilds will determine their own *productive processes* internally, yet the consumer councils will help steer the course of economic development by overseeing the actual *product*. In this way, the jurisdiction of each functional association is clearly demarcated. Only in the rare case of impasse will the local commune be called to adjudicate. This basic specification, that the guild cooperatives control their means of production but not actually own them, provides a solid starting point for democratising the kind of economic relations upon which to build federal structures of coordination, through which quasi-independent local communities can then affiliate.

The undigested stone in social anarchist thought

In an anarchist federation, local communities may withdraw from given policies they regard as insufferable. As indicated above, without this their liberty is impaired in direct proportion to the growth of strong centralising forces. So the freedom to secede is in accord with the key anarchist principles of voluntarism and decentralisation. The belief that production and consumption can take place through local communities has, however, been questioned, even by critics of capitalism. Statist approaches to socialism have been suspicious of anarchism's utopia, pointing to problems in localism and the organisation of self-governance, which suggest a general underestimation of technological complexities. The claim here is that regional autonomy will need interregional bodies to mediate between disputes and monitor solutions to, in geographical terms, the unequal access to natural resources. David Bouchier captures the problem neatly:

> If welfare were decentralised ... the poorest communities with fewest resources would face a catastrophic future. If resources were transferred from one community to another, we would be back to the conflict between local freedom and centralised control ... The fact is that the problem of equality sits like a hard stone, undigested in the body of social anarchist theory and practice. (1996: 111)

In the absence of the state, then, who will assume responsibility for the sets of transfers required to distribute goods according to need (Pepper, 1993: 216; Miller, 1984: 173; Schecter, 1994: 185)?

Associational anarchism makes significant inroads into this 'problem of equality' by weakening its structural tension. It does this by placing control of rare natural resources, those that are not abundant in every region, into the hands of the guilds, and not the local communities themselves. As such, a scarce mineral that naturally concentrates in a given region will not be the exclusive property of that region, as it were. Rather, its extraction and distribution to other regions will fall to, in this case, the mining and distributive guilds respectively. As a corollary, delegated authority is structurally checked in an important way. The functional principle in effect limits the scope of demarcated jurisdictions. The regional bodies of each separate guild will monitor distribution, within their own industries, to neutralise the disadvantage of the regions with fewer natural resources. This will clearly not implicate every guild on every particular distribution. It only entails those directly involved in any given issue, which will change on a case-by-case basis. As such, a given distribution does not affect local communities seen in their totality; it only concerns the regional bodies in the guild responsible for the supply of the item in question. In this sense, the federated forms may be curtailed political authorities, but interregional dissemination is everywhere specific. Although there may be an extensive role for the distributive guild, there is no recourse to undifferentiated centralised

control. The critical issue then is not so much that local communities cannot secede from regional federation, as this is not really what they are being
asked to refrain from. The request to conform is now of a lesser magnitude;
in certain situations, local guilds will be prepared to release an amount of
their home-generated natural resources for redistribution to other regions.
It is true that a local community could no longer exist in total isolation, at
least not permanently. And if a given local community did secede, no appeal
could then be made to the combined power of other communities in cases
of fraud. Bakunin reasoned along similar lines. An unjust association could
not, he thought, enjoy the protection of the wider community against other
associations who fail to respect their voluntary obligations (1973: 82). It is
for these reasons that federal coordination has, as Bakunin puts it, a "powerful mutual attraction".

Voluntarism in absolute terms has then been relinquished, which granted
involves some loss of liberty, but this move can be justified on the anarchist
grounds that in practice it expresses the key principle of mutual aid. In
their capacities as producers, citizens will have strong incentives to seek the
common good of their whole guild; this theme came through strongly in
section one of the previous chapter. Understood in terms of a Rawlsian 'veil
of ignorance', which rules out subjective knowledge of all deliberating parties, who in this case would be teams of functionally demarcated producers,
it would be irrational to object to a particular distribution of an essential
item to all regions, even if it results in one's own local community exporting
more than it imports. Remember, before the metaphysical veil is lifted, no
one knows which community they belong to, as that would fall within the
bounds of subjective knowledge. In this condition, which is adapted from
Rawls's 'original position', individual cooperators are compelled to consider the plight of others.[3] So in the current example, the one natural principle Kropotkin suggests is in every society is invoked. "Treat others as you
would like them to treat you under similar circumstances" (1970: 97). This
moral principle is equality, and the solidarity which stems from it, mutual
aid, is for Kropotkin "anarchism in deed" (1970: 97–105). Consequently,
if an economic agent imagines she is a member of a cooperative in a region
without a particular natural reserve, she would wish for the region which
has to supply it, through the guild system, to the cooperatives in her local
community. Rationally, therefore, she cannot object to this very same distribution if it turns out she belongs to the latter region. In sum, for liberty to be
effectual and of equal value to all agents, the dissemination of rare natural
resources must be placed into the hands of the regional guilds, rather than
local communities.[4]

These then are the self-governing arrangements that begin to digest
Bouchier's metaphorical hard stone. In doing so they effectively fill out in
finer detail Bakunin and Kropotkin's federalist structures in a manner that

does not completely crush the autonomy of local communities, which, along with the self-employed sector outlined and discussed in Chapter 10, are totalities of interacting functional associations.

Radical republicanism

There are two sub-sections to this second section of the chapter. The first, 'Anarcho-republicanism and freedom as non-domination', introduces two republican positions, the 'red republican Knights of Labour' and the classical and contemporary anarcho-republicanism. Both approaches developed critiques of capitalist methods of production, which at the normative level became the basis for an appeal to a 'republicanisation of labour'. The argument of this book draws significantly from their lead, whilst, simultaneously, offering something important in return. The second sub-section, 'Moralised investment plans and the common good', addresses the problematic disjuncture between private investment decision-making and one's will as a citizen, understood as committal to a public common good. The method of democratic investment planning explained in the second section of Chapter 3 is here offered as the necessary corrective. This schema is distinct from the inter-regional distribution of scarce natural resources discussed directly above. But as the former also has a federal structure, it will be worth establishing why, from the radical republican point of view, it is an essential component of democratic republicanisation.

Anarcho-republicanism and freedom as non-domination

From the labour and anarchist republican perspectives, full republicanisation involves abolishing private ownership rights in productive property, and for the latter, it also entails the eradication of the modern state. Very briefly, with an emphasis on both arbitrary authority within the workplace and structural domination, the labour republicans identified a contradiction between republican politics and lack of freedom in economic relationships. Denied access to productive assets, workers were compelled to contract with an employer of some kind. In this sense, their domination precipitated through many agents, rather than through the discretion of any one single individual. For these reasons, the wage-labour contract was regarded as incongruent with the kind of subjective judgment the participatory ethic of republicanism advocates. This demand that economic agents need independent access to productive resources in order to secure material autonomy constitutes a powerful case that republicanism and capitalism are incompatible (Gourevitch, 2013: 591–6; White, 2011: 565–7, 571–2).

As Ruth Kinna and Alex Prichard point out, the equating of non-domination with a renunciation of the constitutional protections of private property and the asymmetries of power established in wage-labour contracts was also of great interest to the major anarchist thinkers. In developing their critiques, they fine-tuned the language of domination during the latter decades of the nineteenth century, amidst debates about the entrenchment of capitalist relations of production, escalating commodification and the appearance of the liberal state. Yet in rejecting statist solutions they went a stage further. As elites are ingrained at the structural level, the constitution the state secures, which is a bastion of class privilege, cannot be democratised. So the republican democratic deficit exists at the constitutional level, within which systems of power operate. A 'democratic republicanisation of property' was therefore demanded as the necessary corrective. Anarchists rejected the constitutional arrangements of their day, but they were democrats, and they did not reject constitutional politics. As section two of Chapter 2 explained, both Bakunin and Kropotkin condemned private property as titles in ownership require a statist legal framework for their protection. For the former, the socialist republican, or 'federalist republican', incorporates the ideals of equality and solidarity, without which liberty will be just an 'empty word' (Bakunin, 1973: 116–19, 123, 130, 144, 336–8). Following in their footsteps, modern-day anarcho-republicanism appeals for an egalitarian control over productive property and a thorough retransformation of work, which would involve fuller participation and new forms of deliberation framed beyond the institutional boundaries of statehood. So, the project to instil 'non-domination as a transformative principle' must question the ideological and structural domination of class-divided societies, whilst retaining a firm republican grounding (Kinna & Prichard, 2019: 222–3, 224–5, 227–8, 233–5).

These, succinctly put, are the central tenets of radical republicanism. There is evident congruence with associational anarchism's mode of production, which to reiterate situates non-dominating relationships within a democratised constitution theorised very much in anti-capitalist and anti-statist terms. It does this whilst retaining the transformative principle of non-domination as a normative reference point. The forthcoming chapters can be read as a defence of these organisational forms that the radical republican argument prefigures. This is especially so in Chapter 9, which will contend that Hayek's conception of coercion captures merely a small fraction of external interference. This is a lengthy chapter and is introduced in more detail at the time; suffice it to say here that my repudiation of Hayek is anarcho-republican in essence. For present purposes, it will be of much value to the overall argument of this book to explain why a democratic republicanisation of labour and property needs to include ethicised collective investment decisions.

Moralised investment plans and the common good

The contemporary republican theorist Stuart White invites his readers to imagine a future society that has realised equality in private wealth. A government then introduces a policy promoting a common good, but it causes a fall in the general rate of profit. This induces property owners to cut back on investment, which precipitates a recession. As a corollary, the government begrudgingly withdraws the policy. White's point is that if elitism is the only thing of concern with the power to make investment decisions, then no republican can object in this case because the withholding property owners are the entire citizenry. This echoes Rousseau's distinction between a citizen's general and particular wills and the internal conflict that emerges between them in the 'egalitarian capital strike' scenario. Voting as a citizen, an individual seeking the common good would favour policy A. Yet as an independent property owner acting from her particular will, which in this case is a concern with profit, she would rationally prefer to withhold investment. If this choice is collectivised, the government will have little option other than to abandon policy A. "The problem is not political inequality – an inequality between property-owners and the wider citizen body – *but the way in which individuals can use their rights as property-owners to subvert their wills as citizens*" (White, 2011: 570, original emphasis). So the concern is not just with an unequal distribution of property, or the control of investment by self-interested elites whose commanding position admits an indirect yet effective undermining of the public good. The crunch is more fundamental – investment decision-making restricts political decision-making. The outcome is that "the polity suffers a diminution in its capacity to form and act on sincere judgments about what the common good requires" (White, 2011: 570). Given policies will be scrapped due to concerns that individuals may debase them through their investment strategies. The real problem then is the separation of investment decision-making from the moral concerns pertinent to the public sphere. A genuine republicanism must, White concludes, find a way to ethicise investment decisions so that they reflect citizens' considerations on the common good (2011: 569–71).

Responding to White's challenge, I would say that only a fully democratised economy, one constituted through functional demarcation in re-politicised local communities, can provide the framework within which conflicts between investment decision-making and ethical concerns can be surpassed. White concludes his article by pointing towards a similar solution. He rejects the state socialist remedy, and for good reason; it merely reproduces the elitism of capitalist forms of investment only in a political context. But he does indicate an alternative approach, "situate control of investment outside of the state itself in independent and democratic associations within civil society" (2011: 571). In this way, investment funds may be socially directed, and decisions taken by independent bodies can fall in line with the common good. Translated into associational anarchist speak, citizens can then be held in their collective higher-selves.

Section two of Chapter 3 explained that the flow of investment funds originates initially from the centre, then to regions, through to local communities and finally to guild banks who will award grants to the cooperatives under their jurisdiction. The bodies at all three tiers are also responsible for financing projects like pollution control, sanitation and the upkeep of transport systems at their respective levels. The national and regional committees will be assimilated into the Industrial Guilds Congress, and at the local level, there is a more thorough functional demarcation, where funds will be allocated to individual guilds. This scheme limits the scope of central administration in four key ways. Firstly, it is only for new investment, and not for the whole economy. Secondly, the national committee only decide the finance required for the maintenance projects mentioned directly above, which on the face of it seems fairly innocuous. Thirdly, finance is allocated to various regions on a per-capita basis, rather than through the self-interests of plutocracies. Fourthly, the projects the regional and local bodies prioritise are not determined from the centre, and as the guild banks have full autonomy over which cooperatives to award grants to, the national and regional committees have little direct influence at the town and township levels, where inclusive modes of participation are ingrained in guild life. So economic decision-making increases in scope and detail the nearer it gets to the local communities. Through these democratic forms, investment decision-making will be a key aspect of political decision-making.

To press the point, providing the bottom-up nature of guild organisation is maintained, decision-making at the central and regional levels will genuinely reflect the common interest. Empirical research has shown that a careful combination of direct and representative forms compensates for each other's weaknesses, as well as mutually enriching the positive attributes of both.[5] I have argued elsewhere, Wyatt (2011), that representative institutions can be purposefully embedded within a vibrant participatory environment. As will now be clear, the guild cooperatives are direct democracies, and the local and regional bodies are representative in form. With regard to investment planning, bodies at all stages are chosen from below. Every cooperative within each guild will elect the personnel to sit on the local committees. The latter will then elect representatives to form the regional committees, who would themselves elect the members of the national committee. In terms of accountability, the largest threat is the potential remoteness of the regional and national bodies, who if left unchecked are liable to perpetuate only their own sectional interests. The near-universal acceptance of this democratic defect is one of the cornerstones of twentieth-century social science. So in order to negate the organisational tendencies that lead to electorate–elected polarisation, what Roberto Michels called the strong theory of oligarchy, the investment planning bodies will, in accordance with all other guild structures, be temporary, continually rotated and part-time. This ensures that for some of the time every representative at all three tiers will continue to work in the cooperative from which they initially came. In this way, rank-and-file members can retain contact with the higher-level bodies, thus preserving the momentum from base to summit. It is through these arrangements that investment funds can be socially controlled through real democratic means.

Conclusion

Schmidt and Van der Walt recognise that pure autonomy at the local level is not really desirable, and in all probability, it would be unsustainable. Varying resource endowments mean that absolute isolation would only reproduce regional disparities in living standards. So in order to ensure equality of economic conditions, production and distribution chains need planning (Schmidt & Van der Walt, 2009: 68). This chapter has discussed the federal structures that serve this purpose. It has outlined the horizontal-ised organisational forms that, in building upon Cole's revision of syndical-ism, add formative detail to Kropotkin's higher form of social organisation. As long as the members of the regional councils of delegates, Bakunin's trailing appendages, are part-time, temporary and continuously rotated, local communities can affiliate without sacrificing their complete autonomy. Finally, it is through this specific cooperative mode of production, where direct and representative democratic forms are attentively combined, that the inclusive planning of investment can be harmonised with citizens' ethical considerations pertaining to the public sphere. Through these measures, the generic desires of the higher-self are well served.

Notes

1 Writing in a contemporary setting, Prichard also observes that to be endur-ing, freedom must be institutionalised; ultimately, there is not a "non-social domain of freedom" (2019: 84).
2 For a factual account covering the origins of the theory of the syndicate, see Cole (1972: 233–51).
3 For Rawls, this category would be the least well off, and is the justification for what he calls the "difference principle". Chapter 8 engages with his conception of justice, "justice as fairness".

4 On a point of clarity, one would imagine these transferences will occur mainly through individual guilds. They are therefore distinct from the operating cross-subsidies (explained in section two of Chapter 3) that may at times be necessary to fix the price of essential goods below cost price. As the latter involve transfers between the guilds, they will be determined by the Industrial Guilds Congress.

5 See, for example, Greenberg (1984: 175, 203–5, 212, 1986: 50–3, 64, 78–9), Gunn (1984: 145–6, 148–9, 151–2, 166–7) and Jackall and Levin (1984: 139–40).

7

The organisational contours of an unorthodox mixed-economy

What is disturbing about contemporary socialists is that they seem to reject both centralised planning and the market mechanism yet suggest no alternative that meets the minimum demands of economic rationality. (Barry, 1979: 182)

Now that the legal framework and free federation of associational anarchism's constitution have been established, this lengthy chapter will show how the 'freedom *to do/become*' strand in freedom as Marxian-autonomy is embodied within a self-determining policy. As the second section of Chapter 3 explained, the product mix is determined by an unconventional combination of non-statist planning and a non-capitalist market system. The goal of economic planning is the deliberate ranking of priorities. In associational anarchism, this translates as a benign ordering of self-actualising forms of labour and inclusive structures of economic decision-making. The other main aims of rational planning are the eradication of market failings like the waste caused by needless duplication, cut-throat competition and imperious advertising; the growth of monopolies and the entrenchment of giant corporations, accompanied by the inevitable huge inequalities in wealth and power; and cyclical fluctuations, economic slumps and periodic unemployment. Associational anarchism pursues these laudable goals through the transparent deliberations between, at the most immediate level, the whole local guild, complete with associated cooperatives, and a corresponding department of the cooperative consumer council; then at the regional levels between the guilds, or the Industrial Guilds Congress (IGC), and the two consumer councils. The following discussion will show how a subordinated market, regulated by the guilds and consumer councils, can fulfil social imperatives. This particular mode of organisation provides a plausible response to the inferred socialist inconsistency Barry finds "disturbing".

There are three sections to the chapter. The first, 'Hayek's sceptical epistemology', establishes his unwavering defence of a market forces economy and his epistemological critique of state socialist planning. The thesis in *The

Road to Serfdom (first published in 1944) argues that as no one body can gather and process efficiently all the particular pieces of information that together form the entire economy, planning is technically impossible. Even the unintended yet inevitable consequences of moderate planning will, he contends, erode the values essential to freedom. Section two, 'The corporate agenda', will argue that the domination of enterprise monopoly, with its irrevocable administration through central planning, in a neo-liberal economy cannot be routinely prevented. From here, the specific ways in which domination by any kind of tyranny will be prevented in the guild system are explained. Section three, 'The associational anarchist product mix', continues where section two left off, only now the argument is developed in finer detail. The basic goods that everyone needs must be provided collectively, irrespective of one's personal bank balance. This can only be met through social planning of some kind. Here particular attention is paid to the consumer councils, who, through continuous deliberations with the local guilds, will play a large role in coordinating agents' interpersonal relations. On a note of clarity, at the local level, the cooperative consumer councils will fulfil their objective through both planning (pre-production) and by perfecting market deficiencies (post-production), including where necessary the blocking of certain products; these distinct yet interrelated tasks will be disentangled as the chapter unfolds. I will conclude that the postulates of Hayek's critique of socialist planning, as penetrating as they are with regard to centralised states, are fallacious with respect to the democratic planning of associational anarchism.

Hayek's sceptical epistemology

There are two interrelating sub-sections to this first section of the chapter. The first, 'The telecommunication system of the market', summarises Hayek's advocacy of a market order. The second, 'The inefficiency of economic planning', outlines his influential critique of the central planning in command socialist societies. Before introducing these two overlapping arguments in more detail, it will be helpful to begin by explaining what he means by the term 'catallaxy'. As the usual meaning of the word 'economy' is misleading with respect to the order he is advocating, he rejects its usage. Strictly speaking, an economy "consists of a complex of activities by which a given set of means is allocated in accordance with a unitary plan among the competing ends according to their relative importance" (Hayek, 1976: 107). Yet for Hayek, in a market order there is no such unitary system of ends. To suppose that activities are governed by a common single scale is, he argues, a "chief source of error". But although the cosmos of the market can never be governed by any particular hierarchy of predetermined outcomes, it does provide coherency with the multiplicity of ends pursued by independent economic agents. It is this overall network of interrelated individual economies which together make up the market order that Hayek calls a catallaxy. As he sees it, this system emerged spontaneously through the mutual adjustments of numerous particular economies competing in an open system (1976: 107–9, 111). We shall see that Hayek's conception of a catallaxy is founded upon a number of highly contestable propositions, some of which I will argue cannot be substantiated.

The telecommunication system of the market

Hayek believes there are special attributes only markets have. Chiefly, they are superior communication systems which digest and disseminate numerous pieces of information more efficiently than any deliberate design ever could. This is because a market economy needs no agreement on the various aims that individuals pursue. Although structured transactions occur through rules of property ownership and contract, any patterned activity is not the outcome of conscious design. It has no single purpose, and is merely the result of numerous individuals pursuing their own particular aims. So according to Hayek, a particular strength of a market economy is that it enables people to live peacefully in mutual benefit even though they frequently disagree, perhaps intensely, on common purposes. Yet the pursuit of non-identical goals can still coordinate. An economic agent can supply items to someone else even though she may not approve of the aims the other is trying to pursue, if indeed they are even known. An economic interdependence of this kind can only take place in a market order:

> It is because in the catallaxy men, while following their own interests, whether wholly egotistical or highly altruistic, will further the aims of many others, most of whom they will never know, that it is an overall order so superior to any deliberate organisation. (Hayek, 1976: 110)

It is not then respective *ends* that connect people, it is *means-relations* that do this. In the sense that everyone stands to benefit from this 'purely instrumental' common purpose, a reconciliation of divergent aims is generated. The role of public policy must, therefore, be to maximise the chances for the great variety of unknown individuals to achieve their respective purposes (Hayek, 1986: 36–7; 1976: 109–16; Butler, 1983: 41–4).

How then does the market reconcile the diverse aims of numerous people in the absence of conscious planning? Hayek identifies in the market system a sophisticated communications nexus for transmitting information in the form of the price mechanism. Fluctuations in price reflect the extent to which people need a given product; in the absence of political coercion, they provide signals which drive individual agents to satisfy the needs of strangers whilst fulfilling their own objectives. When there is a new use for a resource, or perhaps an existing source is reaching exhaustion, it will command a higher price. Changes in the conditions of the market have enabled suppliers, seen along with everyone else as profit-maximisers, to increase the price of their products. Although some consumers will change to substitute materials that are initially cheaper, the new demand will still prompt increases in their supply. So even though few people understand what caused the change, the market allows adjustments to take place to new scarcity and increases in demand. For Hayek, prices are remarkable in that they bring together the many diverse purposes of individuals who are unknown to each other. They achieve this by providing individuals with only the most essential information about the wants of others with relative ease. In his words, the price system "enables entrepreneurs, by watching the movement of comparatively few prices, as an engineer watches the hands of a few dials, to adjust their activities to those of their fellows" (Hayek, 1986: 36, see also 1986: 36–7, 1976: 115–16; Butler, 1983: 45–7).

The inefficiency of economic planning

Hayek makes two main interrelated claims in his prolonged critique of socialist economics, in which he denies the possibility of efficient central state planning. Firstly, the thousands of pieces of economic information, known only in very small detail by individual agents, cannot realistically be amassed and processed by a single body. Secondly, a socialist planned economy will, despite its genuine benevolent intentions, inevitably lead to an excessively authoritarian end, an outcome that may be totally at odds with the initial altruistic vision of the idealist planners.

Hayek denies there can be an efficient socialist method for the distribution and use of scarce resources. The economy may only be effectively steered if the necessary information can be gathered thoroughly. But the determinants involved in the use of resources are huge. In the process of manufacturing, new uses for raw materials, technologies and services will come to light. The frequent transformations in the field of capital goods mean that the conditions through which sources of supply are determined may change at any given moment. As the variables of economic life are forever subject to permutation, all the particular fragments of information that affect trends in supply and demand cannot possibly be conveyed to and then processed by a central authority swiftly enough to make planning viable. This is because the processing of information will be a complicated task, and by the time it is complete, circumstances will surely have changed. If so, a technically sound socialist economy cannot be organised rationally in the absence of the price mechanism. Only the relative price of productive resources can provide an index of scarcity. Hayek's point is that all knowledge is subjective, and in a market forces economy, it is disseminated widely. In discovering fragments of knowledge, agents often unearth unexpected aspects of manufacture and supply, and they may interpret the same discovery in a variety of ways. So it is through experience that manufacturers come to acquire special knowledge that is not fully known to competitors. The market coordinates these personal pieces of individual knowledge into a whole model of economic relations. But it is knowledge that cannot be known in full by anyone, including socialist planners. Some of the information suppliers need so they may calculate product quantities and the selling price depends partly on the plans of others. Competitors will be seeking to exploit similar gaps in the market, and customers may change their plans in light of new opportunities. As such, it is not possible to gather and process all this information centrally (Hayek, 1986: 36–7; Barry, 1979: 179–80; Butler, 1983: 56–7, 71).

It is, then, the belief that economic processes can be rationally planned by political institutions that Hayek opposes. As he sees it, socialist central planning ensures that power concentrates, inevitably, within the structures of controlling authorities. The socialist vision, which has the best of philanthropic intentions, can only be reached by invoking an increasing degree of coercion so that people are made to conform to the contours of a general plan. This in turn allows those who have less benevolent intentions to seize control of the apparatus of coercion and wield it to meet their own selfish ends. The outcome is that the benign socialists engender precisely the opposite of what they initially had in mind. For Hayek this is a great tragedy, "that in our endeavour consciously to shape our future in accordance with high ideals, we should in fact unwittingly produce the very opposite of what we have been striving for" (1986: 4). The real point then is that the arguments between pro- and anti-socialists are not so much about different values; it is more that the means advocated by the socialist constructivists cannot realise the ends they have in sight. A path towards serfdom is set in motion because any intervention in social evolution will engender processes that are inimical to natural spontaneity (Hayek, 1986: 3–4; Butler, 1983: 66–7; Barry, 1979: 182–4).

Summary

Economic factors are so complex, and in such a permanent state of flux, that no centralised planning agency could ever comprehend them all. In order to reconcile the activities of numerous economic agents, state planners must have thorough knowledge of the multiple uses of any given item. This is held to be technically impossible by theorists of the new right like Hayek. For these thinkers, a market order is able to process large quantities of information much more quickly and make better use of it, as there is no need to know all the personal details of market transactions. It is because markets help thousands of individuals to pursue their personal objectives that they are said to be far more efficient than any purposefully devised system.

The corporate agenda

There are two sub-sections to this second section of the chapter. The first, 'Enterprise monopoly and central planning in a catallaxy', argues that the self-perpetuation of enterprise monopoly, with its rapid slide towards internal central planning, cannot be halted in a neo-liberal economy. Consequently, Hayek's argument that a free market system is planned by numerous atomised agents in many separate locations breaks down completely. The second sub-section, 'Beyond bureaucratic tyranny', offers a preliminary account of associational anarchism's particular economic rationalism, which can be distinguished sharply from the authoritarian imposition of command socialism. Section three of this chapter will then analyse in finer detail the functional agencies responsible for coordinating the multiple plans at the local level.

Enterprise monopoly and central planning in a catallaxy

Through his inquiry into the strong tendency for capital to agglomerate in large units, Marx was one of the first canon thinkers to explain how monopolistic corporations had come into existence. His analysis has been a great source of inspiration to critics of capitalism ever since. Although written back in the 1970s, one of the best accounts of the modern corporation is still provided by the influential Marxist, Harry Braverman. His work indicates that the competitive model of capitalism, within which production in every industry is disseminated widely between many different firms, has given way to monopoly capitalism. This process first appeared towards the end of the nineteenth century, with increases in the concentration and centralisation of capital (1974: 251, 257). Agreeing with this critique, Paul Sweezy stresses that although the inner nature of capitalism has remained consistent, its outward manifestations have changed dramatically over the last hundred years or so; not least is the "restless expansion" of capital accumulation (1974: xi). This is because capitalists are driven to accumulate in order to satisfy the self-expanding logic of capital. Otherwise, profits would fall in relative terms. Increases in concentrations of capital and wealth lead quickly to the formation of monopolies, which due to their enormous financial power become largely irremovable. In competitive capitalism, the imperative is to accumulate for the sake of survival, but in monopoly capitalism, it is for oligopolies to invest in order to avoid encroachment (Cowling, 1982: 48). It is this universal tendency that has led to consolidation of new organisational forms.

In highlighting their problematic effect, Braverman points to changes in the scale of management activities within the modern corporation. Along with the considerable growth of the enterprise, the operations of management have correspondingly increased in size, and have demarcated into certain key divisions. This initial development was in the sphere of production. It quickly spread into the organisation of marketing apparatus, especially in terms of transportation and communications, and then likewise into finance. To take the first division, productive activities are typically subdivided, each functional department having a specific role – research and design, planning and control of production, quality control, manufacturing costs, purchase of raw materials, plant maintenance and staff training are the foremost ones that Braverman highlights. The marketing policies of the corporation analyse sales, orders, consumer promotions, advertising, distributions and commissions. The subdivisions within the finance division include borrowing and collecting, questions of credit extension and the general supervision of cash flows. In order to function efficiently, all subdivisions within the main divisions require internal departments, in which case "each corporate division takes on the characteristics of a separate enterprise, with its own management staff" (Braverman, 1974: 264). As a result, there is no longer a single manager or a small managing team, but entire managerial departments. Pivotally, all the major divisions within the private corporation must, as a matter of organisational necessity, be centrally planned. In sum, the advance of modern technological developments has made the growth of private monopolies inevitable. The relentless drive to increase efficiency in order to maximise profit means the most successful firms will become progressively larger. And as competition declines in equal proportion to the rise of monopoly rule, giant corporations will quickly come to dominate the economic landscape (Braverman, 1974: 260–3, 267; Butler, 1983: 68).

Rather than reject this kind of argument outright, Hayek sought to soften its impact. Large companies may be able to minimise their overheads, but, he counters, there are countervailing tendencies in the shape of bureaucratic structures, which may result in a slower response to changes in patterns of demand, especially with minority tastes.[1] If so, only an array of smaller firms can satisfy contemporary consumers, who often demand customised or personalised products. According to Hayek then, there is nothing inevitable about the *continuance* of monopolises. Where they do arise, they are usually sanctioned by governments, and their control is only effective with the assistance of the state. So although he does not look upon enterprise monopoly favourably, he does regard attempts by governments to restrict their size and power as arbitrary, and he remains sceptical about the advantages discretionary policies are likely to bring. "I doubt whether there are any 'good' monopolies that deserve protection. But there will always be inevitable monopolies whose transitory and temporary character is often turned into a permanent one by the solicitude of government" (Hayek, 1960: 266). As a right-libertarian, Hayek is no advocate of monopolies, but he does think that by themselves they are not really the main problem. Rather, it is certain monopolistic practices like preventing other firms from entering the industry that are harmful. He recognises that when a monopolist is the sole supplier of an essential item, they can coerce.[2] This is on the condition that a particular monopolist is able to hold back the supply of something that is indispensable to the survival of others. He adds that "the most expedient and effective method of preventing this is probably to require him to treat all customers alike, i.e., to insist that his prices be the same for all and to prohibit all discrimination on his part" (1960: 136). Nevertheless, it is clear that Hayek is forced to concede that enterprise monopolies are, although supposedly only transient, unavoidable. Indeed, he calls it "unpleasant facts" that there are given capacities that cannot be duplicated (1960: 264–6, 1986: 32–5; Butler, 1983: 68–9).

So whilst Hayek agrees that monopolies are undesirable, as they cannot be avoided in full, he is resigned to the fact that competition will not always be effective, and certain measures will have to be put in place for the purpose of compensation.[3] Any dislike of enterprise monopoly he may have, though, is not down to a belief that they ruin the conditions that preserve *perfect* competition, as these conditions may never exist, or rather no one has any way of knowing whether they exist. He is more inclined to argue that enterprise monopolies cannot dominate the market for long as they are spontaneously erased through the process of free competition. If this is the case then there is no need to prohibit enterprise monopolies by way of legal penalties. Yet in contrast, he regards the monopolies of trade unions and the state as harmful; "it would be disingenuous to represent the existing monopolies in the field of labour and those in the field of enterprise as being of the same kind" (1960: 265). As the former has been purposefully made, they, along with the monopolies of the state, should rightfully be legally curtailed (1960: 265; Papaioannou, 2012: 167).

It is on these points that his reasoning can be called into question. For example, Theo Papaioannou states that Hayek fails to consider the actuality that enterprise monopolies crush the course of spontaneity and the progression of evolution, and as such are far more dangerous to society than he contends. If monopolies are considered in respect of power, then state and enterprise monopolies must be treated on similar grounds. "Since Hayek only disapproves of state monopolies, he appears to hand over the conscious control of the market and society to enterprise monopolies" (Papaioannou, 2012: 168). His argument rests upon an epistemology that denies the market can be consciously planned, but, simultaneously, "it approves of such planning when it comes about through the spontaneous and evolutionary process of the market" (2012: 168). Certainly, major corporations have for some time organised into interlinking oligopolies, from which they quickly seized dominant positions that are virtually impregnable. Cowling prophetically captured this strong tendency some years ago:

> They will remain unassailable partly because these dominant oligopolies will invest in their maintenance in order to secure the benefits of the stream of monopoly profits associated with their position. Competition between and within national oligopoly groups will occasionally break out, but these should be seen as transient elements in the accommodation of different capitals to each other. (1982: 1)

In much the same way, Braverman defines the increasing need for and subsequent growth in marketing strategies. The general purpose of administrative control is to eliminate uncertainty. As the prime area of uncertainty is the market, the corporation will direct its efforts towards reducing what Braverman calls the *autonomous character* of consumer demand, and will direct its efforts towards increasing its *induced character*. So the predominance of marketing organisation throughout the entire corporation is intended to match consumer needs with production needs, rather than the other way round (1974: 264; 265–6). If so, then in contradiction to the famous maxim, the consumer cannot be king. Perhaps the most serious point raised in this debate on the supposedly transitory nature of enterprise monopoly concerns its internal central planning.

The Hayekian perspective recognises that in our own way, we are all planners. All firms must anticipate changes and make plans to deal with them. Successful businesses do this well, even though none will ever possess perfect foresight. Yet in guessing each other's plans, firms reconcile their own purposes. Hayek's point is that an economy without central planning is not actually unplanned. As all economic agents make plans, the free market is planned in many localities and by many individuals (Butler, 1983: 72–4). But this acclaimed asset of the market economy loses all credibility if the above explanation on the longevity of enterprise monopoly holds any weight. Consider briefly the argument of Kieran Allen that the contrast between an idealised market economy with centralised state planning is a false dichotomy. This is because small firms no longer characterise contemporary capitalism. Inevitably, economic activity becomes increasingly internal to large corporations and not through the open market. "The allocation of resources within these corporations and the transfer of goods from one manufacturing unit to another are not based on market principles but are organised through central planning" (Allen, 2011: 190). It is important to underline the sheer scale on which elaborate forms of technical planning are taking place. "[M]ultinational corporations and global supply chain management companies already engage in complex planning for economies that are the size of countries" (2011: 193). The corporate planning of intricate networks proceeds through modern information technologies. Huge retail outlets also rationally plan in order to fill their warehouses with goods destined for markets far and wide. These forms of planning are top-down, with boards of directors at the centre (2011: 177, 190–3). Returning once more to Braverman, he too believes that because capitalist society cannot develop a general planning mechanism to meet the demands of social coordination, a large part of what should be a public function relocates into the internal affairs of huge corporations. "This has no juridical basis or administrative concept behind it; it simply comes into being by virtue of the giant size and power of the corporations, whose internal planning becomes, in effect, a crude substitute for necessary social planning" (1974: 268). Government initiatives of social coordination may be more visible, but "so long as investment decisions are made by the corporations, the locus of social control and coordination must be sought among them; government fills the interstices left by these prime decisions" (1974: 269).

To sum up, as some firms will be more successful than others, they will expand more efficiently than their rivals. From here the entrenchment of large corporations cannot be prevented. For the monopolies and oligopolies, it is business as usual. Of particular importance, within any extensive organisation, political or economic, it reaches the stage where internal decision-making can only be determined through central planning. So if *political* planning is certain to crush the effective freedom of those subject to its decision-making, then much the same can be said about the *economic* planning of the private economic corporation. The remainder of this chapter will address the crucial question of how to piece together a decentralised system of participatory planning that can fulfil the function of coordination, whilst simultaneously correcting market deficiencies, and yet has internal mechanisms built into it through which to prevent the planning agencies from escalating to the point where extensive central administration could not be revoked.

Beyond bureaucratic tyranny

The aim of this sub-section is to present a preliminary sketch of the organisational forms through which associational anarchist structures will fulfil their objective without giving rise to the domineering hierarchical forms common to both corporate capitalism and command socialism. These are the decentralised horizontal links between producers and consumers, through which extra-market and market-regulating schemes will meet the demands of a left-libertarian economic rationalism. Particular attention is paid to how the cooperative consumer councils will operate, as they are, in conjunction with the guild cooperatives, the main agencies of planning, and are hence indispensable to a social anarchist mode of consumption.

Market economies have often been defended for the way they decentralise economic decision-making whilst creating horizontal networks of social relations. In principle, these two tendencies are a valuable asset to any libertarian economy. The problem is, though, that in capitalist society mutual horizontal relations are only open to a small wealthy class; for the rest of us, they diminish in direct proportion to the progression of enterprise monopoly. So in order to operate efficiently, social networks must be set within an alternative constitution where much of the information producers need in order to respond effectively to consumer demand will be provided by neither impersonal market indicators nor hierarchical superiors. Recall that associational anarchism replaces the omnipresent state with numerous different electoral agencies, as many as there are essential social functions. In this unconventional political economy, participatory planning subordinates a market system. The former is a precondition for the latter's efficiency in the sense that it expresses the organised interests of consumers. Some public amenities and primary items are suitable for macro planning. Water, electricity, gas, health care, education, sanitation, public transport, protection of the natural environment and the basic items in diet and dress all fall within the need category. Here prices will be fixed at the regional levels, through the approach explained in the second section of Chapter 3, as they are the minimal requirements for material survival. The committees at the higher echelons of the guilds and consumer councils, who, to reiterate, are part-time, temporary and continually rotated, will assume responsibility for this aspect of social planning. Whilst this is high-level decision-making, their *modus operandi* is as transpicuous as practicality will allow. Firstly, as the previous chapter explained, these organisations are bottom-up in nature, and secondly, regional administration is divided between the interrelating functional bodies, where it becomes less opaque. Following this, at the town and township levels, other needs that vary according to climate, geographic location, demographic curves and simply local taste can be articulated democratically from below through negotiation between all interested parties; the prices of the products requested to satisfy these locally expressed needs will also be fixed in the usual associational anarchist way.

In addition, the cooperative consumer council will have a supplementary role in terms of negating market weaknesses. The methods through which they will approach this important task can be explained through a response to two salient critiques of markets from Branko Horvat and Andrew Sayer. Horvat stresses that acts of consumption can be incorrect, can be irrational, frequently derive no lasting satisfaction, can be informed by custom and frequently lack adequate knowledge. The likelihood is that trends in consumptive choice are often indicative of ideological distortion, as with the internalisation of norms and values that do not serve the long-term interests of consumers; this I have termed the lower-self. Perhaps the most immediate contention is that reflective consumption is dependent upon adequate education and less-imperfect information, the implications of which are clear. "If our choices are socially determined, then we had better consider how to control the forces responsible for this determination and stop flattering ourselves as to how much individual sovereignty we enjoy" (Horvat, 1982: 330, 329–32). Turning now to Sayer's critique, he suggests that markets in which prices are volatile are less common than fixed-price markets, where producers respond to low sales by holding out for custom, rather than lowering the price. He then highlights the difference between standardised goods brought 'off-the-shelf', contracting in which only information on the price is given, and those 'made to order', 'relational contracting', where producer–consumer relations are more personalised. The latter involves the sharing of information and the enhancement of trust. Sayer contends that liberals tend to overestimate the accuracy of information displayed through price signals.[4] Non-price information, which is free to consumers and hence outside market exchange, also needs to be available. In sum, as markets are anything but self-regulating, extra-market modes of coordination are needed to rectify them (2000: 84–6).

It is in response to these critiques that the cooperative consumer councils offer a real improvement to the way markets operate. To help illustrate why, consider very briefly a point raised by Alex Nove. He infers that competition and the use of advertisements have some positive features. They are both a prerequisite and a consequence of free choice, and as they provide a stimulus, they can ensure improvements in quality and service. The aim of advertising is to attract customers; without it, there is the danger of indifference to need. He acknowledges this can degenerate into "pseudo product innovation and differentiation" and "excessive expenditure on garish packaging". But without competition, there is a risk that the momentum of technological progress will stagnate. So in Nove's feasible socialism, glossy catalogues will continue to tempt potential customers (1983: 38, 41–2, 205). In my opinion, this is an inappropriate way to entice the interests of consumers. It is precisely this kind of marketing strategy that gives rise to fetishism and hence does not move beyond this book's account of the lower-self. Excessive competition brings in its wake gimmicky and aggressive advertising, sales-pitch promotions, commercial blurbs and the like, which, consequently, poses a permanent threat to the autonomous character of consumer preference. It is also emblematic of an economy that is dominated by exchange relations, and it obscures the difference between necessary products and the triviality of tacky items. Associational anarchism has an alternative rationale for improving quality and service. The cooperative consumer councils will be the social forums through which to critically appraise product promotions. Rather than appeal to the intemperate vanity of consumers, advertising can assume new forms if it deliberately seeks to disengage the petty and illicit appetites of the lower-self. The intention is that conscientious consumers will be more concerned with questions surrounding the degree of workers' fulfilment externalised in the product and the effect of productive technologies on the environment.

To widen the scope a little, at the local level, the cooperative consumer councils will provide open deliberative forums within which popular opinion can be sought and minority interests voiced. Their subsequent social research will aim to identify unmet demand, and through their advisory capacities, they will be a valuable social force for guiding consumer choice. In these regards, they have extra-market and market-regulating functions. Their main objectives are (1) to determine just prices for essential goods, those required to satisfy locally expressed basic needs; (2) in pre-productive terms, to request items not yet on the market and to provide social forums where promotions for new products can be scrutinised; and (3) in post-productive terms, to negate the kind of market weaknesses mentioned above and, where necessary, intercept in the further sale of a given product already released onto the market.[5] In all these senses, the cooperative consumer councils will fulfil a vital illuminating role which can help recast agents' 'means-relations' along a very different path to that defended in Hayek's catallaxy. Simultaneously, consumers will have the opportunity to participate meaningfully in the determination of the product mix, irrespective of one's personal bank balance, which clearly involves a lot more than merely calculating the price of goods against marginal utility, and in the process activate what I have termed the consumptive higher-self.

In any economy that values freedom of choice, there is no fail-proof way to ensure consumptive preference stems consistently from sound judgement. But associational anarchist consumers can, through formal requisitions of products not yet on the market, help determine the product range rationally before the act of purchase. The cooperative consumer councils will carry out the initial research, through which they can gauge the kinds of demand poorly represented in the price system. They will then supply the resulting data to the guilds. As decentralised functional organisations, they are well placed to respond to particular requests from their neighbourhoods. If direct communications between producers and consumers decide this element of the plan, local economies will not be subject to centralised control. The remainder of microeconomic decision-making will fall to the guild market system. Here producer–consumer relations can wherever possible be determined in person through relational contracting. Beyond this, the cooperative consumer councils will, drawing from their empirical data, provide an outlet for the sharing of both less imperfect and non-price information, which suggests consumers will lack adequate knowledge less frequently than they otherwise would. So in response to the critiques of Horvat and Sayer, these councils are, as market-regulating modes of coordination, in an ideal position to steer the guild market system in a direction that satisfies more efficiently people's needs and wants. As such, there is every indication that irrational consumptive choice will be less frequent than it is in an unshackled market economy, where marketing departments have greater licence to increase hype, often through fierce and invasive strategies that seem to deliberately target the low self-worth of already vulnerable social groups. In sum, whilst price signals will have a significant role in the mediation of supply and demand, as the cooperative consumer councils have a far greater aptness to correct market failures than an intervening state, their direction will take precedence. Hence, they offer far more than just a palliative.

Summary

This then is the general outline of the political economy through which associational anarchism will determine the product mix democratically without engendering the kinds of imposing top-down bureaucracies typically found in both capitalist and statist economies. Hayek provides a devastating critique of the centrally planned economy of state socialism, a polemic that is, in general, shared within the social anarchist tradition. As section two of Chapter 2 explained, for Bakunin the communist state will require immense knowledge as it will centralise control of production, land, factories, commerce and the banking system. A new class hierarchy will form, and it will need armed force to restrain the inevitable discontent of the masses. Its brutal reign will be "the most aristocratic, despotic, arrogant, and elitist of all regimes" (Bakunin, 1973: 319, see also 315). Likewise, for Kropotkin, "in all production there arise daily thousands of difficulties which no government can solve or foresee" (1970: 76). As it is such a complicated task, centralised economic planning inevitably leads to an "absolutely ineffective" party directorship. It is clear then that Bakunin, Kropotkin and Hayek all firmly reject the authoritarian socialist state for similar reasons.

But herein ends the social anarchist congruity with Hayek. He seems to think that the emergence of enterprise monopolies is inevitable, but there is nothing equally inevitable about the effectiveness of their control, as without the 'solicitude of government', they will lose their permanence. I would say he is way off the mark here. His belief that enterprise monopolies display a "transitory and temporary character" as there are countervailing tendencies naturally occurring spontaneously is, in the harsh and unforgiving climate of a real existing market forces economy, wildly unrealistic. There is little reason to suppose that existing monopolies will play fairly by the rules of the market game. Given the hard principle of profit maximisation, it is far more likely that the incentive to outstrip potential rivals at all costs will drive large enterprises to sustain their monopolistic privilege by any means available, including predatory behaviour. It would be incredibly naive to assume otherwise. Besides, irrespective of whether the permanence of given enterprise monopolies is endemic to a market economy, or whether there may be occasions where some will, as highly unlikely as this seems, spontaneously dissolve due to market forces, it is still the case that they will continue to dominate as the latter will simply be replaced by others. Either way, it is plainly evident that enterprise monopolies will not only endure but will also retain their enormous power. For these reasons, it was important to illustrate the structural arrangements through which associational anarchism will avert huge concentrations of both economic and political power. The following section will explain in more detail how social coordination will be mediated efficiently by the decentralised functional bodies.

The associational anarchist product mix

There are three closely interrelating sub-sections to this final section of the chapter. The first, 'Democratic planning and social markets', argues that even though there will always be some unpredictable changes in economic conditions, harmonious adjustments can still be made in the absence of either political or economic imposition. In a similar vein, sub-section two, 'Desire formation and content-neutrality', explains the idea that real autonomy has less to do with the actual content of desires and more to do with the antecedents that inform their historical development. Here I indicate why this claim, when applied to the guild system, is of much value to freedom as Marxian-autonomy. The third sub-section, 'Market externalities', broadens this account of the product mix, only now it is set within a wider context of exposing the sources of externalities. This task is essential to the free society, not least because externalities impose upon the freedom of others 'external' to the initial transacting parties.

Democratic planning and social markets

This sub-section explains why the guild cooperatives and the cooperative consumer councils in the local communities do not need perfect insight into all the essential facts of economic life in order to reconcile the various aims of individual agents; neither do they need to agree on a hierarchy of rational goals. In this case, Hayek's particular claim that universal congruity on a common scale of particular ends is not required for the purpose of integrating the numerous activities of individuals into a peaceful order applies just as much to associational anarchism as it does to a catallaxy.

In contrast to an assumption of the traditional equilibrium theory, Hayek points out that the economy is not static, and precise foresight is unachievable as individual agency is always dependent upon the flexible and temporary plans of other people. Equilibrium can only have meaning for the single individual, but never for society at large. The thousands of individual plans can never exist in perfect harmony as no one can ever predict with certainty how unforeseen alterations in economic circumstances will lead others to change their minds in the future. However, although he rejects the claim that equilibrium can be used as a premise for planning, he does believe that a market may be loosely in equilibrium in the sense that there is a tendency for the plans of numerous individuals to reconcile in the long run. As Butler notes, it may be thought of as a *dynamic equilibrium*, as a constantly evolving process towards equilibrium. For this reason, "we can begin to understand the futility of supposing that this complex process can be arrested, harnessed and planned" (Butler, 1983: 57; 56–7). There are two immediate responses that can be made to this contention. Firstly, the argument that there is a process towards equilibrium only applies to a market sector that is genuinely competitive. Such a process is severely frustrated so long as enterprise monopolies dominate, which, as we have seen, will be all the time. The second point is that for planning to serve its purpose of social coordination and goal fulfilment, the corresponding 'complex process' in the guild market system will be neither 'arrested' nor 'harnessed'. If there can be a tendency for a market to form a loose and 'dynamic equilibrium', then it is more easily guided when interacting functional agencies assume joint responsibility for identifying its general patterns. In this setting, the 'process towards equilibrium' can gather momentum more efficiently due to the absence of monopolies and other market imperfections like those mentioned in the previous sub-section. As this market system is placed within the framework of social planning, let us take a closer look at how the latter will operate.

The previous section outlined the combined roles of the local cooperative consumer councils. The point to add now is that as they will need to focus only on specific sets of confines, they will be internally demarcated so that subdivisions can specialise in given fields. So in terms of their organisation, these councils will be internally divided into distinct departments; how many will depend on local contingencies and will vary from region to region. The demarcation denotes a given department's relevance to just one guild. The latter is a technological homogeneous productive association, and it breaks down into a set of quasi-autonomous cooperatives, each one composed of no more than 500 members. This ensures that the subdivisions within the cooperative consumer councils will not be asked to engage with undifferentiated economic conglomerates. By far the most important and largest volume of communication will take place at the fundamental level. By this I mean relations will be set up locally between a particular department of a cooperative consumer council and the guild with which it is in dialogue.[6] Rather than establish direct relations between a singular guild cooperative and the corresponding department of the former, it is probably fairer for all information to pass through the local committees of each separate guild, where it will be disseminated equally to all affiliated cooperatives. That way no single cooperative is disadvantaged. Crucially, due to the restricted scope of each single department, there is no imperative to process all the information of the entire local economy, and contracts can be freely negotiated without being subject to interference from a central body. It follows that as the members of any given department are not required to decipher the entrails of grand plans, they can circulate fragments of knowledge swiftly and more effectively. To reiterate, these processes are only in relation to local planning and the correction of market flaws; individual consumers are free to purchase directly from given cooperatives of their own volition. In all cases though, as planning of some kind is a requirement of every economy, including Hayek's catallaxy, the decentralised horizontal networks discussed here are considerably less cumbersome than the centralised planning of either statist or market societies. The following two sub-sections will add substance to this claim.

Desire formation and content-neutrality

So far, I have offered reasons why the cooperative consumer councils will, as open deliberating forums, become the new social forces for influencing consumer preference; whilst, simultaneously, their members will be held democratically accountable by the town wards from which they were elected.

This rationale will now be extended to include a particular defence of positive freedom from the wider academic literature. This is the credible suggestion that as an agent's autonomy is historically informed, her freedom does not rest on the actual desires felt in the current moment. When applied specifically to the guilds and consumer councils, this idea will be a worthy addition to freedom as Marxian-autonomy.

For John Christman, positive freedom addresses the mode of desire *formation*, rather than what the desires actually are.[7] This is the idea that a person's autonomy should be treated as essentially historical, that it is dependent on her past. Analysis must therefore focus on the conditions within which preferences were formed, rather than their actual structure at any given moment. Emphasising the origin of desires provides a 'content neutral' theory of positive freedom. Pivotally, the forces that account for the changes in someone's preference set "must be the one's that the agent was in a position to reflect upon and resist for the changes to have manifested the agent's autonomy" (Christman, 1991: 346). As the free person does more than simply choose her own desires, it is important to identify whether they emerge through balanced reflection, or whether they are the outcome of manipulation or interference. This argument for self-reflection asserts that a person who undergoes a lifestyle change is not really free if her decision is a result of indoctrination, deceit or oppression. But she can be considered positively free if her decision was arrived at through rational assessment and is not the outcome of ignorance of other plausible options. So authoritarian bodies cannot coerce people to do a certain thing under the pretence that their freedom is being increased, the very practice Berlin warned of, as holding a particular desire neither enhances nor restricts freedom (Christman, 1991: 346–7, 355, 359; Carter, 2003: 8).

Focusing less on content and more on formation requires subjective acuteness in the perception of social phenomena. In associational anarchism's realm of necessity, the move beyond indoctrination and into informed contemplation will take place through the medium of the guilds and the consumer councils. If, as seems highly plausible, Christman is right that "autonomy is achieved when an agent is in a position to be aware of the changes and development of her character and of why these changes come about" (1991: 348), then this will be more easily realised when demarcated social forums assume responsibility for disseminating information to autonomous agents. Rather than face the daunting prospect of unpicking an indiscriminate miscellany of hugely diverse and unrelated social determinants, the breadth of issues is restricted to the jurisdiction of functional demarcation. With regards to the cooperative consumer councils, the focus is restricted even further to their internal departmental divides. This approach can, as much as can be expected, untangle and disconnect the various social influences that bear heavily upon the career and purchasing choices of individuals. Commenting on a related issue, Swift points out that (a) there is not a singular path that is rational for all individuals, (b) there is no particular way of life that is rational for any single individual and (c) even if a political body could identity rational courses of action, there are good reasons not to invest it with powers of arbitrary intervention (2001: 84–6). The functional bodies will endorse these pluralist principles. Hence, in order to anarchise Swift's claims that "a state helps its members towards freedom not by getting them all to live the same way, but by doing what it can to help them to live in ways which are rational for them" (2001: 84), we need only substitute the word 'state' with the words 'guilds and consumer councils'. And what is rational for economic agents is to pursue the preferences that have been assessed through the kind of informed reflection that for Christman constitutes a key aspect of positive liberty.

In sum, I have stressed that the illuminating role of the cooperative consumer councils can help redirect agents' collective 'means-relations' along a left-libertarian path. I would now like to add that in the process, they will also provide the conditions within which preferences may be realistically assessed through self-contemplation. This constitutes a significant advance towards the associational anarchist higher-self. For these reasons then, the argument that it is desire formation that is most important, rather than just their content, will be a laudable addition to the positive strand in freedom as Marxian-autonomy.

Market externalities

Through a discussion of market externalities, I will now critically evaluate Hayek's argument that a catallaxy satisfies the needs of individuals in a unique way. "That we assist in the realisation of other people's aims without sharing them or even knowing them, and solely in order to achieve our own aims, is the source of strength of the Great Society" (1976: 110). So apparently consumers are, due to the impersonal nature of market transactions, independent of the wills of their suppliers because both parties are so profoundly self-interested that the latter usually care little for what the former may do with the items they provide. If so, in the usual course of economic transactions, agents act as mutual impersonal means, each concerned only for her own personal purpose. This is supposedly a chief asset of a catallaxy; it enables coordination in the absence of shared common aims (1976: 110–11, 1991: 97). It is not just that for much of the time, traders will have no idea of the particular ends of those they serve; Hayek also thinks that even if suppliers are aware of such ends, and of which they thoroughly disapprove, they would still willingly assist them. "We should be very dependent on the beliefs of our fellows if they were prepared to sell their products to us only when they approved of our ends and not for their own advantage" (1991: 97).[8] In what follows, both these interrelated contentions are considered. I will argue that the guild market system can, when required, attenuate the collective ignorance Hayek praises. Then, moving on to the second issue, it seems to me that this claim is exaggerated. In the appropriate setting, people would rather not further the aims of those whose intentions they despise. Here I show how the local guilds, in continuous dialogue with consumer bodies, can address this problem.

One of the immediate problems of impersonal market relations is that if an economic agent is supplying either intermediate goods or finished products to a buyer whose purpose really is unknown, then there is no way of realising, until it is too late, the extent to which the product is the source of an externality in the bad sense. Externalities have long since been recognised as problematic to 'private' market transactions, but they are likely to increase in intensity as capitalism transmutes from its competitive to its monopoly form in the usual way. The first thing to note here is that Hayek's supposition on supplier ignorance is, in the economy he pictures, perhaps not as extensive as it may at first appear. It is of course true that certain consumption and capital goods can be used for numerous ends, and the particular purpose a given buyer has in mind cannot always be assumed by the supplier in advance of sale. It is also plainly evident that commercial secrecy is in the interests of brute self-interest. But by the same token, in the fictional world of non-monopoly capitalism, as suppliers are fiercely driven to outmanoeuvre business rivals, speculation on the likely ends of potential buyers is a key aspect of fine-tuning product design. Hayek's sceptical epistemology does not rule this out. How effectively supplies are able to do this rests, however, on the key premise that the acclaimed decentralised coordination in a catallaxy is sustainable, and as we have seen, this is questionable in light of the strong centralising tendencies that, in the most profitable sectors, are all but omnipresent. The real problem then is that the task of identifying the aims of others becomes increasingly mystified as competition becomes increasingly ineffective. Ironically, it is here that Hayek's claim carries more weight, on the very processes he regards as "unpleasant", and which do not "deserve protection". Decisively, the difficulties in exposing and dealing with a given externality escalate in proportion to the increase in the distance between the site of production and the place of purchase and consumption. The problem intensifies in relation to the scale of technological complexity, and where labour is divided geographically. It is hardly surprising there is such a general level of obscurity if the manufacture of the various specialist parts that eventually form the finished product takes place in isolation from each other, and perhaps by separate firms located on different continents. Adrian Leftwich illustrates this point well through the example of modern sports trainers:

> The raw materials (like rubber) may come from Malaysia, the finance capital from a consortium of European banks, the technology from a machine designed and built in Japan or America, while the labour may be concentrated in a factory in Vietnam, Costa Rica or China. (2004: 108)

This tendency is most acute in globalised monopoly capitalism, where international supply chains are so complex it is harder to see the bigger picture. If the analysis above is accurate, that enterprise monopoly is unavoidable in a catallaxy; any hope of identifying promptly the main causes of externalities, which are not accounted for in the price mechanism, is all but extinguished. This has a special relevance to the increasing concern over ecological ruin, pollution and the exhaustion of finite resources.

It would seem then that transparency is best assured when the vast majority of economic transactions take place mainly within the same locality, and where close relations between the direct producers and consumers are maximised. This is exactly what the guild system provides. We have seen that the guild committees at the town level will disseminate both information and aggregated requests equally to all affiliated cooperatives, and they will democratically plan investment via the grant scheme. Through these structures of decentralised coordination, where production occurs in guild cooperatives and where consumer councils monitor the product range, the causes of externalities can be identified more clearly. The key point to reiterate is that the universalisation of multi-skilled forms of labour is the first priority. From the perspective of any one individual, the value of self-actualisation in all other cooperatives will come before the profit motive of one's own cooperative. As such, supply and demand curves will affect the quantities and range of products, but not the heterogeneous category of de-alienated labour. As section three of Chapter 3 explained, work-teams will assume responsibility for the production of the product in its entirety, from its initial design to its manufacture, through to its eventual supply. This is an essential constituent of self-actualising work. Significantly, as the guild cooperatives will assemble all the parts that collectively make up the finished product, it is obviously easier for the associated members to perceive the purposes their products will serve. Where particular components cannot be made in any given cooperative, those requiring highly specialist technology for example, then external relations with another cooperative will be established. In these cases, communications between cooperatives will be transmitted through the federal structures of either a single guild or the Industrial Guilds Congress, depending on whether the cooperatives are affiliated with the same guild.

The idea is that as supply and demand are mediated openly and by all those immediately affected, it will be less difficult to identify the particular objectives of economic agents. This is because the goods produced and consumed mainly within close proximately will involve more face-to-face communications, especially with the kind of relational contracting discussed above. Despite their monopolisation, market economics have shown that, at least in certain localised sectors, relational contracting does provide producers with more than a few random insights about the ends to which the goods they supply will serve. Clearly, the very nature of the relation intentionally seeks the continuous sharing of information. When these kinds of direct relations are augmented in the guild system, more often than not the general purpose of a given item could at the very least be roughly known, or at least its rudiments guessed. The resulting transparency is a particular asset of the functional mode of organisation. To recall and enhance the argument of the previous two sub-sections, through the information supplied by the cooperative consumer council, the guild cooperatives will have less imperfect knowledge of unmet needs and trends in consumption. It is neither necessary nor desirable to discover every aim of every individual. But for the sake of freedom, it is essential to expose and erase the causes of externalities. The functional principle of demarcation serves this task better than the skewed market signals of monopoly capitalism, where due to the concealing effects of mass privatised global production, collective ignorance is inevitable and, even worse, openly celebrated.

We turn now to the second issue, the serving of others when their aims are known but disapproved of. Hayek is adamant that in a catallaxy Anne will gladly supply Paul with an item she would plainly condemn (1976: 109–11, 1991: 97). This claim is, one would hope, overstated. Given the choice, most people most of the time would not wish to supply goods to others that will be used for purposes they are in principle strongly opposed to. The real issue is that due to the precondition of sheer survival, they do not always have this choice. When traders are compelled, through the imperative to maximise business profitability, to collude in furthering the intentions of others whose aims they hold in contempt, this can hardly be extolled as a method of coordination that apparently establishes mutual benefit. It says even less about the value of freedom. The freedom to respond to market signals is distinct from the freedom to produce and supply as and to whom one would prefer.

So how can the guild system respond to this particular problem? Does the requisite of the guild cooperatives to respond to consumer demand, as expressed through the cooperative consumer councils, compel them to manufacture goods they would otherwise prefer to avoid? The answer is seldom, and even then, not from the outset. There are options open to the members of a guild cooperative who are in principle strongly opposed to a particular end to which their product will serve. If the aversion is shared by all associated cooperatives, their concern would be relayed back to the department of the consumer council who made the initial request. Further dialogue and research would then take place, followed by an amended request. In the rare case of an impasse, the local commune would arbitrate, whose verdict will be final. So it is true that cooperatives may on occasion be asked to produce a product they have reservations over. This is a consequence of the separation of functions that defines the specific democratisation of economic relations articulated in this book, an important aspect of which is that in the usual course of events, organised consumption must determine the product-mix. In this way, the guild cooperatives can be held accountable by the local community, and not just by their direct customers. The likelihood is, though, that major disputes will be relatively infrequent, and even then, there is still more room for manoeuvre and negotiation than in statist or market systems. The general idea is that although conflicts will not disappear, they will become more visible. This is a particular strength of the associational anarchist way of doing things.

Finally, the query may be raised: what would happen to minority rights in consumption? For example, is it right that a majority should hold the power to block the further production of a good that at present is serving the desires of a minority? The Hayekian liberal would argue that this breaches the negative liberty of consumers. In reply, it is worth recalling that although the members of the cooperative consumer councils will consider sets of cases periodically, all citizens have an equal opportunity to influence the agenda, irrespective of majority-minority status. In this way, whilst decisions will ultimately be taken by the elected bodies, local consumers have access to a social forum through which participation will be more than just symbolic. The demarcated departments within the cooperative consumer councils will communicate the final decision to their corresponding guild. On the specific issue of reversing the sale of a particular product, this, and herein lies the main point, is limited solely to cases that undermine an accepted common good, not least of which will be those implicated by serious externalities. In other words, minority rights in consumption will only be affected when the actual use of a product already in circulation has been empirically shown to encroach upon the freedom of others. Otherwise, individual consumers are free to buy whatever and from whomever they like. To the extent that a particular minority taste is not catered for, the problem will be far less extensive than in Hayek's catallaxy, where the determination of all future investment is wholly dependent upon the dispositions of personal wealth.

Summary

For Hayek, the goal of an economic policy is to "provide a multi-purpose instrument which at no particular moment may be the one best adapted to the particular circumstances, but which will be the best for the great variety of circumstances likely to occur" (1976: 115). This chapter has indicated how a corresponding 'multi-purpose instrument' will function in a left-libertarian political economy. Like Hayek's catallaxy, policies are not, with the exception of the heterogeneous category of self-actualising labour, guided by a common scale of concrete ends, and like the intention of Hayek's catallaxy, they are directed towards attaining an abstract general order which will increase equally the chances for everyone to attain their respective goals. But associational anarchist policies will be grounded within a very different set of means-relations. The free market is supposed to bring choice, efficiency and, as its name suggests, above all, freedom. Decision-making takes place in an economic context where separate individuals are said to know little about the intentions of intermediary suppliers, business rivals and consumers, or are mainly indifferent to them. I have suggested that social relations of this nature are problematic and that they intensify as the domination of enterprise monopoly solidifies. Associational anarchism's social planning reduces these uncertainties. In the majority of cases, there is no need to know all the particulars of every single agent for the cooperative economy to run efficiently. But installing consumer interests as a right of citizenship, where they exist alongside the more familiar sets of subjective liberties, provides transparent structures through which to pinpoint quickly the causes of externalities.

There is one pertinent point that is worth underlining before this third section of the chapter ends. A self-actualising mode of labour is more difficult to sustain if consumptive acts are typically self-centred. The salutary mode of consumption discussed in this chapter seeks to resolve this tension. We have seen that its democratic method of operation provides local citizens with equal access to a social forum where the relations between consumers and their representative bodies will be determined through open deliberation. Taking all the ideas discussed here together, it will be apparent that the cooperative consumer councils, who in effect act in some part as the new social determinants, are, in turn, themselves guided by agendas set from below; such is the reciprocal nature of their internal relations. Through these inclusive structures, where the interests of consumers are accounted for in institutional ways that depart radically from both market forces and state planning, decision-making will be as open and transpicuous as is conceivably possible. As such, the kind of informed self-reflection that rationally assesses the stages of desire formation can continue to evolve with increasing degrees of lucidity. Likewise, the continuous dialogue between organised producers and organised consumers ensures that the social determinants that shape purchasing trends will, crucially, be less opaque. This is how the guild system minimises the harmful impact of collective ignorance. Through these organisational forms, a new consumptive consciousness may realistically be sought.

Conclusion

I have contended that the Hayekian reasoning that objective knowledge cannot be known because it only occurs in a diffused form does not rule out the possibility of approximating lesser degrees of inaccurate knowledge. It is probably true that knowledge seldom comes in concentrated form. Even in a cooperative environment, it will still be incomplete and widely dispersed. No economic system can ever acquire precise objective knowledge on a macro scale. But then to be effective, planning agencies do not need to. Of huge significance, the magnitude of the variables involved in any one particular piece of the plan will be infinitely less extensive than the immense central planning of corporate capitalism. The ultimate aim of this book's inclusive approach to social planning is the maintenance of a stable left-libertarian economic order. For this to be possible, it must also continuously reproduce the participatory means through which it attains this end. Coordinating structures should therefore avoid at all costs the kind of giant organisational forms that anarchism has always rightly opposed. By placing control over the means of production into the hands of the guild cooperatives, with the consumer councils on hand to advise and instruct, associational anarchist theory articulates one way of doing precisely this. This chapter has then argued that it is possible to devise a decentralised system of democratic planning alongside and integrated into a pluralised market system, within which domination by public and private tyranny is eschewed, whilst retaining a measure of sceptical epistemology.

On a closing note, taking the arguments of this and the previous two chapters together, I would like to return to the objections directed to anarchism's anti-statist principles mentioned in the introduction to this second part of the book. As effective coordination can be sought coherently beyond the bounds of statehood, the equation is not reduced to a choice between a retransformed state or an inability to confront capitalism. It will now be clear that associational anarchism's anti-parliamentarianism does not extend to anti-organisationalism; it has a distinct mode of organisation, one that contains forms of authority, power and legitimate coercion. In this sense, it follows Alex Prichard's claim that an anarchist society will need to institutionalise and constitutionalise. In brief, he recognises that, as an institution can be seen as a set of norms and codes that are formularised through collective decision-making, this will allow a place for binding rules and power structures of some kind. What makes them anarchist is the ways in which standards and procedures pertain to both negative and positive freedoms, how accepted decision-making policies mutually constrict otherwise free agents and the extent to which participation and inclusivity are maximised (Prichard, 2019: 82–4). The scheme contrived and developed in this book is one attempt to form this coveted anarchist constitution, especially in relation to the key values of meaningful participation, decentralisation, horizontalism and self-governance, which, as the following chapters will argue, procure freedom as conceived by anarchists. In sum, social coordination is most effective when it passes through the horizontal mediation of a functional federalism, rather than through the vertical organisations of socialist states or capitalist markets, both of which are marked by class privilege and immense coercive bureaucracies. It is for this reason I contend that the state, whether principally socialist or liberal, is not the essential prerequisite for the maintenance of social order.

Notes

1 Kropotkin had previously noted this great inconvenience of 'leviathan factories'; "they cannot rapidly reform their machinery according to the constantly varying demands of consumers" (2018: 170), but he obviously sought the solution in distinctly non-Hayekian terms.
2 This point is discussed at more length in Chapter 9.
3 As Hayek always equates coercion with human origin, he does not define freedom as an absence of law. This is on the provision that a set of abstract legal rules are framed generally, and are equally applicable to all agents. Laws forbid certain actions, but unlike the centralised plans of state socialism, they do not intentionally direct individual agents in distinct ways. He rejects the doctrine of *laissez-faire* precisely because law and liberty are not necessarily inconsistent. There is though a tension here with his concession that monopolists should be made to fix their prices so that they cannot over-charge for essential items. As even sympathetic commentators recognise, this would appear to be "a clear case of discriminatory, coercive law" (Barry, 1979: 73, see also 57–8, 64, 71–3; Hayek, 1991: 80, 98–9).
4 Chapter 10 discusses a more appropriate usage of the price mechanism.
5 There is, however, a strict criterion for determining the grounds upon which a given product may legitimately be blocked, a point clarified towards the end of the following section of this chapter.
6 Given that the members of the cooperative consumer councils are, as with all other elected bodies, part-time, temporary and continually rotated, the

particular department they serve in will obviously not be the one that has direct relations with the guild of which they are still part-time associates.

7 John Clark proposes much the same thing (2013: 110–11).

8 Commentating on this point, Terry Eagleton notes that Marx was a "strenuously moral thinker". "Marx believed that the ethic that governs capitalist society – the idea that I will only be of service to you if it is profitable for me to be so – was a detestable way to live. We would not treat our friends or children in this way, so why should we accept it as a perfectly natural way of dealing with others in the public realm" (2011: 158). Kropotkin also shows disdain for the view that agents should only give in order to receive, which has transformed society into a "commercial company" (n.d.: 143).

Part III

The associational anarchist conditions of liberty in the realm of necessity

There are four chapters in this third part of the book. Chapter 8, 'Self-determination, self-realisation and negative freedom', discusses the associational anarchist intermarriage between the idealist (self-realisation), the republican (self-determination) and the liberal (non-coercion) conceptions of freedom, where a particular property of one informs and mutually enhances the others.[1] Chapter 9, 'Freedom in the guild system', returns to the debate with Hayek, where I contend that a central aspect of a progressive conception of liberty is a non-statist system of producer cooperatives, within which all associates have the freedom to participate effectively. Chapter 10, 'Freedom in the guild system and beyond', completes my argument that economic democracy and individual liberty can live together congenially. The chapter will go on to argue that a substantial self-employed sector will be entirely compatible with the guild system. The themes in Chapters 9 and 10 overlap considerably, and they can be read as different strands in the same argument; they are presented in this way only for explanatory purposes. Finally, Chapter 11, 'The civic functional bodies', brings the exposition of this book's specific functional devolution to a close by offering a fairly short account of the organisational forms the civic services will assume.

Note

1 I use the term liberal freedom for the sake of convenience, and to denote the usual cluster of freedoms *from*.

8

Self-determination, self-realisation and negative freedom

The main objective of the two sections of this chapter is to mark out the specific ways in which freedom as Marxian-autonomy brings together ideals from the positive conceptions of freedom and, far from violating the usual set of freedoms *from*, is, for a number of reasons, the optimum means through which to protect them. Section one, 'The political liberties in freedom as Marxian-autonomy: their fair value and equal worth', argues that only a certain rearrangement of the intrinsic properties of political participation can secure the levels of instrumental acts upon which a just constitution rests. Section two, 'Forced to be free', is an elaboration of the above discussion, only now the focus is on the role of civic virtue as the required protector of negative liberty. We begin with a few preliminary details that will help set up the rest of the chapter.

Amalgamating distinct conceptions of liberty

The point has been raised that liberal freedom is a precondition of idealist liberty. In asking whether they can be reconciled, Miller's answer is that as the latter involves action that is in harmony with authentic beliefs and desires, it is reasonable to suppose that liberal freedom is indeed a requirement for the meaningful exercise of idealist liberty. Here Miller is stressing the need for social diversity, where people choose, from an array of various lifestyles, the one that is most fitting to their more deeply felt desires and beliefs (1991: 19–20). Alternatively, the relation between the liberal and the republican conceptions of freedom can be approached from the other way around – by addressing, that is, if the latter is actually a precondition of the former. Adam Swift, for example, notes that one aspect of republican freedom is Berlin's negative freedom. This is because participation has an instrumental role inasmuch as it is the best means by which to secure a general condition of non-restraint. A self-governing collective which encourages political participation does this in the sense that it alerts the electoral to the early stages of tyrannical rule (Swift, 2001: 66–7). It is the contentions thrown up in these intermixtures that are explored in the following two sections. So, what are the main ways in which freedom as political participation and freedom as autonomy are amalgamated in associational anarchism?

Swift stresses that, firstly, if freedom is equated with self-realisation, which in turn is achieved through political participation, then, logically, the latter is a central element of the former. On the traditional interpretation, republicanism holds that to participate politically is to live a good life. This is distinct from the orthodox liberal view that freedom should be regarded as leaving people alone to live according to the wishes they may or may not have at any given moment. Secondly, if laws restrict the freedom of individuals, how can one live within legal bounds yet still be free? The republican response is that autonomy equates with abiding by the laws that have in some way been collectively determined. So these two kinds of republican freedom, both of which stress the importance of political participation, fall within the category of freedom as autonomy (Swift, 2001: 64–6). It will be evident from previous discussions that freedom as Marxian-autonomy does this in a particular way. Recall that in their productive lives, members of work teams in the guild cooperatives will self-elevate into their higher-selves through a democratic determination of cooperative method and policy, including self-legislation, which overlaps with the radical republican notion of liberty (self-determination), and the universalisation of a de-alienated mode of labour, which is a version of idealist liberty (self-realisation). In the sense that control over productive procedures is a key constituent of de-alienation, these two labour processes cannot be separated. It is this specific coalesce that will now be critically evaluated, beginning will a discussion on what is termed the fair worth of the equal political liberties.

The political liberties in freedom as Marxian-autonomy: their fair value and equal worth

The three sub-sections of this first section of the chapter argue that freedom as self-determination and self-realisation is, in the sense in which it is configured in this book, the optimal means by which to secure negative freedom. I defend this statement through an engagement with John Rawls's account of political participation. In his conception of justice, 'justice as fairness', from the basic set of liberties that constitute the first principle of justice (1999: 53), only the equal political liberties are assured a fair value to all citizens. I will agree with the democratic socialist response that, to be effectuated, these specific liberties must be set within a system of workplace democracies. I will though go a stage further and suggest that the political liberties can only be of fair value to all workers if they rest upon a creative and aesthetic intrinsic value, itself an essential component of self-actualising labour, expressed within the guild system; only then can they serve their instrumental purpose.

Equal political participation and the neutrality principle

In *Theory*, Rawls endorses a principle of equal political participation. The political liberties are those of the 'ancients', notably participation in public life, which are distinct from the usual set of personal freedoms, those of the 'moderns'. Some overlap, the freedoms of speech and thought for example, but they are justified on different grounds, depending on whether they relate to personal freedom or the democratic process. Classical liberalism holds that if one were forced to choose between the personal liberties or the political liberties, the former would take preference as they have more intrinsic importance. For Rawls, though, this conflict need not arise as it is possible "to find a constitutional procedure that allows a sufficient scope for the value of participation without jeopardizing the other liberties" (1999: 202, 2001: 143–4; Howard, 2000: 31–2, 37). Perhaps most notably, guaranteeing the fair value of political liberty is essential to a just constitution. Rawls does this by responding to the critique, going right back to the young Marx, that in class-divided societies equal liberties are only formal in the sense that the wealthiest can, through a heavily disproportional influence on the legislator, combine together to effectively control political life (Rawls, 2001: 148). It is in meeting this critique that "justice as fairness treats the political liberties in a special way. We include in the first principle of justice a proviso that the equal political liberties, and *only* these liberties, are to be guaranteed their fair value" (2001: 149). There should, then, be a fair opportunity for all persons to attain positions with status and authority, irrespective of social class. Rawls suggests this may be done through placing limits upon campaign donations, public funding of political parties, equal access to public media and wide dissemination of property and wealth. This adjustment to the basic liberties enables political life to be independent of the power of private capital and wealth, upon which a just constitutional democracy depends (Rawls, 2001: 149–50; Howard, 2000: 31–2, 37). What then does the required arrangement of liberty actually consist of?

Rawls asks whether it would be just to allow an unequal value of political liberty on the grounds that this particular total system of liberty provides more protection to the other liberties. His theory of procedural justice approaches these kinds of questions in a particular way. "An inequality in the basic structure must always be justified to those in the disadvantaged position" (1999: 203). To take the most immediate political inequality, the transgression of the 'one person one vote' principle, Rawls states that if certain assumptions hold, Mill's system of plural voting may be 'perfectly just'. However, even though justice as fairness does treat the equal political liberties as holding less intrinsic value than the basic personal liberties,

> the grounds for self-government are not solely instrumental. Equal political liberty when assured its fair value is bound to have a profound effect on the moral quality of civic life … [and] the effect of self-government where equal political rights have their fair value is to enhance the self-esteem and the sense of political competence of the average citizen. (1999: 205)

And the sharpening of opinions to aid political participation "is an activity enjoyable in itself that leads to a larger conception of society and to the development of … intellectual and moral faculties" (Rawls, 1999: 205–6). In the absence of these more inclusive sentiments, citizens become estranged and come to see one another as rivals. Equal political liberty then is not just a means. "These freedoms strengthen men's [sic] sense of their own worth, enlarge their intellectual and moral sensibilities, and lay the basis for a sense of duty and obligation upon which the stability of just institutions depends" (1999: 206, see also 2001: 143–4). It is clear then that Rawls's principle of equal political participation invokes, to varying degrees, both intrinsic and instrumental properties.

It is important though to understand how this conception of political liberty corresponds with a central maxim of Rawls's theory of justice, liberal neutrality. This is the insistence that just principles must not, through any deliberate objectives of policy, prioritise one way of life over any other. Rawls's theory is neutral in the sense that the public political culture, and its democratic institutions, are not based upon any version of the good. As the state should be an impartial umpire, it is illegitimate for it to judge, even democratically, how citizens should live. So what exactly are neutrality liberals like Rawls neutral about? They distinguish between (a) the commitment of free and equal citizens to act in accordance with principles of justice, together with a capacity to frame, revise and pursue their own conceptions of the good, which they are *not* neutral about; and (b) the chosen particular conceptions, which they *are* neutral about. The state is restricted to providing the background conditions in which freedom and autonomy are secured. As Rawls puts it, justice as fairness is neutral with regard to aims; it is not procedurally neutral. The two principles of justice are clearly substantive (2001: 153).[1] The idea is that neutrality does not apply to justice, equality and autonomy, but to the given ways of life that citizens choose to pursue. This theory of justice does then build upon a fairly minimal conception of the political good, in the sense that state action may be premised upon shared reasons. But it is still a neutral theory, as it builds from a 'common ground' held between citizens. Crucially, Rawls adds that an 'overlapping consensus' on the political values of freedom and equality can still be forged, as different and sometimes incompatible ways of life will, if they are reasonable, subscribe to the basic structure of political liberalism (2001: 18–24, 32–7, 188–9; Swift, 2001: 154–7, 161–5; Howard, 2000: 4, 20, 22, 25, 30–1).

The significance of the neutrality principle comes through strongly in Rawls's discussion on the nature of political participation. He draws a distinction between *civic humanism* and *classical republicanism*. The former contends that people are political beings whose inner nature is realised through participating democratically in political life, which is held to be the 'privileged locus' of the ultimate good. As this is a 'comprehensive philosophical doctrine', Rawls rejects it as "incompatible with justice as fairness as a political conception of justice" (2001: 143). Political participation has, he infers, "a lesser place in the conceptions of the (complete) good of most citizens" (2001: 143).[2] Public engagement is needed, not to express an inner human essence, but to safeguard the usual set of subjective liberties. This for Rawls is the position upheld in the classical republican perspective:

> The idea is that unless there is widespread participation in democratic politics by a vigorous and informed citizen body moved in good part by a concern for political justice and public good, even the best-designed political institutions will eventually fall into the hands of those who hunger for power and military glory, or pursue narrow class and economic interests, to the exclusion of almost everything else. If we are to remain free and equal citizens, we cannot afford a general retreat into private life. (2001: 144)

The idea here is that the political virtues and a willingness to participate in public life are the means to a just constitution. As classical republicanism does not constitute a comprehensive doctrine, it is, he concludes, fully compatible with justice as fairness (Rawls, 2001: 142–5).

For Rawls then, classical republicanism seeks to protect the liberty of the moderns, as "the question is to what degree citizens' engaging in politics is needed for the safety of basic liberties, and how the requisite participation is best achieved" (2001: 144). Participation in public life is not, he infers, ranked at the highest tier of most citizens' conceptions of the good. It can of course be a good, even a great good, but it is not, for all citizens, the chief or the sole good. "[T]he extent to which we make engaging in political life part of our complete good is up to us as individuals to decide, and reasonably varies from person to person" (2001: 144). It is in this sense that civic humanism goes beyond the sanction of political liberalism. Rawls is not, as mentioned, suggesting that the political liberties are only instrumental, it is more that the basic liberties are valued for different reasons. So, an account of democracy which seeks to draw out its intrinsic value can be consistent with Rawls's advocacy of classical republicanism (2001: 143; Howard, 2000: 34).

In sum, an understanding of these four key themes – assuring the fair value of the equal political liberties, the intrinsic and instrumental value of participation, the liberal neutrality principle and an endorsement of the classic republican ethic of participation – are the necessary prerequisites for the discussions that now follow. We will begin with the argument that more extensive democratic measures are required for the purposes Rawls asks of them.

The fair value of the equal political liberties and workplace democracy

In his account of how best to enhance the fair value of political liberty, Michael W. Howard defends the intrinsic worth of workplace democracy through an argument that respects liberal neutrality. This is in sharp contrast to other interpretations of the neutrality principle. In brief, the latter position holds that if a system of worker-managed firms is legally mandated, it would favour some workers above others, those that prefer cooperative labour to all other forms, in which case, it would be sectarian as priority is given to a particular conception of the good. Left-neutrality liberals support egalitarian rights to material resources, but they do not see them in positive terms:

> A neutral liberal will resist the suggestion that one is not 'truly' free unless one is participating in civic life, or exercising essential human capacities, or objectifying one's imagination through work, or realising one's social essence, or, in general, realising some conception of the good life. (Howard, 2000: 25)

The sectarian charge is that one vision of the good, self-actualising work, is imposed upon everyone. If so, the argument that self-managed labour is intrinsically more meaningful when compared to wage-labour contains a perfectionist claim that violates liberal neutrality (Howard, 2000: 23–5).

Howard begins his response by pointing out that almost all theories of justice cannot avoid invoking some theory of the good, however 'thin'. Rawls's neutralist liberalism is no exception:

> Justice as fairness is grounded in a view of moral personality involving a sense of justice and the capacity to develop a conception of the good. This conception of the person defines the 'thin theory' of the good, and the primary goods are needed for these moral powers to unfold. Rawls thus, implicitly at least,

relies on a partial conception of the good that ... asserts the worth of human existence, fulfilment of human purposes, and a commitment to rationality as the chief guide to life. (2000: 31)

In stretching the scope of this thin theory, Howard adapts what has been called 'participatory autonomy' in the literature on Rawls. This term, which also has both intrinsic and instrumental properties, refers to an equal liberty of agents to participate meaningfully in all decision-making procedures that directly affect their lives. In this way, everyone has a fair opportunity to determine their own fate. Howard agrees with Rawls's electoral reforms, but he adds that on their own they are not enough to realise the fair value of political liberty. Even if wealth is distributed more widely through policies of higher inheritance and redistributive taxation, major investment decisions would still be in the exclusive hands of a powerful capitalist class. The omnipresent threat of capital strike/flight can only be negated by subjecting the most pressing investment decisions – where, in what fields and in which quantities – to democratic adjudication. There will always be social and environmental consequences to investment decisions in any society; Howard's argument though is that in a market forces economy, they are depoliticised and made privately behind the doors of corporate boardrooms. In addition, private enterprise generates large inequalities of power that impair the equal value of political liberties for employees in certain ways, two of which are worth highlighting. Firstly, there is a power imbalance within the firm, with owners exercising control over workers; and secondly, employees subject to autocratic power are prone to become cynical and lose hope of gaining any control over work conditions. It is for these reasons that the central aspect of participatory autonomy, equal rights of participation, must be extended into the democratised workplace (Howard, 2000: 32–3, 37–8).

For Howard then, workplace democracies provide more realistic opportunities for ordinary workers to have their say on productive processes, and in a way that refines the sought-after political virtues, which, intrinsically, are certain to have the profound effects Rawls proposes – enhance self-worth, develop intellectual and moral sentiments and engender a sense of duty essential to the longevity of just institutions – only to a richer extent. Howard therefore concludes his argument that workplace democracies can, on grounds acceptable to a liberal neutrality theory of justice, assure the fair value of political liberty (2000: 33, 38–9). Whilst he is operating within a market socialist framework, his defence of workplace democracy is directly applicable to associational anarchism's guild system. The sub-section below will agree fully with his response to Rawls, but it will also indicate why the equal worth of political participation within the cooperative workplace must form the central constitutive of a self-actualising environment.

The fair value of the equal political liberties in the guild system

I firstly argue why it is legitimate to invoke a tighter defined intrinsic virtue, and secondly why associational anarchism puts the instrumental value of political participation to much better effect than is realistically achievable in Rawls's political liberalism. In recognising the permanent fact of "reasonable pluralism" that informs his idea of an "overlapping consensus" (2001: 32), Rawls would regard Marx's claim that productive relations must be arranged in order to give full realisation to the creative essence inherent in all individuals as a comprehensive philosophical anthropology, the prioritising of which he would see as unreasonable. It follows that he would also reject associational anarchism's higher-self for much the same reason. In reply, we might point out that as the general category of labour is universal, it will always be a ubiquitous good of some kind. Labour is the fundamental activity of all societies, none of which can survive without it. So in this most basic of respects, labour is unique, even if its form is context-dependent. But whilst this truism is clearly self-evident, by itself, it would not satisfy the sectarian critique outlined above. Only if one could show that fully skilled and self-enhancing labour secures, optimally, the fair value of the equal political liberties, and as such gains the full support of the shared reasons that form the common ground, could its identification as a basic principle of justice be defended on Rawlsian grounds of reasonableness.

Significantly, despite placing a capacity to frame and revise a conception of the good (the rational) beneath a sense of justice (the reasonable) (2001: 18–24, 32–8),[3] Rawls acknowledges that a strong desire for work to be fulfilling is both widely and deeply felt. He suggests that a just society does not necessarily require "a high material standard of life". What citizens "want is meaningful work in free association with others, these associations regulating their relations to one another within a framework of just basic institutions. To achieve this state of things great wealth is not required" (1971: 290); elsewhere he adds that all citizens should have "at least one community of shared interests to which he belongs and where he finds his endeavours confirmed by his associates" (1971: 442). Too much personal wealth is now said to be a "positive hindrance", "a meaningless distraction" and a "temptation to indulgence and emptiness". Then there is the dynamic captured in his 'Aristotelian principle'. Here individuals are viewed as essentially doers, exercising and enjoying their capabilities, they are not seen simply in consumerist terms (1971: 426). In their capacities as producers then, Rawls believes people have deep interests in using and developing their skills. If this really is what all citizens want, and I think he is right that they do, then integrating the quality of self-actualising labour into participatory autonomy, so that its intrinsic content now fully embraces the profound creative yearnings deep within us all, may, reasonably, form a core element of a neutral theory of justice. If so, how would this effect the value of political participation?

I have inferred that, alongside and integrated into self-actualising forms of labour, the act of participation will serve as the vehicle through which cooperative associates will ascend into their higher-selves. In this respect, the inclusive structures of democratic decision-making integral to the guild cooperatives have an intrinsic value. I will conclude that without it, optimal levels of participation cannot be sustained. Before this, it is important to indicate how the guild system will consolidate and then put to good effect the instrumental value of political participation. Let us say Rawls is right that it is required by a learned and conscious citizenry, and in its absence is it probable that powerful elites will come to seek only their own selfish interests, to the detriment of virtually all else. Translating his warning into associational anarchism's functional mode of organisation, the potential danger would stem from the higher echelons of the guilds and councils, and not of course from the state. But in principle, the problem remains. This idea, that political participation is a precondition for the preservation of negative freedom, claims that through regular acts of participation, people will increase their awareness of the system they would otherwise remain ignorant of. As a direct consequence, they will be alerted to the early stages of tyrannical rule. So the immediate question has to be whether the required levels of participation can be sustained in the market-based societies liberals endorse.[4] There are, it seems to me, good reasons to doubt this. Generally speaking, political participation in these societies is restricted to a public sphere which, due to organisational detachments, is largely removed from the economic domain, and even here it usually denotes only the most minimal acts of citizenship. It is questionable whether the corresponding low levels of interest can invoke and protect the instrumental value of political participation, especially to the extent that the citizen body becomes 'vigorous and informed'.

There is a far greater opportunity for citizens to participate more effectively in associational anarchism. This applies in particular to their economic affairs, not least through the guild cooperatives and the local consumer councils.[5] In order to defend this statement, let us take a moment to highlight the indispensability of economic democracy to meaningful participation. As section one of Chapter 3 explained, Cole thought democracy should apply to industry as well as to politics. Due to the fact that it rests upon an industrial autocracy, political democracy is for the most part impotent. As there is no opportunity to practice the fundamental basics of self-government in a smaller setting, individuals have no control over the larger apparatus of modern politics. For Cole, people's natural desire for self-assertion is suffocated daily through authoritative commands in the workplace. Industrial democracy is, however, an entirely different creature. In industry, individuals understand their surroundings, an environment without the 'vague glamour' members of parliament fabricate in order to imitate their spurious stature. In these circumstances, the guild official will be unable to follow the career politician. Political demagogues are successful only because the electorate has no adequate checks upon them. What, Cole wonders, would be the likely outcome if the electorate choose a poor foreman?

> At every turn, every hour of every day, the workers in the shop will be conscious of the incompetence of the man they have chosen. He will be dealing with matters that they themselves understand, and his interference will soon be resented by men who know his business better than he knows it himself. When the day of re-election comes round they will have had enough of him and his sort to make them choose a more capable man in his place. (1972: 167)

Through their participation, workers would quickly grasp the lessons of self-government. There is every chance this would act as a stimulus upon their interests (Cole, 1972: 157–61, 163–4, 166–7).

The associational anarchist contention that, to be effective, democratic participation must reach into the economic aspects of people's lives is made in the same general spirit. If large numbers of citizens are currently self-absorbed in their capacities to frame, revise and pursue distinct conceptions of the good, which may or may not value highly active engagement in public life (Rawls, 2001: 19, 144), then it is unrealistic to expect them, en masse, to find the time for the continuous levels of participation the protection of individual liberty depends upon. For political participation to fulfil the instrumental function, the subject matter must be accessible and, of equal significance, appear for the most part attractive. That is, a 'vigorous and informed citizen body' can only come into being if one's immediate surroundings are generally held to be intriguing and engaging, and this is far more likely to be the case if democratic politics is, on the provision that the place of work is an enriching and self-confirming environment, extended into ordinary citizens' working lives. The institutionalisation of balanced job-complexes serves this purpose very well. By injecting what are primarily economic bodies with a political content, they bring the democratic issue closer to the average worker's mind and soul. Given what Rawls's Aristotelian principle denotes, there is every chance that workers will be inspired to participate meaningfully in the daily running of their cooperative, and in the process develop the political virtues upon which just institutions rest. So, the more intimately the intrinsic value is felt, the more effective the instrument role of participation becomes.

Summary

Disputes between defenders of negative or positive liberty are not, Rawls thinks, really about definitions, but rather their relative values when they conflict. He follows MacCallum that when any explanation of liberty references the three items of the triadic relation – "this or that person (or persons) is free (or not free) from this or that constraint (or set of constraints) to do (or not to do) so and so" (1999: 177) – all the relevant information will be provided (1999: 176–7). Whilst freedom as Marxian-autonomy is conceptualised within this general framework, the sets of relative values differ considerably. For there to be 'widespread participation in democratic politics', the context of participation is just as crucial as the content. As we have seen, only a certain kind of economic democracy can generate the required levels of instrumental participation. It achieves this vital task because it embodies, in the first instance, a specific and more extensively defined intrinsic participation. To be more precise, the values of justice, equality and autonomy, shared by all reasonable citizens, are reconfigured in order to incorporate self-actualising forms of labour, which give a deeper meaning to the intrinsic value. In the sense that the magnitude of the intrinsic content is now larger than in Rawls's thin theory of the good, this can rightly be seen as a 'thicker' theory. I have argued though that it provides the most effective means through which to secure the fair value of the equal political liberties. Rawls's electoral reforms are not sufficient to do the job he asks of them. The might of the wealthiest class, with their monopoly over the means of investment, would still *de facto* disenfranchise the poorer classes (especially the most disadvantaged). If the political virtues are to be most effective at enhancing self-worth, sharpening moral and intellectual sensibilities and engendering a commitment to engage politically in public life, the 'participatory autonomy' principle requires a wider application; and, crucially, in self-enhancing conditions.

So, for the equal political liberties to be of fair worth, they must be experienced through the guild system, where the requisite inclusive sentiments will form the essentials of an anarcho-constitutionalism. Democratic participation by informed citizens in freedom as Marxian-autonomy will serve to protect the liberty of the moderns, but, in contrast to the left-liberal position explained above, it is also constitutive of their freedom. The intrinsic value of self-actualising labour appeals, however, to neutral values in the sense that it qualifies as a primary aspect of the 'common ground'. My argument in favour of stretching the bounds of the neutrality principle has then used Rawlsian premises to reach a distinctly non-Rawlsian outcome. In accordance with the main argument of this book, associational anarchism's newly formed overlapping consensus enables all citizens to frame, revise and pursue their chosen careers in the realm of necessity, and then their preferred 'ends in themselves' in the realm of freedom, only now on an equal basis. On the strength of these reasons, I conclude that social ownership of productive property must, along with private ownership of personal possessions, be regarded as first principles. The following section of this chapter will add substance to this claim.

Forced to be free

This second section of the chapter engages with the debate on civic virtue as a guarantor of individual freedom. It addresses the defence of negative liberty put forward by Michael Kramer, focusing on his critique of Quentin Skinner. The latter attempts to identify a link between republican institutions, upheld by civic virtue, and the liberal freedoms they make possible.[6] Skinner does not openly embrace the ideal of positive freedom. Rather, his republican notion of freedom is a variant of 'ordinary' negative liberty (1991: 193, 202). But he does take issue with the critiques of positive freedom that stem from the negative liberty position. Kramer seeks to defend the latter from Skinner's riposte. Continuing with the letter and spirit of the previous section, I intersect in this contention by inferring that for the implied link between civic virtue and negative freedom to be robust enough to fulfil its instrumental role, a system of workers cooperatives formed through internal participatory structures is the essential ingredient. In these self-governing conditions, the freedom of citizens will need no formal enforcement from a centralised political authority.

Skinner believes there is an instrumental connection between people's duty to act with civic virtue and the protection of negative liberty. His standpoint may be seen as an 'instrumental republicanism'. He argues that contemporary defenders of negative liberty (CDNL) overlook this connection. The civic-republican tradition and the CDNL both endorse negative liberty, but for Skinner, the difference is that the former promotes an ideal of the common good. He adds that the civic-republican heritage contains two propositions which are at odds with the CDNL. Firstly, citizens must participate actively beyond the private sphere in order to prevent individual liberty from deteriorating into servitude. If people want to be free from interference to pursue their personal projects, this will require a measure of prudence to effectively engage in public life. As individual liberty can only survive in a context of vigorous public service, there is a strong instrumental bond between the performance of civic virtue and the attainment of freedom. People must realise that their duties are serious business and that public obligations should be discharged emphatically. In the second place, there is the 'forced to be free' principle. As there is a strong tendency among people to become immersed in their private projects, political arrangements must discourage the luxury of over-disengagement. So in order not to undermine the common good, people need to be nudged away from their self-engrossed reluctance to participate in public affairs. "Political rationality consists in recognising that this constitutes the only means of guaranteeing the very liberty we may seem to be giving up" (Skinner, 1991: 203). It is therefore necessary to design pressures to induce virtuous behaviour, even if they do not correspond with any natural inclination (1991: 185–6, 198–200, 202–3; Kramer, 2003: 105–6, 108–10).

Kramer agrees that a particular strength of the civic-republican position is its allegiance to negative liberty. It does not claim that a duty to act with civic virtue via political participation actually constitutes freedom. The activity itself is not seen as liberty, freedom is treated as a condition of unpreventedness. But he adds that as Skinner's two propositions are "straightforwardly consistent" with what the CDNL endorse, the present-day civic-republican thesis is more platitudinous than innovative. Civic republicans acknowledge some instances of freedom will perish as the overall liberty of everyone is augmented. But the positive liberty theorists deny this, for them what is lost does not count as freedom. This is because freedom is equated only with a desired objective. For this reason, Kramer stresses that the civic republican view is compatible with the CDNL, both recognise the instrumental role of widespread political participation in protecting each person's overall freedom. With regards to Skinner's second proposition, the notion of being forced to be free, Kramer rejects it if it is construed as a positive liberty theory as suppressed opportunities must count as forfeited freedoms. But as a civic-republican thesis it, again, dovetails neatly with the doctrine of negative liberty. Imposing legal duties of civic virtue will restrict the conjunctive exercisability of certain liberties, but overall freedom will be enhanced as despotism will be avoided. As the dutiful public service cannot be left to people's short-sighted or even enlightened self-interest, they must in some sense be forced to be free. For these reasons, Kramer concludes that Skinner's two propositions are compatible with the CDNL (2003: 109–10, 119–21).

This debate between Skinner and Kramer is of much interest as it not only captures neatly what the preservation of negative liberty requires but also illustrates clearly the degree of congruity between the doctrine of civic-republicanism and liberal political philosophy. Kramer does not dispute the view that there are important differences between the two positions. The former is chiefly concerned with the freedom of the community, often viewed in terms of national autonomy. The value of individual freedom is still important, but it is subservient to an independent community. Liberalism tends to reverse this pattern of priority. How warranted the imposition of a legal sanction is will depend on whether it boosts individual liberty, and only secondarily on how it may strengthen the autonomy of the community. Yet for Kramer, the difference in emphases between civic-republicanism and liberalism should not be overstated. The inference that the value of a duty to civic virtue is fundamental to the maximisation of liberty is not, he observes, incompatible with the individualistic underpinnings of liberalism. "The civic-republican thesis concerning an instrumental connection between popular political participation and the preservation of individual freedom is scarcely something that will strike negative-liberty theorists as a joltingly unfamiliar observation" (Kramer, 2003: 149; 122–4). Others, too, have noticed the affiliation Kramer is drawing attention to. Ian Carter, for example, suggests it is possible that republican arguments on freedom merely point to which particular form of political institutions can best secure negative freedom (2003: 8–9). Likewise, Miller also notes that instead of singling out which of the two is the real version, it may be more accurate to treat the republican conception as essential to the defence of liberal freedom (1991: 6).

To widen the debate a little, it has been claimed that negative liberty need not correlate with any particular political system. Berlin himself recognised that in a dictatorship people may still possess negative freedom all the time the dictator reframes from interfering (1991: 129–31).[7] In contrast, republican freedom is more than just a sphere of non-interference. It is the existence of certain conditions within which interference cannot occur. These may be a democratic constitution, restrictions on a government using state institutions arbitrarily and a shared opportunity for political participation:

> The republican concept allows that the state may encroach upon the negative freedom of individuals, enforcing and promoting certain civic virtues as a means of strengthening democratic institutions. On the other hand, the concept cannot lead to the oppressive consequences feared by Berlin, because it has a commitment to liberal-democratic institutions already built into it. (Carter, 2003: 8)

As Carter puts it, to be free means to live alongside political institutions whose powers of interference are circumscribed (2003: 8–9). Associational anarchism protects the freedoms of thought, speech and expression devoutly, but it does not have the usual liberal-democratic institutions built into it, at least not in the sense that they are customarily perceived. Functional devolution diametrically opposes undifferentiated representative democracy. As such, there is no universal suffrage in periodical elections between competing mass political parties. Neither is there a market forces economy with private ownership of productive resources. Here though the instrumental link between the civic virtue gained through political participation and the preservation of individual liberty can, on the grounds that freedom is forced through self-governing means, be put to optimal use.

The question of how best to initiate and direct the pressures required to induce virtuous behaviour can be placed within the wider context of an anarchist-compatible use of coercion. Schmidt and Van der Walt point out that in anarchist thinking, coercive power is generally regarded as legitimate if it derives from open forms of democratic decision-making, which are used to develop a libertarian socialist system (2009: 67). In this sense, freedom must be regarded as a social product. Recall that for both Bakunin and Kropotkin, freedom is only attainable within the appropriate social context; it cannot exist outside a society. They both equated freedom with solidarity, where there is equal access to the means of production. Section one of Chapter 6 explained that this will require carefully organised federated structures, which will institutionalise certain organisational forms. What makes these structures of power anarchist is how they embody both negative and positive freedoms, how they maximise participation and inclusivity and the ways in which accepted decision-making policies mutually constrict the freedom of agents (Prichard, 2019: 82–4). In associational anarchism, the apparatus of coercion, including its specific usage of forcing people to be free, has been devised through a particular application of these anarcho-constitutional guidelines. The three chapters in Part II of this book discussed these collective rule-making mechanisms in some detail, and the following two chapters will complete the exposition. For the current purpose, let us take a moment to briefly reiterate how exactly the guild system contrives the social conditions of freedom.

At the wider community level, political intermediation takes place through interlinking functional institutions in civil society, especially with price-fixing and the democratic planning of investment. In accordance with Prichard's definition, these inclusive arrangements will evolve through mutually determined rules that will no doubt place equal limits upon the freedom of all agents; they are justified though on the grounds of their essentialness to both the negative and positive ideals in freedom as Marxian-autonomy. Then there are the various forms of political participation within the sphere of production, which, in congruence with the central tenets of anarcho-republicanism, revolve around new forms of deliberation and a complete retransformation of work. The self-legislation of a local guild, constituted through all affiliated cooperatives, can impose legal duties of civic virtue effectively. As section one of Chapter 5 explained, there is an obligation to adhere to the laws of one's own making, but mutual commitments are between fellow associates. Whilst there is a political authority of sorts, it is based upon internal horizontal relationships. In addition, the direct democracy within the guild cooperatives includes the collective design of balanced job-complexes, as monitored by their internal social councils. Seen in this light, an inclusive mode of popular participation is an important component of one's job description. It is in these senses that freedom, and the criterion on which it can be legitimately forced, are addressed through the demands of the specific anarcho-constitutionalism develop in this book.

In sum, continuing the general argument made in section one of this chapter, it is the context of participation that is crucial to its instrumental value. The dutiful engagement and knowledge of political processes will be a result of the democratisation of economic life, where the cultivation of civic virtue takes place within and between the interlocking spheres of production and consumption. This does mean that within the guild cooperatives, the freedom to refrain from political participation of any sort is lost, but in any productive unit workers obviously participate in some ways. All societies are driven by natural necessity to meet their own material needs. This implies that for the vast majority of people, work of some kind is a cardinal aspect of their lives, hence the associational anarchist pledge to universalise meaningful forms of reskilled labour. The general idea then is that associational anarchism will invoke more effectively Skinner's first proposition, instrumental participation, within its democratised economy. Yet with regards to his second proposition, forced to be free, as citizens are democratically active in self-governing local communities, where any use of coercive power is mandated by means of collaborative decision-making, external political imposition is no longer required to prompt the coveted virtuous behaviour. Finally, on a point of clarity, recall that it is a version of the X, Y, Z triadic relation, which blends harmoniously negative and positive ideals, that is developed in this book. This means that whilst there are similarities with the civic-republican/CDNL advocacy of negative liberty, there are also significant differences. With regards to the guild system's self-imposed reframing of the conjunctive exercisability of subjective liberties, suppressed opportunities do count as losses to freedom. There is no disagreement with Skinner and Kramer here. Yet the political participation required to procure the instrumental civic virtue is, now parting company from their position, regarded as a positive ideal; it is not only a means to an end but also a key constituent of liberty itself. This, I contend, is the best route through which to propagate the instrumental connection between the cultivation of civic virtue and the protection of freedom *from*.

Conclusion

Although human agents are forced into work relations by nature, and this applies to all known societies, the force in question may be expressed in a variety of distinct socio-economic formations, each with specific coercive social arrangements and/or political directives. As will now be clear, associational anarchism does this in a certain way. In particular, its non-statist approach to eradicating the class domination of bourgeois society does not endanger the totalitarian menace. On the contrary; piecing together certain elements from the self-determination and self-realisation perspectives in the precise way freedom as Marxian-autonomy does is the most effective means through which to preserve a general condition of non-restraint. In order to fulfil its instrumental role, political participation is far more likely to be effective when grounded within a libertarian economic democracy, where it is frequently liable to be maximised, than when it takes place in a liberal democracy, where it frequently is not. Likewise, on the grounds that political participation reconfigures its precise arrangements of the intrinsic and instrumental values, the proposed link between civic virtue and the protection of negative freedom will for the most part be realised in the self-actualising environment of the guild cooperatives. Extensive participation in the realm of necessity will serve two key instrumental imperatives. It will protect a degree of freedom *from*, and it will secure the freedom for citizens to pursue their personal interests in the realm of freedom. By picking up once again the debate with Hayek, the following chapter will continue this argument.

Notes

1 These two principles of justice are "(a) Each person has the same indefeasible claim to a fully adequate scheme of equal basic liberties, which scheme is compatible with the same scheme of liberties for all; and (b) Social and economic inequalities are to satisfy two conditions: first, they are to be attached to offices and positions open to all under conditions of fair equality of opportunity; and second, they are to be to the greatest benefit of the least-advantaged members of society (the difference principle)" (Rawls, 2001: 42–3).

2 There appears to be different usages for the same term in the literature. Rawls makes it clear he is identifying civic humanism with a form of Aristotelianism (2001: 142), which is what Swift refers to as classical republicanism (2001: 64–5).

3 Rawls calls the 'reasonable', which presupposes and subordinates the 'rational', the two moral powers of free and equal citizens (2001: 18).

4 I should like to point out that Rawls himself is a modern (sometimes called social, or redistributive) liberal. He invokes phrases like "hopelessly hostile", "prejudice and folly", "will to dominate", "oppressive cruelties" and a "corrupt society" to describe neo-liberalism (2001: 38). And as the following endnote indicates, he does not, on the provision that worker-managed firms are

able to develop the democratic political virtues a just constitution depends upon (2001: 178–9), rule out certain forms of market socialism.

5 It is worth noting that not all thinkers with a liberal tone are averse to economic democratisation. Like J.S. Mill and Emile Durkheim before him, Rawls himself believes workplace democracies are worthy of careful consideration. Anticipating Marx's objection that private ownership of productive resources is irreconcilable with his principles of justice, Rawls acknowledges that this "major difficulty" "must be faced". His own response, which rejects both laissez-faire and welfare-state capitalism as well as state socialism (2001: 137–8), is scant, to say the least. But he does indicate that a system of worker-managed cooperatives is, in principle, "fully compatible" with the constitutional regime he advocates, "property-owning democracy", and which could, it turns out, be a form of "liberal socialism" (2001: 138–9, 178–9). Sadly though, probably due to his reluctance to commit to a definitive end-state, he does not pursue these important questions. For a fuller exposition and analyses of Rawls's theory, see Wyatt (2008).

6 Incidentally, Berlin shows some anticipation of this convergence in republican and liberal political though. "Perhaps the chief value for liberals of political – 'positive' – rights, of participating in the government, is as a means for protecting what they hold to be an ultimate value, namely individual – 'negative' – liberty" (1991: 165).

7 Kramer is critical of these kinds of claims (2003: 130–1).

9

Freedom in the guild system

Freedom is not simply the absence of restraint; it assumes a higher form when it becomes self-government. A man is not free in himself while he allows himself to remain at the mercy of every idle whim: he is free when he governs his own life according to a dominant purpose or system of purposes. (Cole, 1972: 157)

The disputes about what counts as interference with freedom have a long and varied history and continue to throw up numerous inciting questions. Following suit, through a contrast between the guild cooperative and the private enterprise economies, both taken in ideal-typical terms, our discussion with Hayek is resumed. In *The Constitution of Liberty* (1960), he argues that coercion exists only when an individual becomes the arbitrary instrument of someone else's will, and freedom is defined simply as its absence. As coercion is always both inter-agential and intentional, freedom is not a function of the array of opportunities open to individuals. Hayek therefore rejects the claim that freedom is dependent upon an egalitarian distribution of material resources (1991: 80, 98–9; Miller, 1991: 14; Barry, 1984: 263–4). The two sections that make up this chapter will critically appraise his position. The sub-sections in section one, 'Negative liberty, positive liberty, and coercive obstructions', are included mainly for the purpose of explanation; they serve as the necessary prerequisites for the analyses that follow in section two, 'A repudiation of Hayek'. The latter section casts serious doubt over Hayek's overly stringent account of coercion. In sharp contrast, I will argue it is only when people have equal and democratic access to the means of production that they can be free from interference and restrictions, deliberate or otherwise.

Negative liberty, positive liberty and coercive obstructions

There are three sub-sections to this first section of the chapter. The first, 'Hayek: freedom and the market', is self-explanatory. The second, 'Positive conditions', provides a review of the most immediate critical responses to the general position Hayek is an ardent exponent of. The task of the third sub-section, 'Hayek's rejection of the republican, idealist and socialist conceptions of freedom', is to indicate why he renounces fiercely all the positive notions of freedom that invoke more extensive accounts of coercion – those that, by definition, go beyond the inter-agential and intentional.

Hayek: freedom and the market

In adherence to classical liberal political economy, Hayek's conception of liberty explores the actions of goal-seeking and purposeful economic agents. His anti-rationalist argument seeks to show how an un-designed yet stable order has arisen from the multi-interactions of 'free' individuals, who are forever adjusting to one another through a series of self-interested initiatives. In a free society, individual liberty exists when a person is not coerced randomly by others. This condition, where people act according to their own decisions, is referred to as "independence of the arbitrary will of another" (1991: 80). He has an equally tight account of coercion. Whilst social situations are often unpredictable, they do not pose a malicious threat to people's personal freedom. Someone may be 'compelled by circumstances' to act in a certain way, but for Hayek coercion always presupposes a human agent. It exists only if a person's actions have been construed in order to serve someone else's will. So for a human act to count as a case of coercion, there must be a threat of causing harm together with the deliberate intention of engendering a given course of action. In these situations, although the coerced can still make a choice, the alternatives available have been shaped by the coercer, which means the outcome will be in the interests of the latter. This implies that the coerced is denied the chance of applying her own knowledge to pursue her independent aims because her plans must fall within the boundaries set by another (1991: 85–6, 88–90; Barry, 1984: 265–6).

Coercion can be prevented solely by securing a private domain, an 'assured free sphere', within which individuals are protected from the interference of others. The possession of private property is the first step in delimitating the private sphere. People may form coherent plans only if they have access to material objects. Yet in market societies, individuals are protected from coercion not so much through property ownership, but because the material means they need to fulfil their plans are not exclusively controlled by a single agent. Hayek believes it is a particular asset of modern societies that people can enjoy freedom even when they own little property, and where the property that meets their needs is managed by others. What is important, and Hayek stresses this unambiguously, is to disseminate widely the required properties. This would ensure that people will not be dependent upon particular individuals who may otherwise be the sole suppliers of resources or employment:

> The decisive condition for mutually advantageous collaboration between people, based on voluntary consent rather than coercion, is that there be many people who can serve one's needs, so that nobody has to be dependent on specific persons for the essential conditions of life or the possibility of development in some direction. (Hayek, 1991: 97)

So for Hayek, it is the sufficient dispersion of property in a competitive market economy that prevents the individual owners of high-demand goods from wielding coercive power (1991: 95–7). This then is the basis of Hayek's defence of a largely untrammelled market economy. The following sub-section will summarise the polar argument that a conception of freedom requires positive conditions, some of which reflect anarchist sentiments.

Positive conditions

Maureen Ramsay claims that freedom is not a separate issue from the value of freedom. This is because freedom as non-interference makes little sense if it is unrelated to what it is that people are left alone to actually do, which is usually valued as more than solitary confinement. If a person is living within a certain domain of unpreventedness together with a strong sense of purpose that is not beyond her capabilities, but it cannot be fulfilled because she is inhibited by external impediments that may not be the direct result of deliberate inter-agential coercion, then this seems a very odd condition of freedom. Once it is realised that there is a logical link between freedom and what gives it value, the association of freedom with ability cannot be denied; or as it is sometimes termed, freedom is irreversibly embedded within the conditions of its exercise. Alex Prichard summarises these themes neatly:

> I may have all the rights in the world, and be free from all immediate acts of interference, but without the means to exercise these freedoms am I really free? Also, without a positive conception of what it means to be a human being, what exactly do my negative freedoms afford me. A pure negative liberty would leave me directionless and treading water. Without the resources to develop, and a sense of what to develop into, in what meaningful sense am I free? (2019: 80)

In particular, if negative liberty is of value because it enables people to achieve their purposes, then it follows that the ability to do so is dependent upon a steady and reliable access to the required means and opportunities. This is actually the whole point of non-interference in the first place. So as nurturing the ability to achieve a given aim may require more than a state of non-interference, simply being left purely to oneself is not enough to be truly free (Ramsay, 1997: 40–5; Prichard, 2019: 80).

A congruous response can also be made to the claim by negative libertarians that impediments to freedom must always be inter-agential and intentional. We have seen that for theorists like Hayek and Berlin, interference is always from others, and for the former, it has to be deliberate.[1] So inabilities stemming from unintentional acts, those that are the indirect outcome of social arrangements, do not constrict freedom. Market outcomes are held to be non-coercive to those who come to own the least resources, who as a result are in no stable position to fulfil their goals because such outcomes are unintentional and cannot be foreseen by particular individuals. Yet for Ramsay, even if the consequences of individual actions are inadvertent, this does not mean they place no limits upon people's freedom. Given the vast gulf in property ownership, economic agents who start with the least will usually leave the market with the least.[2] The resulting outcomes may not be intended, but they are still coercive to the worst off (Ramsay, 1997: 48–50). This point is also of great interest to the labour and anarcho-republicans, a perspective revisited in section two of this chapter.

The two main interconnected claims of positive libertarians outlined here – freedom is irreducibly attached to what gives it value, which implies freedom cannot be disconnected from abilities, and that the cause and form of coercion also occur at a structural level diffusely and through unpremeditated means – lead straight to a powerful critique of an unfettered market economy. We shall return to this argument that positive liberty does not, in contrast to negative freedom, protect capitalist property relations from critical scrutiny further on in the chapter, where the key institutions of capitalism are indeed renounced. In order to provide the context through which to do this, it is first necessary to establish Hayek's critique of positive liberty.

Hayek's rejection of the republican, idealist and socialist conceptions of freedom

Hayek firstly considers political freedom, which, as Chapter 1 explained, includes participation in the choice of representatives, legislation and administration. Whilst extending decision-making into a collective seeks to give organised groups an aggregate liberty, free groups so described may not consist of free people. It is possible that people may 'freely' contract themselves into a condition of complete dependence. As will now be clear, for Hayek freedom belongs to individuals; it is not a property of collectives. The identification of liberty with political participation cannot then be 'an equivalent or substitute for' individual liberty seen as independence of the arbitrary will of another. For neo-liberals like Hayek, the legal protection of individual liberties like free choice in occupation, movement and property ownership meet the condition of liberty irrespective of whether they come with political liberty. Hayek is equally dismissive of inner or metaphysical freedom. Recall this position stresses a person is free when she is guided by her own considered reason, rather than through an illicit impulse to succumb to the irrational passions and appetites of an undisciplined character. Just as he does with political freedom, Hayek draws a distinction between individual liberty and inner liberty. "Whether or not a person is able to choose intelligently between alternatives, or to adhere to a resolution he has made, is a problem distinct from whether or not other people will impose their will upon him" (1991: 84). Seen in this light then, inner liberty confuses liberty with an individual's psychological state of mind, rather than a matter of inter-agential relations (1991: 80–5; Barry, 1984: 275).

But for Hayek, the most dangerous misuse of the term freedom is when it is associated with power or ability – for example, when it appears in the dreams of those who falsely believe they have the capacity to do whatever they like. He juxtaposes the illusory belief that people can rearrange their environment to suit their own wishes with the equally erroneous belief that they can fly like a bird or defy the laws of gravity. Here he is dismissing the argument for socialism:

> Once this identification of freedom with power is admitted, there is no limit to the sophisms by which the attractions of the word 'liberty' can be used to support measures which destroy individual liberty, no end to the tricks by which people can be exhorted in the name of liberty to give up their liberty. It has been with the help of this equivocation that the notion of collective power over circumstances has been substituted for that of individual liberty and that in totalitarian states liberty has been suppressed in the name of liberty. (1991: 85–6)

Hayek's fear is that when freedom comes to be generalised as an 'absence of external impediments' *per se*, the tighter identification of coercion with human agency is obscured (1991: 85–6). In sum, although the same word has been invoked in the senses of 'political', 'inner' and 'power/ability', for Hayek this is nonsensical:

> This is the source of dangerous nonsense, a verbal trap that leads to the most absurd conclusions. Liberty in the sense of power, political liberty, and inner liberty are not states of the same kind as individual liberty, we cannot, by sacrificing a little of the one in order to get more of the other, on balance gain some common element of freedom. (1991: 88)

To speak in terms of a common element because different conditions are described with a singular term through which liberty is increased as a whole is, for Hayek, "sheer obscurantism" (1991: 86–8; Ramsay, 1997: 41–2).

This then is Hayek's stringent conception of freedom, his advocacy of a largely unfettered market economy and his rejection of positive liberty in all its forms. These are the preliminary explanations that are the essential prerequisites for the critical evaluation that now follows. I will refute the opinion stated in the above quote. Continuing the argument made in the previous chapter, the associational anarchist conception of liberty, whilst blending together in a specific way these four main kinds of liberty, is not a "verbal trap" that will lead to "absurd conclusions".

A repudiation of Hayek

There are three sub-sections to this second section of the chapter. The first, 'A return to radical republicanism', contrasts the Hayekian and the labour republican accounts of coercion, where the latter's thesis on domination in both its structural and workplace forms is reiterated, only now particular attention is paid to the destructive dynamic between the former and anonymous interdependence. From here I will argue that this critique of the capitalist mode of production provides solid means through which to strengthen the case against Hayek's tight definition of negative liberty. Sub-section two, 'The limits to Hayek's conception of freedom', contends that an adequate conception of freedom needs to incorporate a more extensive account of coercion. Finally, sub-section three, 'The anarchist voluntary and free communal service principles', completes my argument by weaving together these two principles through an associational anarchist reading of freedom *to do/ become* and freedom *from*.

A return to radical republicanism

Hayek recognises that economic agents may have to reconsider their plans to accommodate sudden changes in the social landscape. But even though their alternatives may now be impoverished or uncertain, as their actions are not determined by the will of another, they are not subject to coercion:

> Even if the threat of starvation ... impels me to accept a distasteful job at a very low wage, even if I am 'at the mercy' of the only man willing to employ me, I am not coerced by him or anybody else ... So long as he can remove only one opportunity among many to earn a living ... he cannot coerce, though he may cause pain. (Hayek, 1991: 92–3)

If so, then it is not power *per se* that is bad, but the power to coerce through an enforceable threat of inflicting harm. "There is no evil in the power wielded by the director of some great enterprise in which men have willingly united of their own will and for their own purposes" (Hayek, 1991: 90). On this analysis, the power possessed by someone like Henry Ford is not the power to coerce. Hayek accepts that at times of high unemployment, opportunities for coercion can arise, but he adds that in a 'prosperous competitive society' these exceptions would be rare. This argument is developed by drawing a clear demarcating line between coercion and the terms on which people offer their services. In a free society, the mutual services everyone requires to satisfy their needs are voluntary. When a producer refuses to supply someone with a given item, all the time the latter can turn to others, the conditions the former demand in return for providing them cannot count as coercion. This is on the key provision that the actions which place people in their predicaments do not intentionally block certain courses of action. Given acts may cause harm, but so long as they do not make someone serve the ends of another, the effect on freedom falls within the same category as all other natural calamities; fires or floods are the examples Hayek cites (1991: 90–3).

In diametrical opposition, the radical republican thesis on domination articulates sharply the omnipresent threat of coercion at the systemic level. Section two of Chapter 6 explained that from this perspective, domination occurs where productive property is unequally controlled, especially where a legally protected class of private investors monopolise ownership.[3] All owners of productive property stand by the institution of private ownership, which is a prerequisite for any of them to put to profitable use their particular resources. Here the non-owners are in a collective condition of economic dependency for their livelihoods. As Gourevitch puts it, wherever structural domination exists, "the labour contract is voluntary but not free; the contract reflects a voluntary agreement, but labourers do not sell their labour freely" (2013: 602). Unfreedom in this sense is caused by an absence of reasonable alternatives to the wage-labour relation. Along with structural domination, the labour republicans were also concerned with the personal dependence of workers upon the arbitrary will of employers as soon as the contractual agreement was signed. Unequal power relations between employers and employees ensure that structural domination is transformed into modalities of personal domination at the place of work. In sum, as long as employers remain, through their disproportional control over productive property, in full control over workplace arrangements, it is doubtful any lasting solutions can be found within the capitalist system (Gourevitch, 2013: 601–2, 607–9).

This then is the wide gulf between Hayek, who argues an agent is coerced only when subject to the deliberate imposition of someone else's will, and radical republicanism, for whom coercion exists more seriously through systemic forms of domination. The discussions that follow in the next two sub-sections will defend the latter view, and they will indicate why the democratic relations and the egalitarian dissemination of productive assets within the guild system provide sound conditions for the free exercise of agency. The remainder of this sub-section will offer some important preliminary remarks.

In what may be seen as something of a concession, Hayek acknowledges that in a certain situation, a particular economic power may be applied coercively. A monopolist, for instance, could exercise coercion if she was the only provider of a basic asset that others are helplessly dependent upon for their survival. The example he gives is the sole controller of the supply of water in a desert. In doing so, he qualifies his claim that the terms through which market exchanges take place cannot result in coercion. Yet even here it is only when a single party, who must be the one source of something that is crucial to the existence of others, is able to retain an indispensable good can coercion be exercised, which is supposedly only in "very exceptional circumstances" (1991: 91–2). For Raymond Plant and Kenneth Hoover, though, if, as Hayek concedes, coercion can be enforced when a fundamental item is controlled, then an explicit conceptual link is established between essential commodities and the exercise of liberty (1989: 206–7). Miller also wonders why, once Hayek has conceded this possibility, he restricts the situation so narrowly to only those cases that involve a total command over a vital resource. It is clearly now the case that possession of resources will bear heavily upon the distribution of negative liberty (1991: 14–15).[4] At the normative level, these critiques point to paths beyond Hayek's catallaxy, of which there are many, and most stay firmly within the bounds of statehood. But they nevertheless appear to offer some support to the radical republican critique of systemic coercion. So, in the interests of fairness, the question now becomes if Hayek's conception of freedom is too extreme, can much the same be said about the former? For instance, it may well be wondered whether the labour republican conception of domination is overly expansive and whether the general interdependence of individuals really is a source of unfreedom. The concern would be that if domination is taken beyond the restriction of personal employers, the important dividing line between unintended consequences and intentional interference becomes blurred; the Hayekian liberal would no doubt make this claim. If so, then the anonymous interdependence of agents, which is their actual social existence, incorporates domination. In this case no one can ever be truly free (Gourevitch, 2013: 604–5).

But as Gourevitch explains, the labour republican account of domination is subtler in its critique:

> Structural domination is an intermediate condition between personal subjection and anonymous interdependence. It is a concept that explains how unequal control over productive assets *converts* anonymous interdependence into the domination of wage-labourers by owners without this domination taking the form of personal subjection. (2013: 604)

The freedom to walk away from a particular job does not move beyond the compulsion to sell one's labour to someone else. The relation between anonymous interdependence and structural domination is that in class-divided societies the former is systematically unequal. At the superficial level, structural domination may seem to be anonymous and unintentional due to the voluntary nature of agreements. But the compulsion of workers is propagated through the repetitive and intentional acts of employers taken as a whole. These macro structures form the backdrop within which specific aspirations of any one employer are carried out. The collective intentionality does not command any particular individual to assume any particular position. This though is not the main point of the labour republican critique. They were more concerned to show that a property system with an unequal distribution of productive assets can be identified with domination in the sense that it is possible to distinguish the agents whose actions reinforce this inequality. This holds regardless of whether given individuals have deliberate intentions about this or that singular transaction. So the labour republican position does not so much object to social interdependence *per se*; rather, it targets the ways in which it comes to be organised (Gourevitch, 2013: 604–7). Keeping all these points in mind, the following two sub-sections will first recognise the very real existence of systemic domination and, second, indicate how to reorganise anonymous interdependency in a way that protects to a greater extent the equal value of personal liberty.

The limits to Hayek's conception of freedom

Although Hayek argued, convincingly, that state socialist strategies of economic planning will ultimately destroy the freedom it hopes to attain, his claim that even when the coerced are still in a position to make some choice they nevertheless lack freedom because the available alternatives have been shaped by the coercer can, with some revision, apply with equal measure to capitalist markets. We have seen that for Hayek "[i]t is competition made possible by the dispersion of property that deprives the individual owners of particular things of all coercive powers" (1991: 97). The problem, though, is that, as section two of Chapter 7 made clear, due to the tendencies integral to the concentration of wealth and power in market forces economies, property universally does precisely the opposite. The immense power that inevitably accumulates in organisations like the MNCs and the TNCs is, in the sense that genuine competition on an even playing field is the last thing they want, just as damaging to freedom. In order for property to be 'sufficiently dispersed', extensive and continuous political intervention is required. This, however, would be to socially engineer, which is clearly at odds with Hayek's neo-liberal critique of socialist constructivism. The assured outcome is that a class of wage-labourers often have only limited opportunities to choose which particular employer to sell their labour-power to. And even when genuine competition does break out, due to the collective lack of ownership of the means of production, the chances of workers applying their own knowledge to pursue their independent aims are entirely dependent upon whatever work employers happen to be offering. The possible options have been shaped by a class bias inherent in the system. Here I would endorse the labour republican claim that whilst wage-labour contracts may be voluntary, they are not free. In capitalist society, employers and employees enter into a relationship. The former control the productive process in the workplace, and workers are 'free' in the sense that they are not subject to the kinds of obligatory bonds that upheld feudal ties of duty and privilege. But, as we saw in Chapter 1, there is a gulf in content between the two commodities they sell each other. The very nature of capital also enables it to change form. Stockholders and owners can, through their boards of directors, close down production facilities and open new workplaces in different regions, or even countries. Conversely, workers are only free to choose which particular capitalist is going to hire their labour-power. In these senses then, the propertied have a vastly superior bargaining power than non-owners (Allen, 2011: 20; Clark, 2013: 114–17).

Once it is accepted that coercion is not reduced to only cases of deliberate intent within inter-agential relations, Hayek's argument can be rejected on the bases that the dependency of employees goes beyond the sole provider of essential material means. If so, the power possessed by someone like Henry Ford, when the focus extends to the wider context of social relations, does amount to the power to coerce. Consider Hayek's claim that in order to form coherent plans, individuals must know they have access to material resources. It is true that wage-labourers may not always be dependent upon a given agent for the supply of material means, but in capitalist societies, they are still dependent on someone. Whether the latter is a sole monopolist makes, in terms of dependence, little difference. The certainty is that wage-labourers cannot avoid the regular position of having to sell their only productive asset, their labour-power, to an employer of some kind, and it is through this contract that they are compelled to accept disadvantageous terms. So whilst economic agents may not, strictly speaking, be forced to do a particular thing, a systemic condition of dependence is built into the system. This situation may be unintended, but it is easily predictable. The ruthless drive to expand capital ensures that within the investment class, individual capitalists are continuously trying to out-strip their rivals. The brute logic of competitive accumulation is inherently unrelenting. The ceaseless pursuit of increased profitability frequently exists in accordance with harsh cost-cutting procedures. Perhaps most significantly, it is in the interests of profit maximisation to reduce the cost of labour-power to the absolute minimum. If the 'many people who can serve one's needs' are, due to the dictates of market signals, supplying virtually identical terms of employment, the end result for employees is much the same. How widely properties are disseminated does not alter the objective fact that the non-owners of productive property remain in a prevailing state of dependence on other parties for the 'essential conditions of life'. *The formal freedom/equality of the wage-labour contract masks a deeper structural unfreedom/inequality.*[5] Hayek's belief that a market economy cannot coerce rests, therefore, upon a definition of liberty that is far too narrow. The freedom to choose who to be dependent on is an impoverished conception of freedom. If freedom cannot be exercised because agents do not possess adequate material assets, in what sense are they free? For these reasons, the radical republican critique of systemic domination is absolutely correct.

To sum up, the opportunity for individuals to enhance the capabilities they hold in high esteem and are not beyond their competencies is unequivocally dependent upon an equal and stable access to essential resources. The unequal distribution of the means of production inherent in capitalist society, therefore, has to fall within the category of coercive obstacles. On the grounds that inequalities in power do not just diminish the conditions of liberty but diminish liberty itself, liberty must be understood as more than an absence of intentional inter-agential constraints. As such, a fuller and more adequate account of external obstructions needs to include the inadvertent and unpremeditated obstructions which are brought about by sets of social arrangements which could be, if we so wished, retransformed. So the claim that it is not the unity of freedom and its conditions that depletes the meaning of freedom but the distinction that divides them that does is coherent. In class-divided societies markets can, it would seem, impede hugely upon individuals. Chapter 1, followed by section two of Chapter 2, explained at some length that workers are forced to work for a particular capitalist through a series of social arrangements that embody inequalities, and which are permanently liable to lead to their exploitation. Hayek's contention that the wealthiest capitalists do not possess the power to exercise coercion must, on these accounts, be rejected. Likewise, his argument that freedom should be understood only as non-interference, that people have freedom whilst lacking the conditions of its exercise, misses completely domination in its systemic form. As wage-labourers are in a collective state of dependence in objective and structural terms, their formal freedom has less effective value in relation to the possessing class. This contention adds substance to the point raised in section one of this chapter that the whole objective of being unprevented is that agents are then free to actually do something. To deny this is to sever the link between freedom and subjective properties like people's feelings and their goals. For these reasons, impersonal market forces must lose their deterministic powers in much the same way the unaccountable authority of the centralised socialist state must be replaced with a libertarian alternative. It is one of the main threads of the argument running through this book that a specific combination of social planning with a guild-regulated market system fulfils both of these intentions. Through a discussion of the anarchist voluntary and free communal service principles, I will now indicate what this entails.

The anarchist voluntary and free communal service principles

Colin Ward notes that central to the anarchist theory of organisation is the 'voluntary' principle, which stresses that agents must have the liberty to choose which organisations they affiliate with, as mandatory membership violates individual freedom (2004: 31). Secondly, Cole, who agrees fully with free choice in occupation (1920b: 75), suggests that within the capitalist system, workers are motivated to work through fear (of starvation) or appeals to their greed (greater financial reward). As he regards both motives as equally inadequate and undesirable, he proposes a new principle in the form of 'free communal service'. It is communal in the sense that goods will have a use value that is determined democratically, and it is free in the sense that freedom is inseparable from the principle of industrial self-government. These two principles of service (to the community) and freedom (in the workplace) are incomplete without each other. The fundamental claim here is that the good of the community, in particular the manner in which it meets its basic material needs, must take precedence over the private interests of the individual, especially with regard to the maximisation of personal profit (1921a: 2–3, 1921b: 2–3). Taken together, the voluntary and the free communal service principles express the dual need for freedom *of* organisation and freedom *within* organisation. This assertion implies that both compulsory membership and the authoritarian workplace transgress individual freedom.[6] It is this account of coercion that an advanced conception of freedom must respond to.

Recall that a key premise of the argument of this book is that freedom cannot be separated from the conditions of its profitable exercise. If a large section of the populace lacks the opportunity to take advantage of formal freedom because they do not possess sufficient material resources, their standing as free beings must be called into question. As we have seen, in capitalist society people's only access to the means of production is often through a singular route, wage-labour. Even though there are no direct political orders enforcing workers to sell their labour-power to any particular employer, in the absence of investment capital they have little option other than to hire out their labour in some way. In these enterprises, workers have no choice but to follow the owner/manager's will, at least if they wish to stay employed. In contrast, within associational anarchism's cooperatives, the only will is the collectives' in which all members share equal democratic rights. When commenting on the benefits of workplace democratisation in general, Howard puts it neatly:

> It is hard not to see the extension of one's democratic rights (into the democratised workplace) as an extension of one's autonomy ... one is not giving up meaningful individual freedoms to the collective but, rather, is restricting the freedom of elites (owners, managers, stockholders) in ways that empower workers as a group and, as a result, protect each worker from oligarchical power. (2000: 30)

It is in this sense that subjective freedoms are protected. Guild cooperators have access to inclusive participatory structures that are, in the main, unavailable to wage-labourers. A conception of liberty on the triadic formula will always involve freedom *from* as well as freedom *to do/become*, which is why neither the negative nor the positive conceptions are, if framed in permanent contradiction, complete. Capitalism may provide some measure of the former, which is all Berlin and Hayek ask of it. But the statement that with very little input into decision-making over productive processes and corporation policies, the liberty of wage-labourers *within* the workplace is at best minimal is not terribly contentious.

Indeed, drawing from the above critique of Hayek's conception of freedom, my contention is that in corporate capitalist regimes, as the option of choosing which particular workplace autocracy to sell one's labour to frequently amounts to very little effective choice, the freedom of organisation on offer is a false paradigm. For the voluntary principle to be meaningful, the form of organisation is paramount. An emphasis on dignified labour, job satisfaction and the opportunity to determine productive issues democratically distinguish the guild cooperatives. The general idea is that a qualified free communal service will be offered willingly as people will, naturally, seek creative fulfilment with their associates. The voluntary principle is a key prerequisite to this desired goal. It does this in the sense that there are no oppressive structures forcing people to associate with any particular guild cooperative. So with regards to Hayek's critique of political (republican) freedom, the guild cooperatives do embody a collective liberty, but as their constitution is compatible with the voluntary principle, they consist of free people. In a cooperative setting, individual liberty can be identified with political participation.

It may initially appear that the voluntary principle is more in line with negative liberty, and the free communal service principle leans more towards the direction of positive liberty. But it is more the case that each principle incorporates elements of both. Put simply, negative liberty is concerned with opportunities, while positive liberty pertains to accomplishments. So the former is an absence of constraint or restriction, and the latter is the exercise of certain faculties or the realisation of particular objectives (Kramer, 2003: 2). Yet with regards to the triadic formula, the actual dispute between the negative and the positive conceptions revolves, as Chapter 1 explained, around the ways in which the three variables in the X, Y and X relation are interpreted. Any liberty anyone can ever think of will always involve both opportunities and accomplishments. In terms of the anarchist voluntary principle, there is freedom *from* compulsory membership, and freedom *to* choose which cooperative to join, start or loosely affiliate with. With regards to the free communal service principle, there is freedom *from* an imperious or even tyrannical enterprise, and freedom *to* participate on democratic terms within the cooperative.

Associational anarchism's specific reading of freedom *from* and freedom *to do/become* accords with the wider doctrine of anarchism. An anarchist society will deliberately seek to attain freedom from arbitrary domination in every sense. But as Prichard explains, it would be incorrect to reduce an anarchist conception of freedom to a sphere of non-interference, as seeking only a condition of "unencumbered isolation" (2019: 80). Raekstad makes exactly the same point, adding that a positive account in the anarchist sense has "organic links to solidarity and equality" (2016: 409). Likewise, going back to the first few pages of Chapter 1, recall Honeywell's informative account of anarchism's advanced selfhood, where negative and positive ideals are thoughtfully combined within a conceptual framework that does not view them in universal contradiction. Freedom for the anarchist is also far more than the freedom to pursue a particular brand of a given commodity, which often boils down to the freedom to choose between predetermined alternatives that only differ in the minutest of ways. It is freedom *from* interference by an outside party, political or economic, and freedom *to do/become*, in particular self-realisation by transcending subtly imposed identities which serve the interests of powerful elites (Shantz & Williams, 2013: 11–12). Associational anarchism embodies these freedoms in a certain way. In the productive sphere, there is freedom *from* corporate capitalist relations which, on the anarchist reading, risk exploitation, unfulfilling labour and workplace autocracy, and in the consumptive sphere there is freedom *from* commodity fetishism and the kind of implacable advertising which stimulates the desires and impulses of the lower-self. In terms of freedom *to do/become*, there is a momentum towards the freedom to produce in self-actualising ways and to participate meaningfully in productive decision-making, and the freedom to consume with a consciousness that is not wholly reductive to the instant gratification of one's personal whims. As such, there are mutually reinforcing freedoms *from* and freedoms *to do/ become* in the interlinking domains of production and consumption.

We are now in a position to conclude this section by returning to the labour republican claim that the way anonymous interdependency is organised in class-divided societies results in a loss of real freedom. In associational anarchism, as there is egalitarian access to productive resources, and because there are no plutocracies exerting disproportionate control over the means of investment, there is no structural domination as conceived by the radical republicans. In complementary terms, as the wage-labour relation has been replaced with salaried labour within a system of workplace democracies, the associated producers are not subject to the arbitrary will of employers. In these conditions, where the voluntary and free communal service principles are of equal value to all citizens, anonymous interdependence is not systematically skewed. It is in this sense that cooperative labour contracts are free as well as voluntary.

Conclusion

This chapter has reviewed Hayek's account of the interrelation between freedom, economics and property. As it has covered a breadth of theoretical ground, it will be useful to reconfirm the key points made. His claim that coercion is always both inter-agential and deliberate is, in the sense that it can exist in this form, not actually bereft of any truth. It is just that his criterion is overly restrictive. I have indicated that his thesis not only leaves many important dimensions of freedom unaddressed, but in the sense that there are external coercive obstructions that cannot be attributed to his minimum criterion, he is in no position to address them satisfactorily. To pass over these kinds of restrictions as examples of inability rather than coercion, or to liken them to natural constraints, is to reduce the parameters of coercion to the point of vacuousness. The activities of workers inside the capitalist enterprise are directed by another's will, and as such the substance of their freedom must be seriously doubted. Hayek's response would be that as employees in capitalist society enter into work relations of their own accord, and can likewise leave as they choose, there is no coercion. This, I have argued, is to overlook systemic and unpremeditated forms of domination. The implications of this are clear. An individual who is "compelled by circumstance", those that are the outcome of hard market forces that are replaceable, "to accept a distasteful job at a very low wage" through "the threat of starvation" can hardly be held up as the epitome of freedom. In the global sweatshop economy, it is doubtful whether similar 'circumstances' are as rare as Hayek imagines. Ultimately, an economic condition in which "I am at the mercy of the only man willing to employ me" in effect amounts to an obliteration of both formal and effective freedom no tyrannical political system could ever wish to emulate. The fear of starvation is no doubt a potential threat to all people at all times, but this is why labour is such an important category. For this reason alone, the elimination of workplace autocracy and alienated labour should be targeted above all else.

A sphere of non-interference is a key component of any plausible conception of freedom, yet it is impoverished without communal control over the material means of existence. In this regard, the belief that the private property relations of corporate capitalism can uphold negative freedom for all individuals equally requires a dramatic leap of faith. From this book's perspective, the opportunities for agents to pursue the capacities they have good reason to esteem are dependent upon democratic and equal access to adequate resources. It was important then to show how the voluntary and free communal service principles in the guild system embody freedom *to do/become* whilst providing optimum protection to a measure of freedom *from*; which, I suggest, is a plausible way of reorganising social interdependency felicitously. Associational anarchism accordingly pursues more than merely political forms of emancipation, the limitations of which were devastatingly exposed by the young Marx. Conceptualising a new theory of liberty in the way freedom as Marxian-autonomy does certainly determines the direction within which liberal freedom is recast, but this is in the interests of liberty taken in its totality. The following chapter will complete this argument.

Notes

1 Miller points out that for Berlin, restrictions on freedom are always attributable to human agency, but he is inconsistent on whether coercion must be deliberate, or if it can also be indirect (1991: 13). Alternatively, Gray indicates

that Berlin's theory can, if certain conditions hold, regard impersonal social forces as imposing upon negative liberty (1984b: 341).

2 Hayek acknowledges this point, although he is uncritical of it (1976: 123).

3 The contemporary communitarian anarchist John Clark also sees domination through processes of impersonal mechanisms as most prominent. "In a techno-bureaucratic, commodified, and mediatised society, domination takes on increasingly more ideological and mystified forms that gave it a quality of *invisibility*" (2013: 105).

4 Even sympathetic observers have expressed scepticism on this point. "The trouble is that those things that are 'crucial to my existence' are necessarily subjective, so that someone could say he 'felt' coerced by the terms of a transaction even though, objectively, the situation did not approach that of the sole owner of the spring in the desert" (Barry, 1984: 273).

5 Callinicos makes this point well (2003: 27, 115, 124).

6 A particular benefit of life in a democratic society is that everyone has the same rights. The alternative is the police state where subjects have no choice but to obey orders, however arbitrary. They are overseen and controlled by official bureaucrats, who punish dissent and disobedience. Although this is a thoroughly wretched state of affairs, it doubles as an accurate portrait of the typical modern workplace, which as Bob Black observes, is structured by a demeaning system of domination (1996: 239–40).

10

Freedom in the guild system and beyond

There are two sections to this chapter, which in various ways substantiate the associational anarchist pledge to safeguard a certain configuration of negative freedoms. The first, 'Rethinking liberal freedoms', develops the argument that although some liberal freedoms have been sacrificed and others revised, freedom as Marxian-autonomy maintains a more general condition of unpreventedness.[1] The second, 'A self-employed sector', explains why a domain within which individual agents and small firms who seek to labour on their own account will not only exist but thrive.

Rethinking liberal freedoms

A likely objection from certain quarters to my argument, that true communism (de-alienation and the abolishment of the wage-labour contract) is compatible with a reinvigorated social anarchism, is likely to be in relation to market-based freedoms. In summarising this kind of critique, Robert L. Heilbroner points out that the political command in a socialist mode of production need not be arbitrary or dictatorial, but it will involve restricting a key bourgeois economic freedom, the right of an individual to privately own productive assets. In the debates that assess whether a socialist transformation can maintain economic rights, a common assumption is that the restriction of property rights, including the right of people to do as they wish with their labour-power, entails a grave reduction of economic freedom (Heilbroner, 1980: 157). Right-liberals, for instance, adhere to a form of freedom in which self-interested individuals are free to profit from the labour of others and accumulate virtually unlimited wealth. As such, they would forcefully reject freedom as Marxian-autonomy. What, the immediate question is certain to be, has happened to liberalism's traditional defence of an inviolable private sphere?

Typically, the liberal concept of freedom is agency as independent self-interested individuals ('X'), the constraint or obstacle is interference through the arbitrary imposition of the will of an external party, social or political

('Y'), and the goal/end is pursued or un-pursued desire-independent wants ('Z'). This concept has something important to add to any account of liberty. In its conceptualisation of freedom, though, associational anarchism proposes certain qualifications. Chapter 1 explained that, ontologically speaking, a single individual is an ensemble of social relations. Yet social relations can be shaped so that a sphere of unpreventedness extends to the maximum degree compatible with the guild economy. On a revised liberal reading, agency in associational anarchism is cooperative individuals who associate distinct aspects of themselves in functionally demarcated economic organisations ('X'), the constraint or obstacle remains interference from external bodies, only now the threat is from the federated bodies of the guilds, the consumer councils and the communes ('Y'), and the goal/ends have been modified to ensure compatibility with a cooperative political economy ('Z'). It does this in order to attain what I have termed the pluralist delimited yet interrelating aspects of the collective higher-self. So although the liberal equation of 'X', 'Y' and 'Z' has been revised in order to accommodate a left-libertarian account of idealist liberty, the liberal emphasis on freedom from constraint, obstacle or interference has been retained. This does mean that the latter will obviously exist within a new politico-economic framework. The private sphere has been re-politicised and is now constituted through participatory democratic forms. There is no place for certain market practices, and individuals cannot make money merely through ownership.[2] Guild cooperatives cannot offer interest payments to private parties in exchange for investment capital, neither are they in a position to hire employees on permanent wage-labour contracts. Guilds can accommodate numerous sole traders and small firms within their ranks,[3] but once they expand beyond a certain size, they are obliged to comply with the cooperative nature of guild production.

Nevertheless, whilst inroads have been made into certain liberal freedoms, others have been retained in their fullness. Recall from the previous chapter that from the Hayekian perspective coercion is always a matter of person-to-person relations. For Hayek, as the range of choice on offer at any one time is distinct from the extent to which people are free to pursue their intentions, it does not impact upon freedom:

> Whether he is free or not does not depend on the range of choice, but on whether he can expect to shape his course of action in accordance with his present intentions, or whether somebody else has power so to manipulate the conditions as to make him act according to that person's will rather than his own. (1991: 82)

Freedom, so understood, requires a protected private sphere within which other people cannot interfere (1991: 81–2). With regards to the specific issue of access to an economic unit of one's choosing, his reasoning can apply equally to cooperative-labour as it does to wage-labour. This is on the pivotal condition that the former is established within a non-statist framework, and is thus compatible with the anarchist voluntary principle. So long as no external party has the power to manipulate the conditions that would effectively determine the course of actions open to economic agents, there is no coercion as conceived along Hayekian lines. The actual number of cooperatives seeking to expand is, at any given moment, likely to differ from region to region and from industry to industry. But for Hayek, and he is adamant on this point, the presence or absence of coercion does not rest upon the range of choices. It depends solely on whether people can frame their actions in accordance with their intentions. In the sense that the choice of entry and the right of exit in associational anarchism are both inviolable, as is the freedom to form a new cooperative or work solely for oneself, a private sphere of sorts will remain. So Hayek's plausible claim that "[a] complete monopoly of employment, such as would exist in a fully socialist state in which the government was the only employer and the owner of all the instruments of production, would possess unlimited powers of coercion" (1991: 92–3), has no relevance to associational anarchism's mode of production.

The same remit of liberty also applies to the sphere of consumption. What are now ethical consumers are free to consume as they please. The interaction between producers and consumers also occurs pre-production as well as post-production. As sections two and three of Chapter 7 explained, consumers may relay to producers information on personal taste through the consumer councils, where they can direct their concerns about given items. In doing so, the request for certain products is determined irrespective of personal bank balances. This is what differentiates associational anarchist consumers from their capitalist counterparts. In order for these liberties to be effective, the freedoms of speech, thought and expression will be both universal and sacrosanct.

Finally, any remaining losses must be assessed against the overall enhancement of freedom. Defenders of neo-liberalism who equate capitalism with liberty and deny the link between socialism and liberty, including for our purposes anarcho-constitutional forms of socialism, often do so by uniting capitalism and the market. But the objection to capitalism upheld in this book is in regards to wage-labour and the private ownership of productive resources. In associational anarchism, as there is only an ultra-minimal role for wage-labour and very little private ownership of the means of production, it is not possible for hostile class divides to form through which the propertied could profit from the labour-power of non-owners. Labour relations have been thoroughly retransformed along participatory and libertarian lines. Some restrictions on liberal freedoms must, then, be balanced against the way overall liberty for the majority is enhanced in the guild system. As mentioned, the constraint or obstacle, the 'Y' in MacCallum's triadic formula, is restriction or interference from the higher echelons of the functional organisations. Drawing from an array of empirical data, I have argued elsewhere that the guild cooperatives will be robust enough to maintain their internal democratic structures, thus negating the opportunity for self-seeking elites to seek only their own segmented interests.[4] The significance of this to the preservation of liberty was noted by Cole long ago. "The best guarantee of personal liberty that can exist is in the existence, in each form of association, of an alert democracy, keenly critical of every attempt of the elected person ... to pass beyond his representative function" (1920: 191). Even Roberto Michels, the paradigm theorist of oligarchic tendencies and arguably the most feared critic of democracy, conceded that the organisations most likely to sustain democratic decision-making are workplace democracies (1999: 162). So in confirmation of the arguments in Chapters 8 and 9, vibrant participation within the guild cooperatives is a precondition for the maintenance of liberal freedom, the liberty of individuals from arbitrarily imposed constraint or interference. It is also for this reason that, in applying the rhetoric of instrumental participation, the loss of the particular liberty to expand beyond the 500 principle, where internal democratic relations would break down, is justified, which, to reconfirm, is an appeal to negative liberty more widely conceived.

A self-employed sector

We now turn to the important issue of production through units which are too small to constitute a cooperative. Where associative effort is required, which is the majority of cases, manufacture and service provision will take place predominantly in the guild cooperatives. Beyond this, there is nothing against self-employed individuals, independent artists, freelance writers and small work teams.[5] In defending his model of 'feasible socialism', Alex Nove infers that producing privately for sale is acceptable if it is just one individual. He would also allow a private entrepreneur to employ a small team of workers and profit from their labour. A family farm, for instance, can employ a few labourers, and a small restaurant may hire seasonal staff. As the entrepreneurs are themselves working, there is no unearned income from mere ownership rights. They could be limited by the number of workers employed, or by the value of capital assets (Nove, 1983: 121, 206–7). Likewise, anarchists have also seen that as *personal* property is defined by *use*, so there is no absentee ownership, it is far removed from the private property relations that distinguish capitalist societies (Shannon, 2019: 94).

A similar reasoning will apply in associational anarchism. True to its libertarian spirit, there may be any number of small businesses and solo traders operating at any one time and place. As we will now see, egalitarian competition within a self-employed sector is not in any sense at odds with the soft competitive ethic monitored by each separate guild. With no elitist extraction of surplus value, and in the absence of immense concentrations and centralisations of capital, wealth and therefore power, inequalities of outcome in both the guild system and the self-employed sector will fall roughly within the same range. In order to show what this entails, it will be useful to begin by considering the salient question of remuneration.

Briefly put, the anarcho-collectivism of Bakunin favours remuneration by output, whereas the anarcho-communism of Kropotkin recommends distribution according to need. For the former, all members of society must earn their living through their own endeavours. In anarcho-collectivism, exploitation will not be possible as each person will enjoy the material means for the enhancement of their humanity, but a share in social wealth will be dependent upon the contribution of one's own labour (Bakunin, 1973: 125–6). Individuals may work alone or in a collective. Bakunin believes the latter will generally be the preferred choice as association multiplies the productive output of each worker. So although a small amount of private ownership will remain, this will only be where the owners work themselves and do not actually employ anybody (1973: 89, 92–3). On this particular point, Kropotkin did not follow Bakunin. He argued that as modern production is a complex collective process, individual input cannot be accurately calculated. Approaching production from a synthetic standpoint, where each person's work is intimately intertwined with the work of others, the collectivist ideal that remuneration should correlate to the number of hours worked by each individual is 'absolutely untenable'. For Kropotkin, the 'mitigated individualism' proposed by the anarcho-collectivists cannot operate smoothly within the 'partial communism' understood as egalitarian ownership of material resources. As it is not possible to calculate individual contributions from the general stock, and then the precise amount due to each person, items produced should be considered common property (Kropotkin, 1970: 47, 58–60; n.d.: 27–8, 133, 136–9, 142; Schmidt & Van der Walt, 2009: 89–92; Marshall, 2008: 6–10; Wetherly, 2017: 129–30; Turcato, 2019: 238).

The associational anarchist method of distribution has something in common with both the collectivist and communist perspectives. The satisfaction of basic material *needs* will be met through the approach to social planning explained in section two of Chapter 3. Here prices will be fixed through democratic means by agencies in civil society, the guilds and consumer councils. It is true that the determination of prices is, strictly speaking, a separate matter from whether the hours worked by each individual can be calculated accurately, or for that matter whether pay scales should be installed. But in the fixing of prices, where essential goods will be sold at standard or below-cost prices, it may in certain circumstances be desirable to provide them free of charge. In both cases, this will be irrespective of the personal contribution of any individual, and as such these primary items can be regarded as common property. Yet in terms of satisfying *wants*, as long as (a) labour is offered freely, (b) the productive unit is a participatory democracy and (c) reward for work done cannot lead to hostile class divides, the guild market system is not, in principle, opposed to remuneration by output. Cole's reasoning is pertinent here. He thought that the new moral and psychological conditions, engendered in the general 'atmosphere of a free society', will not only make equality of remuneration possible but will in time destroy the entire principle of reward through actual labour rendered. He did, though, recognise that initially it is probable the guilds would establish different scales of income based upon the skill content in the various categories of labour (Cole, 1920b: 71–3). As we saw in sections two and three of Chapter 3, the guilds in associational anarchism will do exactly this. It may well be that the Kropotkinian maxim of distribution according to need will be more applicable to a fully developed social anarchist society.[6] But in the early stages of post-capitalist society, with its probable residual egoistic self-interest, it is the Bakuninian ideal of remuneration through contribution that would appear to be more expedient for the 'wants' sector. Likewise, just as a carefully monitored profit motive will provide an impetus to innovate in the guild cooperatives, the self-employed sector will also reward personal effort. On the grounds that this will take place within a widely dispersed and largely equal system of ownership, it will form a core element of association anarchism's political economy.

This claim can be further enhanced by reiterating the way in which the guild quasi-egalitarian incomes policy is combined with enriching relations arranged comparably within each cooperative. Kropotkin rejects the distinction drawn between professional and simple work, with the former in receipt of higher income. He believes this would only maintain the inequalities of the current system. "It would mean dividing society into two very distinct classes – the aristocracy of knowledge above the horny-handed lower orders – the one doomed to serve the other" (n.d.: 137). Here inequalities in pay will not be down to production costs but through monopolies in education and industry. "We are anarchists precisely because these privileges revolt us" (n.d.: 139). Sure enough. But differentiated incomes, restricted to the 6:1 ratio, can avoid the self-perpetuation of minority rule if it is set within an egalitarian scheme of ownership rights. Where there is equal access to the means of production, and where democratic control over the productive process is determined jointly through the participation of each member, society will not be divided into opposing classes. It is here that rotating tasks within the cooperative, so that the workload of all associates is a thoughtful configuration of both the more and the less desirable tasks, will bring real benefits. Not least it ensures that the 'lower orders' will not be compelled to serve the 'aristocracy of knowledge' as the assignments of each individual are, within a certain range that may well differ from cooperative to cooperative, mutually comparable. Whilst there will be pay differentials, they are set within an integrated framework where, through job interchangeability, every member has the opportunity to develop all their physical and intellectual capabilities. This is one of the main attractions of balanced job complexes. Seen in this light, a guild apprenticeship does far more than cover the essentials of a trade. It also introduces trainees to the practices of direct democracy, and through its emphasis on mutual benefit, it engenders benevolent sentiments. It is this wider inclusive and altruistic climate that the self-employed sector is integrated into.

It is for these reasons then that time spent in a guild cooperative, through the learning of a trade, will prepare agents for life in the self-employed sector. Neither is it the case that the latter will be fully independent of the former. The guilds will have regulatory and advisory functions, and they are responsible for setting grades of excellence. Individual artisans and small work teams will also rely on the guilds for the supply of raw materials and parts. In all these ways, the self-employed sector will operate in unity with the values and standards of the organisations that, in terms of the guild constitution, are preeminent. In addition, as the function of the cooperative consumer councils is to represent the interests of consumers, irrespective of where any given individual happens to work, they have an important supplementary role. This is especially so with circulating the information that guides consumer choice, which, as it has not been covertly manipulated through intrusive marketing strategies, will benefit the self-employed just as much as the guilds. With these points in mind, let us now see how this sector will self-coordinate.

As it is planned by numerous independent agents, it does not need macro rational planning. Just as Hayek observed, in a genuinely competitive economy every firm must anticipate change and devise plans accordingly. The key difference between his catallaxy and associational anarchism's self-employed sector is that in the latter, where it is not possible for a plutocrat to extract a surplus through exclusive ownership of a productive unit from afar, without having ever set foot in it, the dissemination of numerous pieces of economic knowledge and the reconciliation of the diverse aims of independent agents is not frustrated by the encroachment of powerful economic cartels. Where there is no unrelenting obsession with self-expansion, capital, understood as the self-expanding tendency of value in motion, does not exist. Some firms will naturally earn more than others, and some may even become relatively wealthy, but restricting their size allows for the widest possible dispersion of property. In a classless political economy, where inequalities of outcome are non-accumulative, single firms are systematically prevented from expanding in size to the extent that they can hoard the flow of oligopolistic profit. In these conditions, as the perpetual mutual adjustments of individuals and small firms can operate without having to grapple with the central plans of economic leviathans, the price mechanism can serve the telecommunication purpose asked of it more effectively. So alongside relational contracting, price fluctuations will help mediate the supply of products and services in a way that genuinely reflects autonomous consumption, rather than its induced character. It also seems likely that, due to the many sources that can potentially serve one's needs, there will be more opportunities for capacities to be duplicated, in which case, there will be fewer 'unpleasant facts', as Hayek calls them. For all these reasons then, self-employed markets can more realistically decentralise and form horizontal networks of social relations.

Conclusion

We have seen that a restriction on some specific liberty is exactly that; it does not amount to an attack on liberty *per se*. Despite the curtailment of certain bourgeois freedoms, other liberties cherished by negative libertarians will remain. As individuals are free to seek and change work as they desire, the freedoms of movement and association are as absolute as they are, purportedly, in liberal democracies. With regards to the self-employed sector, I have indicated that the micro-plans of self-reliant individuals and small businesses can mutually adjust through sequences of initiatives far more easily than when they are confronted with ridged class divides. To return to a key theme of the second section of the previous chapter, the guild system does all it can to transcend systemic and unpremeditated coercion. Likewise, the anonymous interdependency of the self-employed sector cannot be converted into the intermediate condition of structural domination. It is in these senses that the interrelations within the self-employed sector will mirror those in the guild system. I conclude then that although the guilds and their cooperatives are the central components of associational anarchism's mode of production, individual and smaller groups of producers will be as unobstructed as they would be in any libertarian society.

Notes

1 To reiterate, the term 'liberal freedom' is used in a very general sense, and to denote freedom *from*.

2 On a closely related point, David Bouchier infers that sacrificing a degree of negative liberty is the price to pay for the positive liberty a democratic community needs. "Unlimited accumulation, unlimited consumption and the unlimited exploitation of others are just three of the things which would have to be curbed" (1996: 115). It will be clear by now the specific ways through which associational anarchism does this.

3 This issue is discussed in the following sub-section.

4 See Wyatt (2011).

5 Cole also recognised the merit of sole traders and small family firms (1920b: 93–4, 167–9).

6 Deric Shannon notes that Bakunin's close friend, James Guillaume, also recognised the merits of anarchist pluralism. Guillaume thought that anarcho-collectivism and anarcho-communism are not in principle distinct, and that the former can be seen as a transitional phase towards full anarchism, where, in line with Cole's thought, remuneration through work performed may well be abolished (2019: 101).

11

The civic functional bodies

As soon as ... material wants are satisfied, other needs, of an artistic character, will thrust themselves forward the more ardently. Aims of life vary with each and every individual; and the more society is civilized, the more will individuality be developed, and the more will desires be varied. (Kropotkin, n.d.: 91)

Providing an account of what the realm of freedom in associational anarchism will entail can only be a speculative task. The two interrelating sections of this chapter are therefore on the brief side. In many cases, there will be little call for formal organisation in this realm, as agents pursue their own goals in their unique ways without the need for specific forms of representation. But where uniform procedures do emerge, they will be accommodated within the civic sphere of a functional mode of organisation. One way of explaining their methods of operation is through an inquiry into whether liberal freedom has any role in Marx's communism. This will include a discussion on the contrast between the values of pluralism and monism. I will argue that this book's redirection of Marx's critique of capital along an associational anarchist path has profound consequences for life in the realm of freedom, which departs radically from how it turns out wherever the realm of necessity is planned and administered through a centralised authority. Certain conjectures are put forward that suggest in their procurement of anarchist values, the realms of necessity and freedom will embody authentic value-pluralisms, although as we shall see, not in equal measure. Of particular pertinence, the realm of freedom will engender a very different set of values to those typically endorsed in bourgeois society. In order to make this argument, it will be worth establishing in very concise terms the organisational forms that will distinguish the civic sphere.

In the realm of freedom, desires are not ranked in any order in the sense that no reference is made to the collective or individual higher-self, which, as will now be clear, is in contrast to the realm of necessity. The responsibility to sustain aim-independent ways of life in the former realm will, at the local level, fall to the cultural and health councils, who, as outlined in section one of Chapter 3, are required to work in cooperation with the corresponding education and health guilds. In Cole's guild socialism, the cultural councils will engage closely with the education guild. They will provide the opportunity for people to have their say on local curriculum, yet also on matters relating to art galleries, museums and other 'kindred spiritual services'. The health councils, who will assume direct relations with the medical guild, have within their sphere parks, open spaces, various public institutions and other amenities of physical life.[1] These two civic councils may establish close relations for addressing jointly any problems that are common to both (Cole, 1920b: 108–10). Drawing from this schema, while the education and health bodies in associational anarchism will continue to provide the services that are essential to the proficient running of both the realms of necessity and freedom, they will assume an additional role. In the process of stabilising a cooperative and complementary relationship with the education and health guilds, the civic councils will also maintain the public arenas through which the physical and spiritual pursuits of local populations, the manifold 'ends in themselves', will take place.

Marx and liberal freedom

Despite their fundamental differences, the question has been raised whether there is any common ground between the Marxian and the classical liberal understandings of freedom. As Chapter 1 explained, the two key forms of the Marxist account of freedom *to do/become* – an increasing command over nature by the rapidly developing forces of production and a collective control over social relations through rational planning – are, for the mature Marx, only necessary conditions for the realisation of authentic freedom, which is an absence of enslaving pressures. The final outcome of communist production will provide people with an amount of time that will not be regulated as all their basic material needs will be satisfied. Here people can pursue their unique individual preferences. Freedom conceived in this sense is distinct from the form of freedom within the realm of necessity; it is indefinite in content, and not subject in the same way to the demands of rational planning (Marx, 1977: 166–7, 180–1, 496–7). As this seems to incorporate a kind of negative freedom, it appears to move closer to what is commonly held to be the liberal view. Walicki therefore asks whether Marx's apparent concern with individual freedom coexists with his condemnation of capitalist class domination. His answer is that although Marx does see individual freedom as an important component of true freedom, it is only to the extent that it coincides with his vision of a historically determined self-actualised human essence. Marx was concerned not so much with individual freedom as with the 'liberation' of the superior capacities inherent, as he thought, in the species nature of man. In his view 'true freedom' was the unhampered development of all the faculties of man as a 'species being'. (Walicki, 1984: 239–40)

Recall Marx was highly critical of bourgeois individual freedom. In capitalist society, humanity's species essence is twisted and distorted through the productive process. Freedom conceived in its negative sense is, he thought, inadequate for people to realise their creative greatness. It is the positive power to collectively self-actualise that can only come with inclusive control over advanced material means that Marx was interested in (Marx, 1977: 52, 475; Walicki, 1984: 232, 238–40, 1983: 50–3; Sowell, 1963: 120).

In response, Walicki suggests Marx failed to recognise that bourgeois values may continue in a communist regime. It is true that Marx did believe the egoism of bourgeois society would die with it (1977: 183). Yet for Walicki, this is no certainty; people may have little interest in being liberated from the features Marx held to be antipathetic to their true nature. "This is why even Marx's vision of the final ideal – of the total liberation of humankind – was only *apparently* compatible with the liberal idea of individual freedom" (1984: 239–40). Others have raised similar concerns. Socialist (including, I would add, social anarchist) freedoms will be distinct from capitalist freedoms, and its main vision of social life will depart sharply from bourgeois ideals. Heilbroner adds it may be wished that the petty and narcissistic elements of bourgeois individuality would be left behind, and the intellectual and aesthetic qualities retained, but this is more hope than expectation (1980: 170–1). So inasmuch as associational anarchism protects explicitly a set of liberal freedoms, will this give rise to greed, vanity and the egoism of possessive individualism? Through a discussion on value-pluralism, the following section will argue there are strong reasons to doubt this.

Value-pluralism

Berlin renounces the single criterion held in monism that he associates with positive liberty. Monism contains a singular formula that promises to harmonise the various ends people have. Its main claim is that society can be forged into a fixed pattern. In rejecting this position, he endorses the pluralism liberals generally attribute to negative liberty:

> Pluralism, with the measure of 'negative' liberty that it entails, seems to me a truer and more humane ideal than the goals of those who seek in the great, disciplined, authoritarian structures the ideal of 'positive' self-mastery by classes, or peoples, or the whole of mankind. (1991: 171)

It is the monist doctrine that for Berlin has led to totalitarianism. In contrast, pluralism recognises that people's goals are not only many but often in rivalry. To suppose there is an ultimate fully reconciling synthesis is "to throw a metaphysical blanket over either self-deceit or deliberate hypocrisy" (1991: 170–2).[2] As I will now show, the positive dimension of freedom as Marxian-autonomy does not, in terms of its pluralist ethic, pull in opposite directions to its negative element.

With regards to its organisational contours, it will now be clear why the associational mode of anarchism is a socio-economic formation that is qualitatively distinct from capitalist and command socialist societies, and as such it offers an alternative account of social life. As the previous three chapters have indicated, liberal freedoms in the realm of necessity have been recast in order to assure compatibility with cooperative modes of production and consumption, which are the democratic means that will satisfy people's basic material needs. The kind of liberties that will remain are those that are indispensable to the ideals of self-actualising labour and ethical consumption, which are realised through a decentralised self-governance distinguished by egalitarianism, horizontalism and functionally demarcated authorities. In other words, a revised liberal freedom forms an integral element of a conception of liberty that in the main has prioritised a left-libertarian reading of self-determination and self-realisation. Understood as such, the realm of necessity constitutes numerous and divergent ends within the two main interrelating heterogeneous categories of the higher-self. I have argued that these social relations are not only in line with certain liberal freedoms but also offer them optimum protection. Just as importantly, this realm also serves as a means to another end, an end of diversity and explorations in a multitude of ways of life. Freedom is now indefinite in content, and distinct from the kind of self-regulation carried out in the realm of necessity. Clearly, the realms of necessity and freedom must be congruous, and there are evident comparisons in their organisational structures. The education and health guilds and the cultural and health councils are no less demarcated in line with the functional principle than the economic guilds and councils. They obviously have distinct subject matters, but they are constituted through internal direct democracies in much the same way. In this sense, they all embody participatory and cooperative values.

Two key points can be established here. Firstly, in the realm of freedom, there will be a range of anarchist-sensitive pursuits open to inquisitive agents. Although freedom *from* in the realm of necessity will centre on the values clarified directly above, in the realm of freedom its aim-independence has a wider field of reference. It is the collective dual higher-self that is organised in the realm of necessity, in the realm of freedom no appeal is made to it. The latter realm is comprised of a maximum degree of non-interference and is in principle non-discriminatory. This is to say that real freedom is premised upon the unhampered development of citizens' binary faculties nurtured in the realm of necessity. This realm will do everything it can to develop the selfhood of agents, where their deeper yearnings to self-actualise as sentient and innovative beings are ranked above all else. The second point is that within the value-pluralism of the realm of freedom, there are life choices that in all probability will be amongst the most popular. At the risk of over-speculation, these are the values that, as a direct corollary from the creative and aesthetic values in the realm of necessity, correlate with the qualities of unity, belonging, self-discovery and the appreciation of beauty. If so, the intrinsic and instrumental goals in the realm of necessity and the predominantly intrinsic pursuits in the realm of freedom will be largely congruous. It is in this sense that associational anarchism does not seek to merely retain the least unattractive of bourgeois aspirations, with its almost exclusive emphasis on undiluted self-interest, and relocate them in a new economic infrastructure. In the absence of empirical experience, little more can be inferred with any degree of certainty. But it is reasonable to conclude that where work is expansive and self-confirming, and where direct democratic structures engender new forms of deliberation, recreation takes on a whole new meaning. Life in the realm of freedom then will be far more than simply recovering from exhausting toil.

I have contended that Marx was right to focus on the realisation of the superior capacities inherent within each person, those of a creative and social nature. To this, I would only add that if Walicki is correct that Marx had in mind a kind of individual liberty that is consistent only with a self-actualised human essence, then this need not impede upon liberal freedom in the realm of freedom. This is because in associational anarchism, 'liberation by reason' does not equate with totalitarianism. Once direct forms of economic democracy and de-alienated labour are institutionalised, given the range of interests open to innovative cooperators, it is probable that experiments in productive projects will, precisely because they are deliberative and creative, branch out into numerous fields, all with potentially unlimited permutations in product design. As the democratic and creative categories cannot be compressed into a singular rigid model, they are not reducible to any kind of homogeneous monism. The realm of freedom takes this a stage further; here value pluralism does not correspond directly to any particular category, including the higher-self, and as such the scope of the 'ends in themselves' has a wider reach. With regards to the unhindered development of diverse potentialities in each realm then, there is a strong affinity between both freedom *from* and freedom *to do/become* with value pluralism; the only difference is in the extent of their range. This is not to throw a "metaphysical blanket" over "self-deceit or deliberate hypocrisy".

Conclusion

The organisational forms of associational anarchism's modes of production and consumption indicate that the realm of necessity is a *gemeinschaft* community. In their working lives, citizens will realise freedom as self-direction and self-realisation through the arrangements that will by now be familiar, and this will also serve to protect a measure of negative freedom. Following this, drawing from the new social relations of production and any subsequent increase in free time beyond the workplace, the freedom of the individual will be preeminent in the realm of freedom. I have cautiously surmised that certain values in this realm will be more compatible with a functionally demarcated direct democracy. My reasoning is that as social anarchists we cannot suppress the worst of bourgeois freedoms through centralised imposition, but we can engender the self-governing social conditions through which they are least likely to emerge. Significantly, lifestyle diversity is not, as previous chapters have argued, threatened in the sense that there is no dominant economic or political elite with the power to impose its will upon subordinate classes; neither are there ideological blind spots or mystification through the fetishisation of economic categories. Here the range of values is not restricted to the imperatives of profit maximisation and commodified forms of consumption. By virtue of an egalitarian control of productive resources, there can be no structural domination along class lines. This, the abolishment of economic divides without invoking a political leviathan, upon which proceeds a more extensive aim-independence in the realm of freedom, is one of the main attractions of a left-libertarian system of cooperative labour.

Notes

1 One cannot help but think the idea of running a health service through open dialogue between civic guilds and councils offers a vast improvement on the current class-divided system, where, as the Marxist perspective adopted in this book contends, the commercial interests of the pharmaceutical giants bear heavily upon, if not largely determine, governmental welfare policies.
2 For a neat account on why Berlin is wrong on both accounts, see John Clark (2013: 87–90).

Conclusion: associational anarchism and human emancipation as developed selfhood

> Libertarian throughout modern European history meant socialist anarchist. It meant ... an antistate branch of socialism, which meant a highly organised society, nothing to do with chaos, but based on democracy all the way through. That means democratic control of communities, of workplaces, of federal structures, built on systems of voluntary association, spreading internationally. That's traditional anarchism. (Chomsky, 2014: 107)

Coming from distinct perspectives, political theorists have frequently defended either an authoritarian or a liberal minimal state, or they have endorsed some kind of middle path between the two. I have approached the question from a different angle. In recognising that freedom should not be kept apart from the conditions of its profitable exercise, a conception that blends congenially positive and negative ideals must, in my opinion, propose a mode of organisation that moves beyond the imposition of both statist and private corporatist control of economic life. This book accordingly contends that post-capitalist society needs to draw equally from the libertarian potential of Cole's guild socialism, the sub-schools of social anarchism and contemporary anarcho-republicanism, which together serve to complement Marx's critique of classical political economy. The outcome is a conceptual constellation that pictures a new mode of egalitarian property rights that, fundamentally, is very much 'based on democracy all the way through'. Demarcated labour processes, when horizontally aligned with other equally differentiated functions, are the most enriching form of production and the optimal method of social provision.

Freedom as Marxian-autonomy in context

It has been the aim of this book to theorise a reconfigured anarcho-constitutionalism that, by placing certain attributes from both the negative and positive paradigms within a conceptual framework that does not cast them

as eternal antagonisms, dichotomises sharply from both the negative freedom of right-libertarianism and the positive freedom of welfare statism. As
will now be clear, this method draws together certain principles that are
also found in three particular political traditions. Generally speaking, in
MacCallum's triadic formula the republican position is that citizens ('X')
are free from domination ('Y') to participate in the legislation of their own
laws, either directly or through elected representatives ('Z'); the liberal position is that independent individuals ('X') are free from the arbitrary interference of others ('Y') to pursue given wants, which are always revisable ('Z');
and the idealist position is that the autonomous and rational higher-self
('X') is free from ignorance and the uncontrolled trivial desires of the lower-
self ('Y') to self-actualise ('Z'). I have indicated throughout the previous
chapters the ways in which associational anarchist ideals have something in
common with all three positions; yet, in coherence with twentieth-century
anarchism, they are arranged in new forms.

Herein lays my rebuttal of pure negative liberty. Berlin claims the questions 'Who governs me?' and 'How far does government interfere with
me?' are separate matters. It is this distinction that, he argues, ultimately
accounts for the gulf between the negative and the positive conceptions of
liberty (1991: 129–31). Liberalism as a doctrine theorises appropriate *limits*
to government action, whereas democracy as a doctrine articulates the particular *form* a government should assume. In the latter, ultimate power rests
with the popular will; in the former, legitimacy is met when a private sphere
is immune from state intervention, irrespective of its source. I would say an
advanced conception of freedom must indicate where it stands on both contentions. In doing precisely this, associational anarchism rephrases the key
terms. Its democracy is plural in the sense that decentralised self-governance
is modelled upon interdependent differentiated agencies. The neo-liberal
retreat of economics from politics has been replaced with a direct democracy in a functional mode of organisation, which deliberately sets out to
raise the social consciousness of citizens. By eliminating the alienation and
coercion of capitalist society through a pervading new outlook, the guild
system echoes Marx's understanding of self and society, where self-realisation is achieved by confirming one's unique and independent standing as a
fully evolved social being. And yet, whilst individuals are able to develop
pre-eminently by living as self-conscious and autonomous members of re-
politicalised communities, they will not be subordinated to the tyranny of
the collective. This is because the realm of necessity, where a certain amal
gamation of freedom as self-determination and self-realisation is pursued
through structures that recast yet ultimately protect a set of freedoms *from*,
will hence defend strenuously the inviolability of a sphere of life within
which the individual is sovereign.

More so, far from violating subjective liberties, as there is a strong instrumental connection between participatory structures and the protection of individual freedom, these are the most favourable means through which to secure a general condition of unpreventedness. As I argued in Chapter 8, it is legitimate to sacrifice *singular* cases of freedom *from* in order to secure the kind of freedom *to do/become* that is itself a prerequisite for the preservation of the *wider* category of freedom *from*; this is one of the reasons why the guild cooperative 500 principle is fully consistent with real freedom. Chapters 9 and 10 added to this the contention that, in certain cases, a revision of *economic* liberty can be justified if in doing so it assures the equal value of *political* liberty. So the demand for self-government and the call for a domain of life independent from interference are not separate pleas; they are distinct yet interrelating components of the same conception of freedom. The lasting value of Berlin's essay is its caution that positive liberty is fraught with totalitarian dangers. It is true that the emancipation of economically oppressed classes can coexist with compulsion in social life. There are historical examples where authoritarian creeds have ruled in dictatorial ways, thus crushing negative liberty under the guise of political liberty. But his mistake was to regard them as particular cases of the inevitable. As this book has argued, a contemporary left-libertarian mixed-economy can determine the product range efficiently through new forms of deliberation, whilst at the same time upholding an overall condition of non-interference to a far greater extent than could reasonably be expected of either statist or neoliberal societies. It is within this framework, which deliberately targets the self-development of all citizens, that a contribution to the twentieth-century anarchist project of advanced selfhood is made.

Social anarchism remodelled

A democratic regulation of the most basic necessities of life must be the key concern of a stable self-governing community. Associational anarchism does this by proposing a libertarian path beyond the state civil-society paradigm. The commune system is constituted through elected members from all the guilds and consumer/civil councils. Its federal structure is analogous to the latter two organisations, i.e. it has a staggered rotation of part-time personnel who will continue to work or live within the functional bodies from which they came. The local communes are not legislating bodies, and they determine neither economic regulation nor public services, at least not directly. As they are constitutionally restricted from intervening arbitrarily in the decision-making autonomy of the guilds and consumer councils, the substance and scope of what is left of their sovereignty have been thoroughly redefined. To reiterate, their only purpose is to adjudge in cases of impasse between the functional agencies brought before them. They are therefore the most ultra-minimal of body-politics conceivable. This is in stark contrast to bourgeois society, where power stems from vast concentrations of capital and wealth, the legal protection of which is the *raison d'etre* of the modern state. My claim then is that a formidable hierarchic structure with a privileged minority at the helm, the kind that is incompatible with a genuine self-organised society, is not a precondition for social stability. In place of the centralised state, there is recourse to a reinvigorated political pluralism to meet the demands of coordination, especially in terms of reconciling individual freedom with communal solidarity. Here there are uniform systems of laws, each one applying to the jurisdiction of an individual guild, but as they are self-legislated and freely accepted by all voluntary members, legal mandates are under popular control.

It will by now be apparent that political intermediation proceeds via a complex web of interlinking voluntary associations, which operate within a decentralised system of revitalised communities. It will be equally apparent that along with the organisational configuration of guild socialism and social anarchism, the works of Marx and Hayek have figured extensively. I have suggested their competing critiques of the general perspective the other one defends sets up a compelling dualism. The argument of this book recognises the merit of Marx's critique of the capitalist mode of production as well as Hayek's critique of authoritarian socialism, but it does not follow Marx into state communism, for all the reasons Hayek (following tacitly in the footsteps of the classical anarchist thinkers) goes into, and it does not follow Hayek into a largely unfettered market economy, for all the reasons Marx (followed explicitly by the classical anarchist thinkers) goes into. If Marx was naïve on 'the withering away of the state', then so too is Hayek on the transient lifespan of private monopolies; with historical hindsight, both have proved to be as equally durable as the other. But taking them both as the most sophisticated representative theoreticians of their respective doctrines, their combined polemics point to a libertarian path beyond the structural constraints of centrally administered economies. The outcome is a new mode of social anarchism that has the following distinctions: (1) egalitarian control over productive resources through plural networks of economic relations; (2) the social unit is the functional group, rather than sovereign states or atomised individuals; (3) alienated labour is to the greatest possible extent transcended and replaced by self-fulfilled, autonomous and civic-minded cooperators; (4) direct and representative democratic forms will consist of consensus decision-making and general will voting; (5) local communities are not under the control of unaccountable central bodies; and (6) the sovereignty of the communes has been hollowed out to the extent that they are the least imposing of political bodies imaginable. As there is no body-politic analogous to the coercive institutions of the socialist state, and no economic bodies analogous to the coercive institutions of the private corporation, there is neither a political nor an economic leviathan. It is upon these twin premises that associational anarchism develops the organisational forms that fill out in finer detail the categories that class-struggle anarchism has always rightly endorsed.

Finally

Recall that for Marx, full emancipation will only be complete when there is no divide between people's standing as citizens and their lives as economic agents. In its proposition that citizens need to have their interests formally represented in terms of production, consumption, education, health and culture, associational anarchism embodies Marx's belief that a truly liberated society develops individuals in a multitude of ways. In doing so it invokes a particular notion of autonomy. Free individuals will operate within and between their functional associations, all of which are founded upon a general context of cooperation and interdependency. Autonomy requires freedom from both direct and indirect constraints and from obstructions that are internal to individuals, such as strong neurotic impulses or illicit cravings that may have a deeper momentary intensity. This entails certain enabling conditions such as the opportunities to refine intellectual and critical capacities, so that beliefs and principles can be subject to reasoned deliberation. Blockages can also be through servitude to conventional norms and values, which lead agents to misidentify their more meaningful purposes. Indeed, if people's interests are determined by social forces they have little control over, their preferences cannot be said to be independently chosen (Ramsay, 1997: 53–5, 59–60). On these grounds, the turn to collective participation in localised systems of workers cooperatives and consumer councils, where agents can be 'held' in their higher-selves, seems fully warranted. The freedom of citizens in these two essential activities initiates, in the language of the young Marx, the move from political to human emancipation.

As de-alienation is at the pinnacle of this transition, it seems only right the closing word should go to it. The subjectivity of the direct producers in capitalist society is an ensemble of uncontrolled and alienated social relations. The subjectivity of the direct producers in associational anarchist society, where labour processes are under the control of re-empowered cooperators, will be an ensemble of mutually integrative and self-actualising social relations. As I have said before, in associational anarchism "the essence of the products of creative labour is immediately apparent because they will be comprehended in terms of the actual relations that produced them.

The outward appearance directly coincides with the essence of things. In this way social attributes are not mistakenly conferred to the commodity" (Wyatt, 2011: 214). And if products are not manifested with autonomy and independent powers, so there is neither a personification of the inanimate nor a thingification of the subject; they will not exist as alienated entities, and neither will the workers who produced them. It has then been the ultimate objective of this book to conceptualise a left-libertarian higher-self, where, in terms of its organisational contours, fulfilment through aesthetic work is made available to all citizens. Labour is analytically unique, it is the one category that is ubiquitous in all societies. For this reason alone, there is every incentive to engender to the greatest possible extent dignified vocations that are gratifying in their performance.

Bibliography

Adams, M.S. (2013) 'The Possibilities of Anarchist History: Rethinking the Canon and Writing History' *in* Kinna, R. & Evren, S. (Eds) *Blasting the Canon: Anarchist Developments in Cultural Studies*, New York: Punctum.

Albert, M. & Hahnel, R. (1991) *Looking Forward: Participatory Economics for the Twenty-First Century*, Boston, MA: South End Press.

Allen, K. (2011) *Marx and the Alternative to Capitalism*, London: Pluto.

Arthur, C.J. (1970) *The German Ideology*, London: Lawrence & Wishart.

Avrich, P. (1973) 'Preface' *in* Dolgoff, S. (Ed.) *Bakunin on Anarchy: Selected Works by the Activist-Founder of World Anarchism*, London: George Allen & Unwin.

Bakunin, M. (1973) *in* Dolgoff, S. (Ed.) *Bakunin on Anarchy: Selected Works by the Activist-Founder of World Anarchism*, London: George Allen & Unwin.

Baldwin, R.N. (1970) *Kropotkin's Revolutionary Pamphlets: A Collection of Writings by Peter Kropotkin*, New York: Dover.

Barry, N.P. (1979) *Hayek's Social and Economic Philosophy*, London: Macmillan.

Barry, N.P. (1984) 'Hayek on Liberty' *in* Pelezynski, Z. & Gray, J. (Eds) *Conceptions of Liberty in Political Philosophy*, London: Athlone.

Bellamy, R. & Mason, A. (2003) *Political Concepts*, Manchester: Manchester University Press.

Benello, G. (1996) 'The Challenge of Mondragon' *in* Ehrlich, H.J. (Ed.) *Reinventing Anarchy, Again*, Edinburgh: AK Press.

Berlin, I. (1991) 'Two Concepts of Liberty' *in* Miller, D. (Ed.) *Liberty*, Oxford: Oxford University Press.

Black, A. (1984) *Guilds and Civil Society in European Political Thought from the Twelfth Century to the Present*, London: Methuen & Co.

Black, B. (1996) 'The Abolition of Work' *in* Ehrlich, H.J. (Ed.) *Reinventing Anarchy, Again*, Edinburgh: AK Press.

Bookchin, M. (1996) 'Anarchism: Past and Present' *in* Ehrlich, H.J. (Ed.) *Reinventing Anarchy, Again*, Edinburgh: AK Press.

Bouchier, D. (1996) 'Hard Questions for Social Anarchists' *in* Ehrlich, H.J. (Ed.) *Reinventing Anarchy, Again*, Edinburgh: AK Press.

Bradley, K. & Gelb, A. (1983) *Cooperation at Work: The Mondragon Experience*, London: Heinemann.

Braverman, H. (1974) *Labour and Monopoly Capital: The Degradation of Work in the Twentieth Century*, London: Monthly Review.

Butler, E. (1983) *Hayek*, Hounslow: Maurice Temple Smith.

Callinicos, A. (2003) *An Anti-Capitalist Manifesto*, Cambridge: Polity.

Callinicos, A. (2007) *Social Theory: A Historical Introduction*, Second Edition, Cambridge: Polity.

Campbell, M.M. (2013) 'Voltairine de Cleyre and the Anarchist Canon' *in* Kinna, R. & Evren, S. (Eds) *Blasting the Canon: Anarchist Developments in Cultural Studies*, New York: Punctum.

Carter, A. (1971) *The Political Theory of Anarchism*, London: Routledge.

Carter, I. (2003) 'Liberty' *in* Bellamy, R. & Mason, A. (Eds) *Political Concepts*, Manchester: Manchester University Press.

Chartier, G. (2013) *Anarchy and Legal Order: Law and Politics for a Stateless Society*, Cambridge: Cambridge University Press.

Chitty, A. (2011) 'Freedom and Community in Marx', Paper given at the Re-Thinking Marx Conference. Berlin, 20–22 May.

Chomsky, N. (1970) 'Introduction' *in* Guerin, D. (Ed.) *Anarchism: From Theory to Practice*, New York: Monthly Review.

Chomsky, N. (2005) *in* Pateman, B. (Ed.) *Chomsky on Anarchism*, Edinburgh: AK Press.

Chomsky, N. (2011) 'Noam Chomsky: Anarchism, Council Communism, and Life after Capitalism' *in* Lilley, S. (Ed.) *Capital and Its Discontents: Conversations with Radical Thinkers in a Time of Tumult*, Oakland, CA: PM Press.

Chomsky, N. (2013) *On Anarchism*, London: Penguin.

Christman, J. (1991) 'Liberalism and Individual Positive freedom', *Ethics*, Vol. 101, No. 2, January.

Christman, J. (2014) *The Inner Citadel: Essays on Individual Autonomy*, Brattleboro, VT: Echo Point.

Cladis, M.S. (2007) *Public Vision, Private Lives: Rousseau, Religion, and 21st Century Democracy*, New York: Columbia University Press.

Clark, J.P. (1975) 'On Anarchism in an Unreal World: Krammick's View of Godwin and the Anarchists', *The American Political Science Review*, Vol. 69, No. 1, March.

Clark, J.P. (1978) 'What is Anarchism?' *in* Pennock, R. & Chapman, J.W. (Eds) *Anarchism: Nomos XIX*, New York: New York University Press.

Clark, J.P. (2013) *The Impossible Community: Realizing Communitarian Anarchism*, New York: Bloomsbury.

Clayre, A. (1980) 'Some Aspects of the Mondragon Co-Operative Federation' *in* Clayre, A. (Ed.) *The Political Economy of Co-Operation and Participation*, Oxford: Oxford University Press.

Cole, G.D.H. (1914) 'Conflicting Social Obligations', *Proceedings of the Aristotelian Society*, XV.

Cole, G.D.H. (1919) *The Guild Idea*, Cole Collection. Nuffield College. Box A1/48/1–5.

Cole, G.D.H. (1920a) *The Social Theory*, London: Methuen & Co.

Cole, G.D.H. (1920b) *Guild Socialism Restated*, London: Leonard Parsons.

Cole, G.D.H. (1920c) May 6th. Kingsway Hall. Lecture. Cole Collection. Nuffield College. Box A1/49/1-8.

Cole, G.D.H. (1921a) January 12th. Mortimer Hall, Lecture. Cole Collection. Nuffield College. Box A1/50/1–6.

Cole, G.D.H. (1921b) Unnamed paper, Cole Collection. Nuffield College. Box A1/50/1–6.

Cole, G.D.H. (1958) *A History of Socialist Thought: Volume IV, Part 1*, London: Macmillan.

Cole, G.D.H. (1972) [1917] *Self-Government in Industry*, London: Hutchinson Educational.

Colletti, L. (1975) *Karl Marx: Early Writings*, London: Penguin.

Corina, J.G. (1972) 'Preface' *in* Cole, G.D.H. [1917] *Self-Government in Industry*, London: Hutchinson Educational.

Cowling, K. (1982) *Monopoly Capitalism*, London: Macmillan.

Davis, L. (2014) 'Anarchism and the Future of Revolution' *in* Kinna, R. (Ed.) *The Bloomsbury Companion to Anarchism*, London: Bloomsbury.

Davis, L. (2019) 'Individual and Community' *in* Levy, C. & Adams, M.S. (Eds) *The Palgrave Handbook of Anarchism*, Basingstoke: Palgrave Macmillan.

DeLeon, D. (1996) 'For Democracy Where We Work: A Rationale for Social Self-Management' *in* Ehrlich, H.J. (Ed.) *Reinventing Anarchy, Again*, Edinburgh: AK Press.

Dolgoff, S. (1973) *Bakunin on Anarchy: Selected Works by the Activist-Founder of World Anarchism*, London: George Allen & Unwin.

Eagleton, T. (2011) *Why Marx Was Right*, New Haven, CT: Yale University Press.

Ehrlich, H.J. (1996) *Reinventing Anarchy, Again*, Edinburgh: AK Press.

Ehrlich, H.J. (1996) 'Anarchism and Formal Organisations' *in* Ehrlich, H.J. (Ed.) *Reinventing Anarchy, Again*, Edinburgh: AK Press.

Elliott, W.Y. (1925) 'Sovereign State or Sovereign Group?', *The American Political Science Review*, Vol. xix, No. 3.

Elliott, W.Y. (1968) *The Pragmatic Revolt in Politics*, New York: Howard Fertig.

Elliss, E.D. (1923) 'Guild Socialism and Pluralism', *The American Political Science Review*, Vol. xvii.

Feiten, E. (2013) 'Would the Real Max Stirner Please Stand Up' *in* Kinna, R. & Evren, S. (Eds) *Blasting the Canon: Anarchist Developments in Cultural Studies*, New York: Punctum.

Fetscher, I. (1973) 'Karl Marx on Human Nature', *Social Research*, Vol. 40, No. 3.

Firth, R. (2019) 'Utopianism and Intentional Communities' *in* Levy, C. & Adams, M.S. (Eds) *The Palgrave Handbook of Anarchism*, Basingstoke: Palgrave Macmillan.

Fleetwood, S. (1995) *Hayek's Political Economy: The Socio-Economics of Order*, London: Routledge.

Franks, B. (2012) 'Between Anarchism and Marxism: The Beginnings and Ends of the Schism ...', *Journal of Political Ideologies*, Vol. 17, No. 2.

Franks, B. (2014) 'Anarchism and Analytic Philosophy' *in* Kinna, R. (Ed.) *The Bloomsbury Companion to Anarchism*, London: Bloomsbury.

Franks, B. (2019) 'Anarchism and Ethics' *in* Levy, C. & Adams, M.S. (Eds) *The Palgrave Handbook of Anarchism*, Basingstoke: Palgrave Macmillan.

Freeden, M. (1996) *Ideologies and Political Theory: A Conceptual Approach*, Oxford: Clarendon.

Freeden, M. (2003) *Ideology: A Very Short Introduction*, Oxford: Oxford University Press.

Gardiner, P. (1984) 'Rousseau on Liberty' *in* Pelezynski, Z. & Gray, J. (Eds) *Conceptions of Liberty in Political Philosophy*, London: Athlone.

Giddens, A. (1971) *Capitalism and Modern Social Theory: An Analysis of the Writings of Marx, Durkheim and Max Weber*, Cambridge: Cambridge University Press.

Glass, S.T. (1966) *The Responsible Society: The Ideas of the English Guild Socialist*, London: Longmans.

Gorz, A. (1988) *Critique of Economic Reason*, London: Verso.

Gorz, A. (1999) *Reclaiming Work: Beyond the Wage-Based Society*, Cambridge: Polity.

Graeber, D. (1993) *Fragments of an Anarchist Anthropology*, Chicago, IL: Prickly Paradigm.

Graham, R. (1996) 'The Anarchist Contract' *in* Ehrlich, H.J. (Ed.) *Reinventing Anarchy, Again*, Edinburgh: AK Press.

Graham, R. (2013) 'Black Flame: A Commentary' *in* Kinna, R. & Evren, S. (Eds) *Blasting the Canon: Anarchist Developments in Cultural Studies*, New York: Punctum.

Graham, R. (2017) 'Anarchy and Democracy', *Syndicalist Review*, Vol. 69, winter.

Graham, R. (2018) '(Mis)Conceptions of Anarchism', *Anarchist Studies*, Vol. 26, No. 2.

Gray, A. (1946) *The Socialist Tradition*, London: Longmans.

Gray, J. (1984a) 'J.S. Mill on Freedom' *in* Pelezynski, Z. & Gray, J. (Eds) *Conceptions of Liberty in Political Philosophy*, London: Athlone.

Gray, J. (1984b) 'On Negative and Positive Liberty' *in* Pelezynski, Z. & Gray, J. (Eds) *Conceptions of Liberty in Political Philosophy*, London: Athlone.

Greenberg, E.S. (1984) 'Producer Cooperatives and Democratic Theory: The Case of the Plywood Firms' *in* Jackall, R. & Levin, H.M. (Eds) *Worker Cooperatives in America*, London: University of California Press.

Greenberg, E.S. (1986) *Workplace Democracy: The Political Effects of Participation*, New York: Cornell University Press.

Greenleaf, W.H. (1983) *The British Political Tradition*, Vol. 2, London: Methuen.

Greenwood, D.J. & Santos, J.L.G. (1992) *Industrial Democracy as Process: Participatory Action Research in the Fagor Cooperative Group of Mondragon*, Stockholm: Arbetslivscentrum.

Grubacic, A. (2011) 'Andrej Grubacic: Libertarian Socialism for the Twenty-First Century' *in* Lilley, S. (Ed.) *Capital and Its Discontents: Conversations with Radical Thinkers in a Time of Tumult*, Oakland, CA: PM Press.

Gourevitch, A. (2011) 'Labour and Republican Liberty', *Constellations*, Vol. 18, No. 3.

Gourevitch, A. (2013) 'Labour Republicanism and the Transformation of Work', *Political Theory*, Vol. 41, No. 4.

Guerin, D. (1970) *Anarchism: From Theory to Practice*, New York: Monthly Review.

Guillaume, J. (1973a) 'Michael Bakunin: A Biographical Sketch' *in* Dolgoff, S. (Ed.) *Bakunin on Anarchy: Selected Works by the Activist-Founder of World Anarchism*, London: George Allen & Unwin.

Guillaume, J. (1973b) 'On Building the New Social Order' *in* Dolgoff, S. (Ed.) *Bakunin on Anarchy: Selected Works by the Activist-Founder of World Anarchism*, London: George Allen & Unwin.

Gunn, C. (1984) 'Hoedads Co-Op: Democracy and Cooperation at Work' in Jackall, R. & Levin, H.M. (Eds) *Worker Cooperatives in America*, London: University of California Press.

Hampsher-Monk, I. (1992) *A History of Modern Political Thought: Major Political Thinkers from Hobbes to Marx*, Oxford: Blackwell.

Harrison, R. (2013) *People over Capital: The Co-Operative Alternative to Capitalism*, Oxford: New Internationalist.

Harvey, D. (2005) *A Brief History of Neo-Liberalism*, Oxford: Oxford University Press.

Harvey, D. (2010) *The Enigma of Capital: And the Crises of Capitalism*, London: Profile.

Hayek, F.A. (1949) *Individualism and Economic Order*, London: Routledge & Kegan Paul.

Hayek, F.A. (1960) *The Constitution of Liberty*, London: Routledge & Kegan Paul.

Hayek, F.A. (1976) *Law, Legislation and Liberty: The Mirage of Social Justice*, Vol. 2, London: Routledge and Kegan Paul.

Hayek, F.A. (1986) [1944] *The Road to Serfdom*, London: Routledge & Kegan Paul.

Hayek, F.A. (1991) 'Freedom and Coercion' *in* Miller, D. (Ed.) *Liberty*, Oxford: Oxford University Press.

Heilbroner, R.L. (1980) *Marxism: For and Against*, London: Norton.

Heywood, A. (2012) *Political Ideologies: An Introduction*, 5th Edition, Hampshire: Palgrave.

Hirst, P. (1990) *Representative Democracy and Its Limits*, Cambridge: Polity.

Hirst, P. (1994) *Associational Democracy*, Cambridge: Polity.

Honeywell, C. (2011) *A British Anarchist Tradition: Herbert Read, Alex Comfort and Colin Ward*, London: Bloomsbury.

Honeywell, C. (2014) 'Bridging the Gaps: Twentieth-Century Anglo-American Anarchist Thought' *in* Kinna, R. (Ed.) *The Bloomsbury Companion to Anarchism*, London: Bloomsbury.

Horvat, B. (1982) *The Political Economy of Socialism: A Marxist Social Theory*, Oxford: Martin Rabertion.

Howard, J., Ehrlich, H.J., Ehrlich, C., DeLeon, D. & Morris, G. (1996) 'Questions and Answers about Anarchism' *in* Ehrlich, H.J. (Ed.) *Reinventing Anarchy, Again*, Edinburgh: AK Press.

Howard, M.W. (2000) *Self-Management and the Crisis of Socialism: The Rose in the Fist of the Present*, Lanham, MD: Rowman & Littlefield.

Hsiao, K.C. (1927) *Political Pluralism*, Torquay: Devonshire Press.

Jackall, R. & Levin, H.M. (1984) *Worker Cooperatives in America*, London: University of California Press.

Jamil Jonna, R. (2015) 'Monopoly Capital and Labour: The Work of Braverman, Baran, and Sweezy as a Dialectical Whole', *Labour Studies Journal*, Vol. 40, No. 3.

Jun, N. (2013) 'Rethinking the Anarchist Canon: History, Philosophy, and Interpretation' *in* Kinna, R. & Evren, S. (Eds) *Blasting the Canon: Anarchist Developments in Cultural Studies*, New York: Punctum.

Jun, N. (2019) 'The State' *in* Levy, C. & Adams, M.S. (Eds) *The Palgrave Handbook of Anarchism*, Basingstoke: Palgrave Macmillan.

Karatani, K. (2005) *Transcritique: On Kant and Marx*, London: MIT.

Kasmir, S. (1996) *The Myth of Mondragon: Cooperatives, Politics, and Working-Class Life in a Basque Town*, Albany, NY: SUNY Press.

Kinna, R. (2005) *Anarchism: A Beginner's Guide*, Oxford: Oneworld.

Kinna, R. (2014a) *The Bloomsbury Companion to Anarchism*, London: Bloomsbury.

Kinna, R. (2014b) 'Where to Now?/Loose Ends' *in* Kinna, R. (Ed.) *The Bloomsbury Companion to Anarchism*, London: Bloomsbury.

Kinna, R. & Evren, S. (2013) *Blasting the Canon: Anarchist Developments in Cultural Studies*, New York: Punctum.

Kinna, R. & Prichard, A. (2012) 'Introduction' *in* Prichard, A. Kinna, R. Pinta, S. & Berry, D. (Eds) *Libertarian Socialism: Politics in Black and Red*, Basingstoke: Palgrave.

Kinna, R. & Prichard, A. (2019) 'Anarchism and Non-Domination', *Journal of Political Ideologies*, Vol. 24, No. 3.

Knight, R. (2013) 'Mikhail Bakunin's Post-Ideological Impulse: The Continuity between Classical and New Anarchism' *in* Kinna, R. & Evren, S. (Eds) *Blasting the Canon: Anarchist Developments in Cultural Studies*, New York: Punctum.

Kramer, M.H. (2003) *The Quality of Freedom*, Oxford: Oxford University Press.

Kropotkin, P. (1970) *in* Baldwin, R.N. (Ed.) *Kropotkin's Revolutionary Pamphlets: A Collection of Writings by Peter Kropotkin*, New York: Dover.

Kropotkin, P. (2009) 'Communism and Anarchy', flag.blackeded.net. Retrieved on 25 February 2009.

Kropotkin, P. (2014) *Mutual Aid: A Factor in Evolution*, CreateSpace Independent Publishing.

Kropotkin, P. (2018) *Fields, Factories and Workshops*, jonathandavidjacksonwrites .com. Retrieved on 15 November 2021.

Kropotkin, P. (n.d.) *The Conquest of Bread*, jonathandavidjacksonwrites.com. Retrieved on 15 November 2021.

Kukathas, C. (1989) *Hayek and Modern Liberalism*, Oxford: Clarendon.

Kukathas, C. & Pettit, P. (1990) *Rawls: A Theory of Justice and Its Critics*, Cambridge: Polity Press.

Leftwich, A. (2004) *What Is Politics?*, Cambridge: Polity.

Levine, A. (2002) *Engaging Political Philosophy: From Hobbes to Rawls*, Oxford: Blackwell.

Levy, C. & Adams, M.S. (2019) *The Palgrave Handbook of Anarchism*, Basingstoke: Palgrave Macmillan.

Levy, C. & Adams, M.S. (2019) 'Introduction' *in* Levy, C. & Adams, M.S. (Eds) *The Palgrave Handbook of Anarchism*, Basingstoke: Palgrave Macmillan.

Lilley, S. (2011) *Capital and Its Discontents: Conversations with Radical Thinkers in a Time of Tumult*, Oakland, CA: PM Press.

Lukes, S. (1967) 'Alienation and Anomie' in Laslett, P. & Runciman, W.G. (Eds) *Philosophy, Politics and Society*, Third Series, Oxford: Blackwell.

McCain, R. (2001) http://william-king.www.drexel.edu. Retrieved on 15 March 2002.

MacCallum, I. (1991) 'Negative and Positive Freedom' *in* Miller, D. (Ed.) *Liberty*, Oxford: Oxford University Press.

Macpherson, C.B. (1973) *Democratic Theory*, Oxford: Oxford University Press.

Marshall, P. (2008) *Demanding the Impossible: A History of Anarchism*, London: Harper Perennial.

Martin, B. (1996) 'Democracy without Elections' *in* Ehrlich, H.J. (Ed.) *Reinventing Anarchy, Again*, Edinburgh: AK Press.

Marx, K. (1959) 'Afterword' to *Capital*, Vol. 1, Moscow: Foreign Language Publishing House.

Marx, K. (1973) *Grundrisse*, Harmondsworth: Penguin.

Marx, K. (1975) *in* Colletti, L. (Ed.) *Karl Marx: Early Writings*, London: Penguin.

Marx, K. (1977) *in* McLellan, D. (Ed.) *Karl Marx: Selected Writings*, Oxford: Oxford University Press.

McKinley, C.A. (2019) 'The French Revolution and 1848' *in* Levy, C. & Adams, M.S. (Eds) *The Palgrave Handbook of Anarchism*, Basingstoke: Palgrave Macmillan.

McLaughlin, P. (2016) 'Anarchy and Legal Order: Law and Politics for a Stateless Society, Written by Gary Chartier', *Journal of Moral Philosophy*, Vol. 13, No. 3.

McLellan, D. (1977) *Karl Marx: Selected Writings*, Oxford: Oxford University Press.

Meikle, S. (1985) *Essentialism in the Thought of Karl Marx*, London: Duckworth.

Meltzer, A. (1996) *Anarchism: Arguments For and Against*, Edinburgh: AK Press.

Michels, R. (1999) *Political Parties: A Sociological Study of the Oligarchical Tendencies of Modern Democracy*, London: Transaction.

Mill, J.S. (1991) *On Liberty and Other Essays*, Oxford: Oxford University Press.

Miller, D. (1984) *Anarchism*, London: Dent & Sons.

Miller, D. (1991) *Liberty*, Oxford: Oxford University Press.

Morrison, R. (1997) *We Build the Road as We Travel: Mondragon, A Cooperative Social System*, Writers Pub Cooperative.

Newman, S. (2012) 'Anarchism and Law', *Griffith Law Review*, Vol. 21, No. 2, 307–29.

Nicholls, D. (1994) *The Pluralist State*, Second Edition, Hampshire: Macmillan Press.

Nimtz, A.H. (2015) 'Marxism versus Anarchism: The First Encounter', *Science & Society*, Vol. 79, No. 2, April.

Nove, A. (1983) *The Economics of Feasible Socialism*, London: Allen & Unwin.

Nozick, R. (1974) *Anarchy, State, and Utopia*, Oxford: Blackwell.

Oakeshott, R. (1990) *The Case for Workers' Co-Ops*, Second Edition, Hampshire: Macmillan.

Ollman, B. (1998) *Market Socialism: The Debate Among Socialists*, London: Routledge.

Papaioannou, T. (2012) *Reading Hayek in the 21st Century: A Critical Inquiry into His Political Thought*, Hampshire: Palgrave Macmillan.

Parry, G. (1969) *Political Elites*, London: George Allen & Unwin.

Pateman, B. (2005) *Chomsky on Anarchism*, Edinburgh: AK Press.

Pelezynski, Z. & Gray, J. (1984) *Conceptions of Liberty in Political Philosophy*, London: Athlone.

Pennock, R. & Chapman, J.W. (1978) *Anarchism: Nomos XIX*, New York: New York University Press.

Pepper, D. (1993) *Eco-Socialism: From Deep Ecology to Social Justice*, London: Routledge.

Persky, J. & Madden, K. (2019) 'The Economic Content of G.D.H. Cole's Guild Socialism: Behavioural Assumptions, Institutional Structure and Analytical Arguments', *The European Journal of the History of Economic Thought*, Vol. 26, No. 3.

Pettit, P. (1997) *Republicanism: A Theory of Freedom and Government*, Oxford: Oxford University Press.

Pettit, P. (2006) 'Freedom in the Market', *Politics, Philosophy & Economics*, Vol. 5, No. 2.

Pettit, P. (2007) 'A Republican Right to a Basic Income', *Basic Income Studies*, Vol. 2, No. 2.

Pinta, S. & Berry, D. (2012) 'Conclusion: Towards a Libertarian Socialism for the Twenty-First Century?' *in* Prichard, A. Kinna, R. Pinta, S. & Berry, D. (Eds) *Libertarian Socialism: Politics in Black and Red*, Basingstoke: Palgrave.

Pittman, J.P. (2015) 'Introduction: Red on Black Marxist Encounters with Anarchism', *Science & Society*, Vol. 79, No. 2, April.

Plant, R. (1991) *Modern Political Philosophy*, Oxford: Blackwell.

Plant, R. & Hoover, K. (1989) *Conservative Capitalism in Britain and the United States: A Critical Appraisal*, London: Routledge.

Prichard, A. (2019) 'Freedom' *in* Levy, C. & Adams, M.S. (Eds) *The Palgrave Handbook of Anarchism*, Basingstoke: Palgrave Macmillan.

Prichard, A., Kinna, R. Pinta, S. & Berry, D. (2012) *Libertarian Socialism: Politics in Black and Red*, Basingstoke: Palgrave.

Raekstad, P. (2016) 'Understanding Anarchism: Some Basics', *Science & Society*, Vol. 80, No. 3, July.

Ramsay, M. (1997) *What's Wrong with Liberalism? A Radical Critique of Liberal Political Philosophy*, Leicester: Leicester University Press.

Rawls, J. (1971) *A Theory of Justice*, Cambridge, MA: Harvard University Press.

Rawls, J. (1993) *Political Liberalism*, New York: Columbia University Press.

Rawls, J. (1999) *A Theory of Justice*, Revised Edition, Cambridge, MA: Harvard University Press.

Rawls, J. (2001) *Justice as Fairness: A Restatement*, Delhi: Universal Law.

Rocker, R. (2004) *Anarcho-Syndicalism: Theory and Practice*, Edinburgh: AK Press.

Rothbard, M. (1978) *For a New Liberty: The Libertarian Manifesto*, Revised Edition, London: Collier.

Rousseau, J.J. (1998) *The Social Contract*, Hertfordshire: Wordsworth.

Rousseau, J.J. (2005) *The Social Contract, A Discourse on the Origin of Inequality, and A Discourse on Political Economy*, Stilwell: Digireads.com Publishing.

Ryley, P. (2019) 'Individualism' *in* Levy, C. & Adams, M.S. (Eds) *The Palgrave Handbook of Anarchism*, Basingstoke: Palgrave Macmillan.

Sale, K. (1996) 'The "Necessity" of the State' *in* Ehrlich, H.J. (Ed.) *Reinventing Anarchy, Again*, Edinburgh: AK Press.

Saunders, P. (2011) *When Prophesy Fails*, New South Wales: The Centre for Independent Studies, Special Publication 12.

Sayer, A. (2000) *Realism and Social Science*, London: Sage.

Sayers, S. (2005) 'Why Work? Marx and Human Nature', *Science & Society*, Vol. 69, No. 4, October.

Schecter, D. (1994) *Radical Theories: Paths beyond Marxism and Social Democracy*, Manchester: Manchester University Press.

Schecter, D. (2000) *Sovereign States or Political Communities?* Manchester: Manchester University Press.

Schmidt, M. & Van der Walt, L. (2009) *Black Flame: The Revolutionary Class Politics of Anarchism and Syndicalism*, Edinburgh: AK Press.

Schweickart, D. (1993) *Against Capitalism*, Cambridge: Cambridge University Press.

Schweickart, D. (1998a) 'Market Socialism: A Defence' *in* Ollman, B. (Ed.) *Market Socialism: The Debate Among Socialists*, London: Routledge.

Schweickart, D. (1998b) 'Criticism of Ticktin' *in* Ollman, B. (Ed.) *Market Socialism: The Debate Among Socialists*, London: Routledge.

Schweickart, D. (1998c) 'Response to Ticktin' *in* Ollman, B. (Ed.) *Market Socialism: The Debate Among Socialists*, London: Routledge.

Shannon, D. (2019) 'Anti-Capitalism and Libertarian Political Economy' *in* Levy, C. & Adams, M.S. (Eds) *The Palgrave Handbook of Anarchism*, Basingstoke: Palgrave Macmillan.

Shantz, J. & Williams, D.M. (2013) *Anarchy and Society: Reflections on Anarchist Sociology*, Leiden: Brill.

Skinner, Q. (1991) 'The Paradoxes of Political Liberty' *in* Miller, D. (Ed.) *Liberty*, Oxford: Oxford University Press.

Smith, G.W. (1984) 'J.S. Mill on Freedom' *in* Pelezynski, Z. & Gray, J. (Eds) *Conceptions of Liberty in Political Philosophy*, London: Athlone.

Sowell, T. (1963) 'Karl Marx and the Freedom of the Individual', *Ethics*, Vol. 73. No. 2, January.

Springer, S. (2017) 'The Limits to Marx: David Harvey and the Condition of Postfraternity', *Dialogues in Human Geography*, Vol. 7, No. 3.

Staples, C.L. & Staples, W.G. (2000) 'Rereading Harry Braverman's Labour and Monopoly Capital After Twenty Years', *Social Thought and Research*, Vol. 23, Nos 1–2.

Sweezy, P.M. (1974) 'Foreword' *in* Braverman, H. (Ed.) *Labour and Monopoly Capital: The Degradation of Work in the Twentieth Century*, London: Monthly Review.

Swift, A. (2001) *Political Philosophy: A Beginners Guide for Students and Politicians*, Cambridge: Polity.

Taylor, C. (1991) 'What's Wrong With Negative Liberty' *in* Miller, D. (Ed.) *Liberty*, Oxford: Oxford University Press.

Taylor, M. (1982) *Community, Anarchy and Liberty*, Cambridge: Cambridge University Press.

Thomas, H. & Logan, C. (1982) *Mondragon: An Economic Analysis*, London: George Allen & Unwin.

Turcato, D. (2019) 'Anarchist Communism' *in* Levy, C. & Adams, M.S. (Eds) *The Palgrave Handbook of Anarchism*, Basingstoke: Palgrave Macmillan.

Ulam, A.B. (1951) *Philosophical Foundations of English Socialism*, New York: Octagon.

Van der Walt, L. (2013) '(Re)Constructing a Global Anarchist and Syndicalist Canon: A Response to Robert Graham and Nathan Jun on *Black Flame*' *in* Kinna, R. & Evren, S. (Eds) *Blasting the Canon: Anarchist Developments in Cultural Studies*, New York: Punctum.

Van der Walt, L. (2019) 'Syndicalism' *in* Levy, C. & Adams, M.S. (Eds) *The Palgrave Handbook of Anarchism*, Basingstoke: Palgrave Macmillan.

Vernon, R. (1980) 'Introduction' *in* G.D.H. Cole (Ed.) *Guild Socialism Restated*, London: Transaction.

Von Mises, L. (1951) *Socialism*, London: Bradford & Dickens.

Wainwright, H. (1994) *Arguments for a New Left: Answering the Free Market Right*, Oxford: Blackwell.

Walicki, A. (1983) 'Marx and Freedom', *The New York Review of Books*, Vol. 30, Part 18.

Walicki, A. (1984) 'The Marxian Conception of Freedom' *in* Pelezynski, Z. & Gray, J. (Eds) *Conceptions of Liberty in Political Philosophy*, London: Athlone.

Ward, C. (1996) 'Anarchism and the Informal Economy' *in* Ehrlich, H.J. (Ed.) *Reinventing Anarchy, Again*, Edinburgh: AK Press.

Ward, C. (2004) *Anarchism: A Very Short Introduction*, Oxford: Oxford University Press.

Wetherly, P. (2017) *Political Ideologies*, Oxford: Oxford University Press.

White, S. (2011) 'The Republican Critique of Capitalism', *Critical Review of International Social and Political Philosophy*, Vol. 14, No. 5.

Whyte, W.F. & Whyte, K.K. (1991) *Making Mondragon: The Growth and Dynamics of the Worker Cooperative Complex*, Second Edition, Ithaca, NY: Cornell University Press.

Williams, L.A. (2013) 'The Canon Which Is Not One' *in* Kinna, R. & Evren, S. (Eds) *Blasting the Canon: Anarchist Developments in Cultural Studies*, New York: Punctum.

Wokler, R. (2001) *Rousseau: A Very Short Introduction*, Oxford: Oxford University Press.

Wolff, J. (2006) *An Introduction to Political Philosophy*, Revised Edition, Oxford: Oxford University Press.

Wolff, R.P. (2015) 'On Being Both an Anarchist and a Marxist', *Science & Society*, Vol. 79, No. 2, April.

Wright, A.W. (1979) *G.D.H. Cole and Socialist Democracy*, Oxford: Clarendon.

Wyatt, C. (2006) 'A Recipe for a Cookshop of the Future: G.D.H. Cole and the Conundrum of Sovereignty', *Capital and Class*, Vol. 90, autumn.

Wyatt, C. (2008) *The Difference Principle Beyond Rawls*, New York: Continuum.

Wyatt, C. (2011) *The Defetishised Society: New Economic Democracy as a Libertarian Alternative to Capitalism*, New York: Continuum.

Zvesper, J. (1987) 'Liberalism' *in* Miller, D., Coleman, J., Connolly, W., & Ryan, A. (Eds) *The Blackwell Encyclopaedia of Political Thought*, Oxford: Blackwell.

Index

Note: 'n.' after a page reference indicates a note on that page.

EU authorised representative for GPSR:
Easy Access System Europe, Mustamäe tee 50,
10621 Tallinn, Estonia
gpsr.requests@easproject.com

www.ingramcontent.com/pod-product-compliance
Lightning Source LLC
Chambersburg PA
CBHW052005270326
41929CB00015B/2791